PSYCHOHISTORY

AMERICAN UNIVERSITY STUDIES

Series XIX
General Literature

Vol. 30

PETER LANG
New York • Washington, D.C./Baltimore • Boston
Bern • Frankfurt am Main • Berlin • Vienna • Paris

JACQUES SZALUTA

PSYCHOHISTORY
THEORY AND PRACTICE

PETER LANG
New York • Washington, D.C./Baltimore • Boston
Bern • Frankfurt am Main • Berlin • Vienna • Paris

Library of Congress Cataloging-in-Publication Data

Szaluta, Jacques.
Psychohistory: theory and practice / Jacques Szaluta.
p. cm. — (American university studies. Series XIX, General literature; vol. 30)
1. Psychohistory. I. Title. II. Series.
D16.16.S93   901'.9—dc21   97-39959
ISBN 978-0-8204-1741-7 (hardcover)
ISBN 978-0-8204-4967-8 (paperback)
ISSN 0743-6645

Die Deutsche Bibliothek-CIP-Einheitsaufnahme

Szaluta, Jacques.
Psychohistory: theory and practice / Jacques Szaluta.
–New York; Washington, D.C./Baltimore; Boston; Bern;
Frankfurt am Main; Berlin; Vienna; Paris: Lang.
(American university studies: Ser. 19, General literature; Vol. 30)
ISBN 978-0-8204-1741-7 (hardcover)
ISBN 978-0-8204-4967-8 (paperback)

The paper in this book meets the guidelines for permanence and durability
of the Committee on Production Guidelines for Book Longevity
of the Council of Library Resources.

© 1999, 2001, 2010 Peter Lang Publishing, Inc., New York

All rights reserved.
Reprint or reproduction, even partially, in all forms such as microfilm,
xerography, microfiche, microcard, and offset strictly prohibited.

Printed in the United States of America

For Alice and Elizabeth

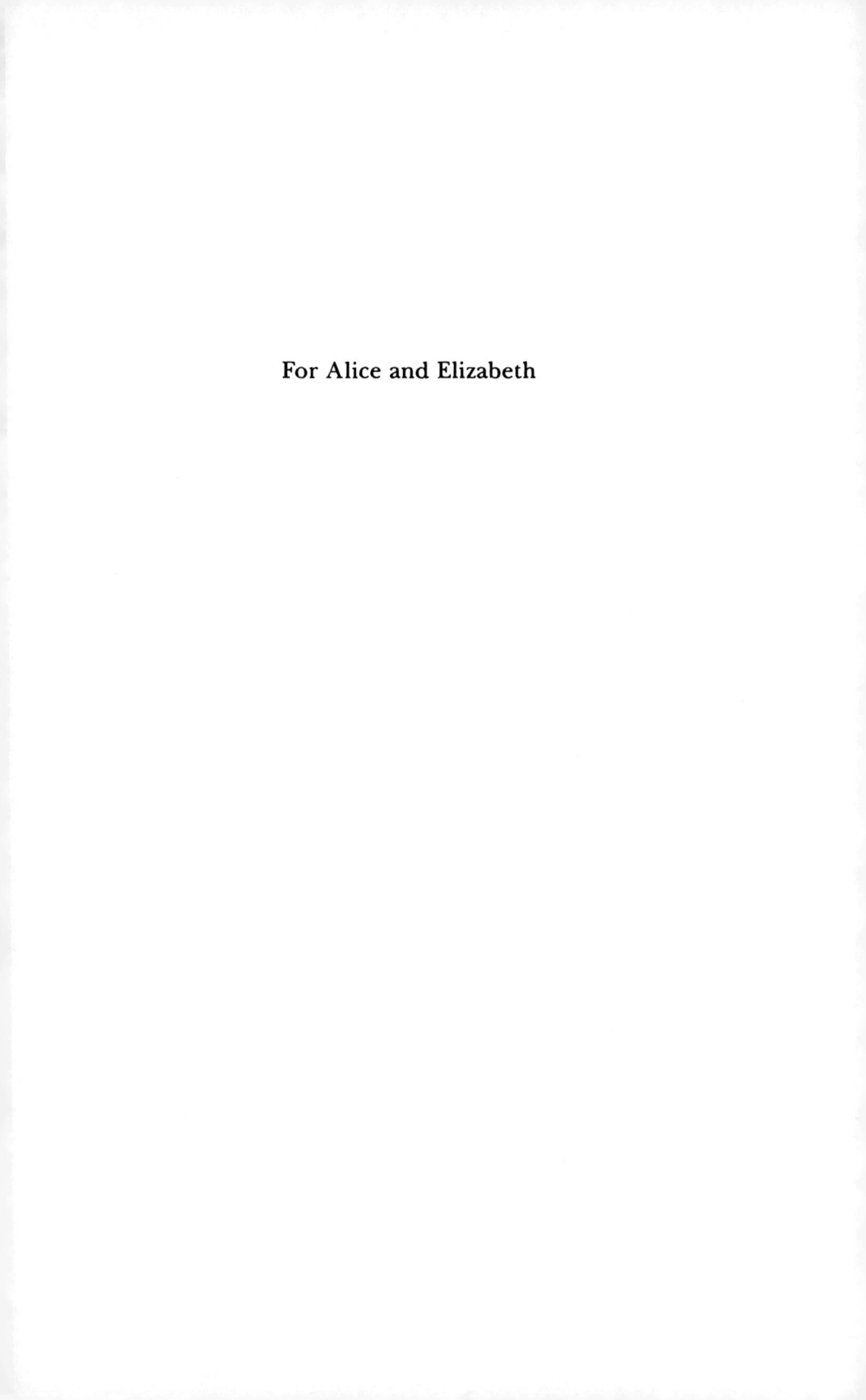

Table of Contents

Acknowledgments   ix

1. **Psychohistory: A Definition**   1
   1. Methodology   1
   2. Issues and Growth in Psychohistory   5

2. **Sigmund Freud: The Fundamentals of Psychoanalytic Theory**   17
   1. Formative Influences   17
   2. Dreams   22
   3. The Development of Personality   25
   4. The Psychical Apparatus   31
   5. Philosophy of History   34

3. **Psychohistory: For and Against**   49
   1. The Critics   49
   2. The Case for Psychohistory   59

4. **Erik H. Erikson: Contributions to the Development of Psychohistory**   83
   1. The Concept of Identity   83
   2. *Young Man Luther*   91
   3. Assessments of Erikson   98

5. **Psychoanalytic Theory: Post Freudian Developments**   117
   1. Ego Psychology   117

2.	The British School	127
3.	The French Interpreters	139
4.	Kohut and Self Psychology	148

6. Psychohistory: Genre and Interpretations — 171
1. Biographical Studies — 171
2. Group Dynamics — 188
3. Childhood — 197
4. The Family — 203

7. Conclusion: The Future of Psychohistory — 227
1. Toward a New Understanding of the Past — 227
2. Psychoanalysis and Psychohistory — 229

Bibliography — 247

Index — 271

Acknowledgments

The present work is an outgrowth of my previous book, *La psychohistoire*, in the *Que sais-je* series, published by Presses Universitaires de France in 1987. This volume expands the original book both in length and scope and includes contemporary issues in psychohistory.

I am indebted to many friends, colleagues, and institutions who have been supportive in this endeavor. First, I would like to thank the administration of the U.S. Merchant Marine Academy, Admiral Thomas T. Matteson, The Superintendent of the Academy, and Dr. Warren F. Mazek, the Academic Dean, for facilitating my work on the manuscript in a number of ways. Thanks also go to Dr. George J. Billy, the Library Director at the Academy, who read and commented on the manuscript.

I am indebted to the psychohistorians who read my manuscript and who have made significant contributions to the field of psychohistory. In particular, I would like to thank Professors Rudolph Binion, David J. Fisher, Peter Gay, Peter Loewenberg, Bruce Mazlish, and William M. Runyan, for reading the manuscript, making insightful comments, and recommending additional literature. I also wish to acknowledge with cordial appreciation Dr. Walter and Eva Heimer who read my manuscript from a clinical perspective.

I want to express my profound appreciation to those whose personal encouragement has been ongoing for many years. I am especially grateful to Professor Laurie Adams, with whom I have collaborated on many projects, and to Professor William S. Omeltchenko, my colleague at the U.S. Merchant Marine Academy, with whom I have worked closely. Heartfelt thanks to Dr. Richard I. Harrison, Director of Research of the New York Center for Psychoanalytic Training, who has been my teacher and mentor. And my wife, Susan, I thank for always being there for me. Whatever errors of fact or interpretation there may be, they are mine alone.

Jacques Szaluta
United States Merchant Marine Academy
Kings Point, New York

Chapter 1

Psychohistory: A Definition

1. Methodology

Psychohistory is a relatively new field and it is interdisciplinary, as the name indicates. It has grown in methodological sophistication and popular acceptance since the late 1950s, the period of its establishment and institutionalization in professional academic circles in the United States. To give it its fundamental definition, psychohistory is the application of psychology, in its broadest sense, or psychoanalysis in a specific sense, to the study of the past, of history. The benefit and the promise of the application of psychoanalysis to the study of history are that it enriches our understanding of the dynamics of the past, adding new dimensions to our perspective of historical processes.

Although psychohistory, as it has come to be called, is a new field, the attempt to understand the past by the use of "psychology" is an old one, but the method heretofore employed by historians was based on a subjective personal judgment known as "common sense." Traditionally, then, historians, in conjunction with their stress on what they thought were objective, verifiable, and documentary data, have depended on their intuition for understanding and interpreting individuals, collective behavior, and events. In other words, factors of causation were considered to be political, military, social or economic. But the development of psychohistory is changing this personal and traditional approach by providing a more systematized method of studying the past. Moreover, psychohistory deals with issues, subjects and topics hitherto neglected, if not avoided. Psychohistory is concerned with the question of motivation in human behavior, whether of the individual or of the group. Psychohistory, as will be shown, has revolutionized the study of history, and hence has been very controversial and continues to meet with much opposition. To be sure, from Herodotus to Ranke, historians have striven to find scientific laws for penetrating the past, and many certainly have made invaluable contributions. However, with Sigmund Freud's discoveries in the early twentieth century, a whole new way of probing man and his past was founded. What has not changed to this day, however, despite the availability of the new tools, is that the historical product, or narrative, still depends ultimately on the ability, training, sources, and openness of the individual historian.

This new interdisciplinary field has its genesis in the psychoanalytic theories founded and developed by Freud. Not only did he develop psychoanalysis, but he was also one of the first to show its application to the study of culture in its broadest sense by applying it to the study of the past.[1] Psychoanalysis, to give it an abbreviated introductory definition, is a body of knowledge about the psychology of human behavior, a scientific discipline concerned with mental functioning, both normal as well as pathological, that is based on an understanding of unconscious processes and motivations. Employing this approach, Freud set the example, demonstrating in numerous works the revealing insights that psychoanalysis as an investigative tool could achieve for understanding society and the development of civilization. The study *Totem and Taboo*, to cite just one work, is such an example, remarkable for its brilliant insights and protean dimensions.

Just as psychohistory is revolutionizing the study of history today, and has accordingly been meeting with much opposition—and downright hostility—so too psychoanalysis was met with much objection. Just as Copernicus' and Darwin's theories were controversial because they changed man's perception of himself, so too the acceptance of psychoanalysis, sharing the customary fate of non-conformist ideas, was initially marked by vociferous resistance to it. Although Freud was a scientist, like some of his predecessors just mentioned, his observations and findings were controversial for many reasons; for one, because they disturbed man's narcissistic views of himself, and, ultimately, for their political and social ramifications. In time, Freud's major contributions were verified clinically and empirically,[2] and today psychoanalysis enjoys a wide—if at times still critical—acceptance.

The themes sketched here will be elaborated more fully in the following chapters, so it will suffice for now just to note additionally about psychoanalysis, that it is a method of investigating the mind by the process of free association, with emphasis on the unconscious manifestations that these productions have. It is also a method of treatment, in which the psychoanalyst interprets the latent and unconscious meaning of the analysand's verbal productions. Freud's discovery of the centrality of sexuality in mental development led to his formulation of the libido theory, with its stress on the psychosexual maturation of the individual. According to the libido theory, there are several maturational phases, going from childhood to adulthood. The outcome of these stages of growth will have a bearing on the individual's formation of his personality. If successful, the outcome will be a normal social adaptation to society; if not, it may cause neurosis or psychosis. Although in his theoretical exposition of psychoanalysis Freud addressed himself mainly to the psychic aspects, he also recognized the importance of heredity, of the personal constitutional factors.

Psychoanalysis and history have much in common, and in their approach have many parallels. Both are concerned with development through time, with antecedents, with their outcome in human actions. To continue with the definition of what is psychohistory, which is to contrast the traditional approach with the psychohistorical one, the psychohistorian Rudolph Binion makes a pithy statement about it when he notes in his *Introduction à la Psychohistoire* that he "takes as his point of departure the elementary distinction between an event or the state of things passed and its causes—between the *what* and the *why* of history."[3] For the psychohistorian, "the *why* of history necessarily comes back entirely to a *why* psychologically. Seen from this optical angle, history is what men have done; to know why men have done what they have, one must look for the deeper motives, not more nor less."[4]

What further distinguishes psychohistory, and what is its debt to psychoanalysis, is the recognition that motives for actions cannot be detected by just searching for what is logical and materialistic. Irrationality exists, and not only that, but much of what occurs is, at certain times, even self-destructive. As Peter Loewenberg, a theoretician of psychohistory notes, psychohistorians use the same sources as other historians; namely memoirs, newspapers, official government documents, the gamut of primary and secondary sources, but they study them from a different perspective.[5]

The fundamentals of psychohistory are concisely presented by Loewenberg who describes the three essential features of the field. He says that to study history psychologically, the first point is to find the role of the unconscious "in human behavior as evidenced by life styles, adaptations, creativity and sublimations, character, slips of speech, hearing, and writing, errors, accidents, dreams, neuroses and psychoses, and human action or inhibition."[6]

The second point is known as the genetic approach, which is historical in nature. He writes: "It emphasizes the importance of origins, antecedents, and patterns of repetition. Thus it is developmental—stressing the longitudinal growth and adaptation of the person, including events and learned behaviors from infancy, childhood, adolescence, and young adulthood. Psychohistory is oriented to dynamic psychology in which the present reality interacts at all times with and is related to the personal and social past of the person in the unconscious."[7]

The third feature of psychohistory is the recognition of the personal and subjective experiences of the individual and "gives due place to the aggression, sexuality, passions, fantasy, and emotional states of the inner world of its subjects. It rejects the myth of the asexuality and innocence of child or adult, man or woman. Psychohistory recognizes that the fantasies of the subject rather than meaning externally ascribed, constitute the relevant determinant of the emotional meaning of an event, symbol, or image."[8]

However, the writing of psychohistory is not just the acquisition of psychoanalytic theory as a technique of investigation, but it is also dependent on the nature of the practitioner, and his emotional make-up. Among the tools and skills necessary for this field is the quality of empathy. In reconstituting an event, that is the selecting and interpreting of an event, the writer has subjective feelings that play a paramount role. Many psychohistorians have drawn attention to the role of empathy in assessing historical information and how this feature has a link between psychoanalysis and history. The historian's work is necessarily psychological because it requires an understanding of people's motivations, their ideas and feelings. As Hans Meyerhoff in "On Psychoanalysis as History" says, the historian's work is "of a highly introspective nature; for it is his task to discover the inner and hidden 'meaning' behind the overt sequence of events."[9] H. Stuart Hughes, in *History as Art and as Science*, also considers the quality of being empathic as essential to the historian.[10] In this book, he gives numerous examples of his students being able to decipher historical questions, or riddles, because the students were able to reach into their own unconscious feeling. Hughes even admonishes the reader, saying: "Unless there is some emotional tie, some elective affinity linking the student to his subject of study, the results will be pedantic and perfunctory."[11] Peter Loewenberg, in "Why Psychoanalysis needs the Social Scientist and the Historian" further elaborates on how the historian "is himself the primary instrument of research" because "he uses himself as the perceptor and interpreter of data."[12] Loewenberg takes the position that not only is there a "common empathic method" between the two fields, but that the richness of social science methodologies "can buttress and fortify the intuitive and empathic realms of affect and expression which are the stuff of psychoanalytic evidence and clinical practice."[13]

The recognition of the importance of empathy is not just a feature of the historian's craft, but parallels the work of the psychoanalyst. Psychohistory grows out of psychoanalysis, but the two fields dovetail each other. Even if they differ in their outcome, they are similar in their approach inasmuch as they share the same theoretical base, they are both historical in nature, and they both demand a personal emotional involvement in their respective tasks. In effect, psychohistorians can and do employ their feelings as tools for understanding and interpreting their subjects.[14]

2. Issues and Growth in Psychohistory

To illustrate the aforementioned, examples of differences in approach to history and to psychohistory will now be presented. These vignettes will demonstrate the varieties that are extant and indicate the nature of the controversy. The great historical figure of Napoleon lends itself to such a demonstration, with the focus on the questions of leadership and motivations.

The eminent French historian of the French Revolution and Napoleon, Georges Lefebvre, internationally recognized for his pioneering studies which advanced our understanding of this momentous era in history, explains the development of Napoleon's leadership in the following way:

> Ever since his military schooldays at Brienne, when he was still a poor and taunted foreigner, timid yet bursting with passion, Napoleon drew strength from pride in himself and contempt for others. Destined to become an officer, his instinct to command without having to discuss could not have been better served. Although he might on occasion have sought information or opinion, he alone was master and judge. Bonaparte's natural propensity for dictatorship suited the normal practice of his profession.[15]

On the other hand, the American historian Harold T. Parker, who takes a psychohistorical approach to the question of Napoleon's leadership, and the basis for its motivation, after reviewing his childhood and early career, concludes:

> In this psychological-social process in which Napoleon's personality was formed, one is impressed by the importance of rejection—the relative inattention of the mother, which the infant might interpret as rejection and which provoked self-assertiveness for applause without associated reciprocal warmth and closeness; the harassment of the Brienne classmates, which fixed the patterns of control of rage, work accomplishment, and proneness to dreams, fantasies, and plans; Paoli's antagonism, which killed the adolescent Corsican dream and focused his energy on a career; and Josephine's infidelity, which closed out his one serious attempt to reach trustful sexual intimacy with a woman. Napoleon was badly hurt four times.[16]

The two above statements by Lefebvre and Parker serve as an illustration of contrast. Though they use similar data and deal with similar events, they make distinctly different interpretations of Napoleon.

Another area still, of psychohistorical investigation, is the matter of group psychology, that is the behavior of groups and responses of a group to a leader. On such a topic, a subject of universal interest is certainly the question of how Napoleon was able to achieve his legendary feats of leadership.

Franklin S. Klaf examines Napoleon's relationship to the Grand Army of 1812 by utilizing the hypotheses and concepts developed in Freud's *Group Psychology and the Analysis of the Ego*. Accordingly, noting that groups are held together by libidinal ties, that the commander-in-chief is like a father who should love all his children equally, and that the bond between the group and its leader has its basis in identification, Klaf finds that Napoleon accomplished these expectations because he served as an ego ideal, a model, who portrayed himself as being infallibly guided by fate.[17]

Klaf explains that, "Napoleon was such a skilled practitioner of an effective variety of mass paternalism that he might almost be termed an artificer. He epitomized the great father, caring equally (or seeming to care equally), for all of the 'children' of his army."[18] Therefore, Napoleon, "by his intuitive understanding of group dynamics, was able to bind together the armies of many nations and drive them toward the conquest of the Russian Empire," and "in an effort to spread identification with himself through the army, he appointed members of his own family as his chief subordinates, and favorite sons as superior officers."[19]

The interpretations just cited are a sample of the historiography on Napoleon, serving as an introduction to the various approaches to this particular person. In the case of Lefebvre, however, who has a more traditional approach, he was guided by his intuition and "common sense" in his appraisal of Napoleon. One might ask how does Lefebvre know that Napoleon had an "instinct to command," and that he was "destined to become an officer."[20] What Lefebvre has done is to assume these qualities on the bases of what seemed to have occurred. Parker and Klaf, on the other hand, arrive at their conclusions informed by formulations derived from psychoanalytic concepts which are based on clinical and empirical data. By probing for Napoleon's motivations, Parker and Klaf have provided a more insightful answer than Lefebvre to the question of *why*.

This leads us now to bring into relation the position of psychohistory within the historical profession. From its inception to the present, psychohistory has met with controversy and heated opposition. Despite the great contributions made by this interdisciplinary field in the last several decades, the historical profession initially did not accord it a warm reception, and not only that, but to this day there is much condemnation of it. Although psychohistory developed and first took hold in the United States, it is here too that the dispute raged in intellectual circles. In this respect, psychohistory has shared the fate with which psychoanalysis was greeted; an opposition that included religious and political organizations. As with psychoanalysis, growth and acceptance did occur, and now perhaps even legitimacy, but it came very slowly and was granted grudgingly. As psychohistory grew and gained prestige, a literature arose to oppose it, to discredit it, to block it from making inroads into the traditional approach to the study of history. Paradoxically, the critics served to bring even greater attention to psychohistory, but some opponents were so vituperative—and irrational—that they served to discredit themselves. One critic, on the faculty of a leading university, in his polemic against psychohistory called it a "cancer that is metastasizing through the whole body of the historical profession."[21] Others have been more moderate.

One example of this controversy, but characteristic of the contending positions, appeared in the pages of the prestigious journal, the *American Historical Review*, in 1972. The eminent cultural historian Jacques Barzun of Columbia University sounded the alarm against psychohistory in an article entitled "History: The Muse and Her Doctors," which was expanded into a book, *Clio and the Doctor: Psycho-History, Quanto-History, and History*. Again, Barzun's very stature ensured wide attention. The article being what may be considered a manifesto against psychohistory, touched off a debate on the pros and cons of the new specialty. Barzun objected to psychohistory because, in his opinion, it did not accord with the traditional study of history, it did not have the basic criteria of writing history, which is to first of all tell a story. Barzun is against psychohistory because it has the intention of being a science; therefore, it is incompatible with the usual definition of what is history. Written with capital letters, he states that there are four criteria of history: Narrative, Chronology, Concreteness, and Memorability.[22] In accordance with these tenets, historians who turn to psychohistory depart from the field of history because they "mingle" their former training with a "type derived from clinical practice." To give a fair representation of Barzun's position, an extensive selection from the article will be quoted: He writes:

> Throughout this essay I have shown or implied the kind of incompatibility I believe to exist between history and psychohistory. The one is not a desirable progression out of the other: they are different undertakings altogether. What is called psycho-history is one of a whole class of efforts, only some of which have names—socio-history, quantitative history, interdisciplinary history. Their common intention is analytic, generalizing, formulary in the spirit of science. They can all be recognized by their frequent mention of 'new tools' being used to create 'new disciplines.' Indeed, a certain use of the word 'method' suffices to disclose their difference from history properly so called.
>
> Other identifying marks of that difference now claim our attention; for the excitement about new hybrid genres has inevitably confused both laymen and professionals as to the spirit of history. The difference itself is fundamentally that between two orientations of the human mind, the intuitive and the scientific.[23]

The rebuttals to Barzun's charges were quick and sharp. The leading exponents in the field of psychohistory, in replying to the criticisms explained the methodology and merit of psychohistory, and challengingly justified the new discipline. For instance, to Barzun's contention that psychohistory was a resorting to "technical jargon" that did not add to understanding, John J. Fitzpatrick replied trenchantly that "This objection is invalid. Concepts such as sublimation, reaction-formation, identification, the self, character defense, etc., have specialized meanings that incorporate new insights into personality functioning. It is time for historians to understand this."[24]

William L. Langer, who was cited in this article for being an exponent of psychohistory, and, when president of the American Historical Association in 1957 had urged historians in a presidential address boldly entitled "The Next Assignment," to turn to modern psychohistory as an additional tool for studying history, in his rebuttal accused Barzun of trying to denigrate psychohistory. As for Barzun's complaint that psychohistorians "tend to put all their eggs into the Freudian basket,"[25] Langer retorted without apology that "If the Freudian doctrine is still preferred, it is chiefly because it alone provides a coherent theory of personality development. It does not advance formulas or attempt conclusions, but it tries to show the wide variety of unconsciously determined reactions to external events and the many defense mechanisms to which human nature resorts."[26]

And with good logic, Langer further said that "After all, there is no reason why, where the sources and the evidence permit, the student should not weigh the psychological as well as the economic, military, religious, or other components of a historical problem."[27]

Peter Loewenberg also replied, accusing Barzun of being an intellectual reactionary. To Barzun's claim that William James' work of 1890, *The Principles of Psychology* is "the classic of psychology perhaps most useful to the historian and biographer," Loewenberg rhetorically asks: "Are we to infer that all that has been developed in the clinical practice and theory of psychology in the last eight decades is of less value to the modern historian than the work of James?"[28] Facetiously, Loewenberg adds, "Some new things have been learned since 1890, including of course the insights of Sigmund Freud. . . ."[29] With further irony, he asks: "But I wonder whether Barzun would also use the anthropology or the linguistics of 1890 as his research models? Or, more to the point, would he select for his family a surgeon, a pediatrician, or a gynecologist whose thought had not developed in eighty-two years?"[30]

As the above statements demonstrate, the debate over psychohistory has been intense, with the defenders taking up the challenge by replying with constructive, thoughtful, and incisive comments. The dialectic has been fruitful, and has served to enhance psychohistory.

Despite the opposition, the field of psychohistory has continued to make important strides, and the psychohistorical literature has been growing exponentially since the 1950's. In recognition of this growth, and a measure of its acceptance, the American Historical Association, at its annual meeting in 1988, held a landmark session, pertinently entitled "Psychohistory and Psychohistorians: The First Fifty Years."[31]

Indeed, periodic studies of the state and growth of the field of psychohistory demonstrate its vitality and proliferation.[32] Two such studies, which amply demonstrate the prodigious development of the field are by William J. Gilmore, *Psycho-*

historical Inquiry: A Comprehensive Research Bibliography (1984), and the essay by William M. Runyan, "A Historical and Conceptual Background to Psychohistory," in the book edited by the same author *Psychology and Historical Interpretation* (1988).[33] Gilmore's study aptly uses the adjective "comprehensive" in the subtitle, because it is such an exhaustive overview of the expansion of the field. What recommends his book is that the bibliography has the effect of dramatically illustrating the accomplishments in the field. In this compendium, which concentrates on publications written in English, but has a sampling of foreign language sources, there is a listing which runs in the thousands, of dissertations, books, articles, essays and papers which were published or presented in the course of only a few decades from approximately 1965 to 1981. The book is divided into two major parts, the first containing a bibliography that is annotated because it deals with the methodologies used by psychohistorians, and the second is largely a bibliography, grouped by geographical area, time period and subject manner, such as childhood, family, and psychobiography. However, Gilmore is also cognizant of the methodological issues, theoretical differences, and problems in the field of psychohistory. Gilmore makes it evident that there are multiple approaches and different "wings" in the field, which means that a degree of fragmentation exists.[34] Among the numerous issues and concerns Gilmore lists, only a sampling will be cited. This will suffice to bear out his contentions; the one that leads his list is on the issue of psychobiography "moving beyond pathogenic personality theory which places primary emphasis on the unconscious rather than on the conscious developments of the self."[35] Others of note are "group behavior and the possibility of pyschohistories of groups," and "how to study the history of emotional life within different societies in the past."[36] A last one, which has drawn much criticism from historians, is "standards of evidence and inference in psychohistory in relation to accepted standards within history."[37]

As one peruses this cornucopia of publications contained in Gilmore's work, one can't help but be impressed by the richness and abundance of the literature in this new field, the problems and issues within and without the field. In the decade that followed the publication of Gilmore's work, studies in psychohistory have continued apace.

Runyan's essay, cited above, dovetails Gilmore's extensive study. In a section of his essay, entitled "A Quantitative Analysis of the Growth of Literature in Psychohistory," the author provides a statistical assessment and shows the accretion of the number of doctoral dissertations, books and articles on psychohistory and psychobiography, which makes the field appear to be very promising in its future. Concentrating overall on the years 1920 to 1980, Runyan makes a special note of the growth of doctoral dissertation in the United States within that period. His findings are revealing. Whereas the growth of dissertations for the field of history in general was four-fold, from 1958 to 1978, the increase in dissertations in psychohistory was thirty times as many. In numbers, 2 dissertations in psychohistory were written between 1955 and 1959, but between 1975 and 1979, 65 dissertations appeared. To look at these statistics in percentages, they become even more striking. From 1968 to 1978, in the entire field of history, there was a 14 percent growth, from 754 to 862 dissertations. But in psychohistory in the same period, there was a more than 500 percent increase. Again, in numbers they went from 12 in 1965-1969 to 65 in 1975-1979. And furthermore, the number is even larger, for Runyan tabulated only those dissertations that explicitly described themselves as psychohistorical or psychobiographical.[38]

This growth has been accompanied by an institutionalization of the field. Many historical journals now accept psychohistorical papers for publication, but there are also journals that are devoted primarily to the field. These are the *Psychohistory Review*, the *Journal of Psychohistory*, both founded in the early 1970s, and *Political Psychology: Journal of the International Society of Political Psychology*, founded in 1979. *Political Psychology* casts its net widely and draws on diverse fields in psychology and the social sciences, which of course includes psychohistory. Still another journal is *American Imago*, founded by Sigmund Freud and Hanns Sachs in 1938, a journal of applied psychoanalysis, focusing on culture, literature and social theory, but which also publishes psychohistorical papers. Although psychoanalytic journals abound internationally, there are few psychohistorical journals published in foreign languages.[39]

Commensurate with the growing number of psychohistorical studies there has been an emplacement of psychohistory courses taught in colleges and universities. Here too, the growth has been impressive. The beginnings were certainly quite modest, for as late as 1966, Bruce Mazlish, a pioneer in the field, said that at that time only two such courses were offered, one by himself and the other by Erik Erikson. However, only a decade later, approximately 200 such sources were offered in academia in the United States.[40] In the first part of this decade, the 1990's, it is probably around 400 courses. Although these figures seem substantial, psychohistory still has to struggle with becoming established in higher education. In practice, the major Ph.D. producing universities only exceptionally have an established systematic training program in psychohistory. Generally, the interest and work in the field is individualistic, supported where there happens to be a sympathetic faculty member willing to sponsor a graduate student.[41] A reason for this equivocal situation is that the production of Ph.D.'s in this field is notably decentralized. Runyan provides a possible explanation for this situation, observing that "although the field may be gradually becoming an *intellectual* discipline, with a defined set of problems and approaches, it has not yet become an *academic* discipline, with well-defined and well organized academic programs."[42]

In sum, in its brief history, psychohistory has moved from being peripheral in academia to a more central position. Nevertheless, serious problems and unique challenges remain for the psychohistorian, which will be addressed in the concluding chapter.

Notes

1. See for example the following works by Sigmund Freud, "The Future of an Illusion," *Standard Edition*, Vol. 21, 1961; "Civilization and its Discontents," Vol. 21, *S.E.*, 1961; "Moses and Monotheism," Vol. 23, *S.E.*, 1978. For a discussion of the early contributors to the theory of crowd psychology, by the Frenchmen Gustave LeBon and Gabriel Tarde, whose works were integrated by Freud, see the essay by David J. Fisher, "An Intellectual History of Crowds," in *Cultural Theory and Psychoanalytic Tradition*, Transaction Publishers, 1991, pp. 227-235.

2. For a voluminous and valuable evaluation of Freud's work, see Seymour Fisher and Roger P. Greenberg, *The Scientific Credibility of Freud's Theories and Therapy*, Basic Books, 1977. A critique of behaviorism, which is called "bankrupt," is discussed by Reuben Fine in *The Logic of Psychology: A Dynamic Approach*, University Press of America, 1983. See also *Diagnostic and Statistical Manual of Mental Disorders*, Fourth Edition, *DSM-IV*, Published by the American Psychiatric Association, 1994, a compendium of the categorization and description of mental disorders for diagnostic purposes. Compiled by the American Psychiatric Association, it is a standard reference work for broad use in the field of mental health. To some degree, this work draws upon psychoanalytic theory.

3. Rudolph Binion, *Introduction à la psychohistoire*, Presses Universitaires de France, 1982, p. 7.

4. *Ibid.*, p. 11.

5. Peter Loewenberg, *Decoding the Past*, Knopf, 1983, pp. 17-18.

6. *Ibid.*, p. 15.

7. *Ibid.*

8. *Ibid.*, pp. 15-16.

9. Hans Meyerhoff "On Psychoanalysis as History" in *Psycho/History: Readings in the Method of Psychology, Psychoanalysis and History*, Ed. by G. Cocks and T.L. Crosby, Yale University Press, 1987, p. 19.

10. H. Stuart Hughes, *History as Art and Science*, Harper and Row, 1964, pp. 52-58.

11. *Ibid.*, p. 56.

12. Peter Loewenberg, "Why Psychoanalysis Needs the Social Scientist and the Historian," in *Psycho/History: Readings in the Method of Psychol-*

ogy, *Psychoanalysis and History*, Ed. by G. Cocks and T.L. Crosby, Yale University Press, 1987, p. 38.

13. *Ibid.*, p. 31.

14. For the necessity of empathy on the part of the biographer, see Alexander L. and Juliette L. George, *Woodrow Wilson and Colonel House*, Dover Publications, 1964, pp. viii–xii.

15. Georges Lefebvre, *Napoleon*, trans. by H.F. Stockhold, Columbia University Press, 1969, p. 64.

16. Harold T. Parker, "The Formation of Napoleon's Personality: An Exploratory Essay," *French Historical Studies*, Vol. II, 1971, p. 25.

17. Franklin S. Klaf, "Napoleon and the Grand Army of 1812: A Study of Group Psychology," *The Psychoanalytic Review*, Vol. 47, 1960, pp. 69–71.

18. *Ibid.*, p. 71.

19. *Ibid.*, p. 75.

20. Lefebvre, *Napoleon*, p. 64.

21. See the biased article by Kenneth S. Lynn, "History's Reckless Psychologizing," *Chronicle of Higher Education*, Vol. 15, number 18, January 1978, p. 48.

22. Jacques Barzun, "History: The Muse and Her Doctors," *American Historical Review;*, Vol. 77, 1972, p. 55.

23. *Ibid.*, p. 54.

24. *Ibid.*, Vol. 77, 1972, p. 1194.

25. *Ibid.*, p. 1195.

26. *Ibid.*

27. *Ibid.*, p. 1196.

28. *Ibid.*

29. *Ibid.*

30. *Ibid.*

31. American Historical Association, *Program of the One Hundred Third Annual Meeting*, Session 138, "Psychohistory and Psychohistorians: The First Fifty Years," p. 89. Another major session was held in 1992, in Washington D.C., see American Historical Association, *Program of the One Hundred Seventh Annual Meeting*, Session 85, "Sigmund Freud and Historians: New Interpretations and Directions," p. 98.

32. For an extensive compilation of works in the already burgeoning field of psychohistory in the mid-1970s, see Faye Sinofsky, John J. Fitzgerald, Louis Potts, and Lloyd de Mause, "A Bibliography of Psychohistory," *History of Childhood Quarterly*, Spring 1975, Vol. 2, No. 4, pp. 517–562.

33. William J. Gilmore, *Psychohistorical Inquiry: A Comprehensive Research Bibliography*, Garland Publishing, 1984. William M. Runyan, "A Historical and Conceptual Background to Psychohistory" in *Psychology and Historical Interpretation*, Ed. by W.M. Runyan, Oxford University Press, 1988.

34. Gilmore, *Psychohistorical Inquiry*, p. xv.

35. *Ibid.*

36. *Ibid.*

37. *Ibid.*

38. Runyan, in *Psychology and Historical Interpretation*, pp. 3–60.

39. In French, there is *Or le temp: Revue Française de Psychohistoire*. The editor in chief of this journal is Robert Liris, who is also the founder and president of the French Psychohistorical Society. *Mentalities/Mentalités* is an interdisciplinary journal published in New Zealand and publishes articles in French and English. Paul H. Elovitz the editor of *Clio's Psyche*, founded in 1994, which is both a newsletter and a journal, reports that there is a Spanish journal, *psicologia politica*, which publishes articles in Spanish and English. See Elovitz, "Special Theme: Publishing in Psychohistory," *Clio's Psyche*, Vol. 3, No. 1, June 1996, p. 3.

40. Runyan, in *Psychology and Historical Interpretation*, p. 30.

41. *Ibid.*, p. 31.

42. *Ibid.*, p. 32. Among the exceptions are the University of California, Los Angeles, Princeton University, Yale University, and MIT.

Chapter 2

Sigmund Freud: The Fundamentals of Psychoanalytic Theory

1. Formative Influences

The classical education that Freud received in the Gymnasium he attended in Vienna served as the indispensable foundation for his eventual discovery and formulation of psychoanalysis. It led Freud thereafter to range widely intellectually. His education provided him with a comprehension of the sources, the cultures, and the history of Western Civilization. One example, for instance, indicative of the cosmopolitan influence it had on him was his strong interest in languages. In this school, the Sperl Gymnasium, which he entered at the age of nine and graduated from at the age of seventeen, he learned Latin and Greek, and then went on to study English, French, Spanish, and Italian. In addition to his native German, he had learned Hebrew even before his entrance to the Gymnasium.[1] As for German, he became a master of this language, and in recognition of his felicitous writing style he received no less than the Goethe Prize for Literature in 1930. His works widely reflect his knowledge of the languages cited and the cultures they represented.

From his humanistic education Freud gained an appreciation of ancient history, a subject which fascinated him his entire life. When he became an adult and traveled to Athens and first saw the Acropolis, he exclaimed in wonderment, "So all this really *does* exist, just as we learnt in school!"[2] The Greek influence on Freud was profound, as much of the terminology of psychoanalysis demonstrates; a key concept being the Oedipal Complex which stems from Greek mythology and is the universal psychological condition. Another case in point, more sublime, is the Socratic adage "Know thyself," which Freud accepted and of which psychoanalysis is a fruition.

Even before Freud entered the Gymnasium, he showed a precocious interest in history and literature, as well as contemporary political events. Born in 1856 in Freiberg, which was then a part of the Austrian Habsburg Empire, Freud moved to Vienna with his family when he was four years old. One of the first books he read was Adolph Thiers' *Consulate and Empire*, and later, at the age of eight, he was reading Shakespeare. Freud was familiar with Napoleon's marshals, and one of his favorites was Masséna, Freud noting that they had the same birthday exactly one hundred years apart. Freud appreciated the achievements of the French Revolution of 1789 and the Napoleonic reforms in Europe. He was affected in his youth by their influence in the course of events which consequently developed in Europe, notably the Austro-Prussian War of 1866 and the Franco-Prussian War of 1870. Fourteen years old at the time of the Franco-Prussian War, Freud took a strong interest in this conflict by closely following its course, and thereafter directed his attention to the leading statesman of this period, Prince Otto von Bismarck.

Freud's sense of history developed early, and served many functions, whether satisfying his intellectual curiosity, answering humanistic concerns, or being a personal search for heroes. In his periods of adversity, and when trying to formulate or gain a hearing for psychoanalysis, the particular heroes Freud selected for himself were useful in helping him to overcome isolation and opposition. What is so significant about Freud's search for heroes, or models, is that it additionally led him to make seminal theoretical contributions in the area of the psychology of identification with a particular person, what is known as an ego ideal.[3] Freud developed this concept in his work "On Narcissism: An Introduction" in 1914, in which he explained that "Idealization is a process that concerns the *object*; by it that object, without any alteration in its nature, is aggrandized and exalted in the subject's mind."[4]

Freud had many ego ideals, and the figures he selected came from a variety of professions, including the military, medical, and political fields. In addition to the personages just mentioned, his other historical ego ideals were Oliver Cromwell, the Puritan leader during the English Civil War; Giuseppe Garibaldi, the Italian nationalist leader; and Ferdinand Lasalle, the German democratic socialist organizer, to name but a few.

While a young man, Freud had many career interests, but he made the decision to go to medical school after being inspired by a reading aloud of Goethe's essay on Nature at a public lecture. Actually, Freud had not been attracted to medicine as such, but Goethe's lecture, which dealt with comparative anatomy, presented "a romantic picture of nature as a beautiful and bountiful mother who allows her favorite children the privilege of exploring her secrets."[5] This prospect which attracted Freud, which was fortuitous, and as he himself was to write, "After forty-one years of medical activity, my self-knowledge tells me that I have never really been a doctor in the proper sense. I became a doctor through being compelled to deviate from my original purpose; and the triumph of my life lies in my having, after a long and roundabout journey, found my way back to my earliest path."[6]

Freud's self-appraisal is instructive because it is indicative of his feelings, his intentions, and is decisive for the originating of psychoanalysis. Again, in his own words:

> "In my youth I felt an overpowering need to understand something of the riddles of the world in which we live and perhaps even to contribute something to their solution. The most hopeful means of achieving this end seemed to me to enroll myself in the medical faculty; but even then I experimented—unsuccessfully—with zoology and chemistry, till at last under the influence of Brücke, the greatest authority who affected me more than any other in my whole life, I settled down to physiology. . . ."[7]

The conjuncture of Freud's ambition with his educational background, and the sequences of relationships he had at critical moments in his life and career with talented men of remarkable character, became the progression in Freud's ultimate realization of the development of psychoanalysis. Ernst Brücke, whom Freud credits for influencing him so much, was the Director of the Physiology Institute at the University of Vienna, and one of the leading physiologists of his time. Freud's association with Brücke lasted six years, which corresponds to the period that he spent in medical school. What is so noteworthy about Brücke is that he advocated the radical scientific concept of dynamic physiology, meaning that the principles of physics and chemistry could be applied to living organisms. Freud became so imbued with Brücke's instruction that he later assiduously tried to apply the master's theories to the study of psychological disorders in people. In this particular respect, Freud's initial attempts to do so were not productive, but he succeeded when he was "able to apply them empirically to mental phenomena while dispensing with any anatomical basis."[8] Ultimately, Freud created a dynamic psychology, demonstrating that scientific laws could be applied to man's personal development.

A most fortunate occurrence in Freud's life was his receiving a fellowship in 1885 to study in France with Jean-Martin Charcot, a foremost authority on diseases of the nervous system. Charcot's influence was to be decisive at this juncture in Freud's life, for Freud too had become interested in the phenomenon of hysteria. Charcot had established a large medical complex at the Salpêtrière in Paris, a treatment, research, and teaching center, for neurological disorders. So prominent was Charcot that his stature in French medicine was compared with that of Louis Pasteur. Charcot, in addition to studying the "hysterical crisis" (grande hystérie), also concerned himself with the manifestations of epileptic convulsions, the uses of hypnosis, and with the subject of traumatic paralysis. Charcot further demonstrated that paralysis varied in etiology, those stemming from mental trauma were unlike symptomatically from the organic ones. Indeed, Charcot was a pioneer and bold researcher in the study of the causes of mental disorders, achieving for it world-wide recognition and respect in his own lifetime.[9]

Freud was profoundly impressed by Charcot, writing exultingly at that time about Charcot's teaching to his fiancee that "I sometimes come out of his lectures as from Notre Dame, with an entirely new idea about perfection. . . . Whether the seed will ever bear fruit, I don't know but what I do know is that no other human being has ever affected me in the same way."[10] The significance of Charcot's medical discoveries, which served to advance Freud's thinking, is that he proved that hysteria was psychogenic in nature, that it was governed by a hidden mechanism, and that it was not unique to women.

During the many months that Freud was in Paris he was opportunely able to establish a personal relationship with Charcot, which was to profit both professionally. Freud's interest in Charcot's work was so marked, that, with Charcot's approval, Freud translated one of Charcot's books, *Leçons sur les maladies du système nerveux* into German. The German title was *Neue Vorlesungen über die Krankheiten des Nervensystems insbesondere über Hysterie* (New Lectures on the Diseases of the Nervous System, Particularly on Hysteria). Some years later, reflecting on the profound impression that Charcot's experiments had made on him, Freud noted about them that he came to recognize "the possibility that there could be powerful mental processes which nevertheless remained hidden from the consciousness of men."[11] Moreover, in honor of Charcot, Freud named his first-born son Jean Martin after the great man.

The last person to be considered as being of special significance to Freud will be Joseph Breuer, a Viennese physician of considerable standing. Unlike the other figures cited, he was a colleague to Freud, both having met in Brücke's Physiology Institute. They became close personal friends and collaborated professionally for many years. However, despite their mutual interests, and the benefits they derived from them, Breuer became estranged from Freud when Freud increasingly stressed the importance of sexuality as a cause of neurotic disturbances.

Nevertheless, the work that Freud and Breuer pioneered in was epochal in the annals of psychoanalysis. The key figure in their collaboration was a patient, a young woman twenty-one years of age, known in the psychoanalytic literature by the pseudonym "Miss Anna O." In effect, she was the first psychoanalytic patient. Moreover, she was remarkable, in that she was gifted intellectually.

Indicative of both her intelligence *and* the forces of her repression, although her native tongue was German and her treatment took place in Vienna, she lost the ability to speak German and resorted to speaking English. This caused Breuer to conduct her treatment in English. Even when asked to read aloud from a French or Italian book, she would immediately translate the text into English.[12]

Miss Anna O, who was suffering from hysteria, which included paralysis, loss of speech and sight, as well as other disturbances, had been attended to by Breuer, starting in 1880. Breuer used hypnosis, with some success, and in 1882 began to discuss and share this case with Freud. Freud then developed a strong interest in Miss Anna O's condition, to the extent that he became Breuer's collaborator in the writing up of the case. In time, many of Miss Anna O's symptoms were relieved, and although there is some question about her physical coordination and speech, she became able to work at a profession productively.

Breuer's and Freud's consultations resulted in the publication of a joint paper in 1893, "The Psychical Mechanism of Hysterical Phenomena," which was then followed by their book *Studies on Hysteria* in 1895.[13] This book marked the beginning of psychoanalysis, providing case histories and a theory of neurosis.

Certainly, there were many other men who influenced Freud, but they are beyond the scope of this study. The three persons mentioned above were important and decisive for Freud in that they were leading authorities in their fields, that he respected them, and that he was stimulated intellectually by them. This formative period was marked by Freud's increasing focus on the etiology and treatment of neurosis, culminating in his *magnum opus*, *The Interpretation of Dreams* in 1899.

2. Dreams

The cornerstone of psychoanalysis is the interpretation of dreams. Freud called the interpretation of dreams the "royal road to the unconscious." Freud's work *The Interpretation of Dreams* is a work of momentous importance, for by unlocking the riddle of dreams he discovered the mental working of the mind.

The meaning of dreams has been of interest to people in eras other than our own, dating from antiquity and until the nineteenth century, when Freud started to study dreams scientifically. As Freud shows, by providing an extensive review of the literature on dreams, especially in his first chapter of *The Interpretation of Dreams*, many peoples, including the Greeks and the Hebrews, sensed that dreams had a special significance. Whereas people in antiquity regarded dreams as a form of divine intervention, Aristotle believed that they should be the subject of psychological study. In the Old Testament there is the story of Joseph's interpretation of the Pharaoh's dream, this ability bringing him prestige and power. Historically, dreams have been a source of serious concern to people.[14]

In a comprehensive presentation, Freud discusses the technique by which dreams are interpreted, and their meaning revealed, but only the fundamental points can be touched on here. Essentially, Freud explains, dreams have intended meaning for the dreamer, and are not just responses to physical stimuli, as some researchers have held. The meaning of dreams, as a formula for them, is that every dream contains the fulfillment of a wish, often of a frustrated wish, that it is the guardian of sleep, that it is significant psychically, and that it shows that mental activity continues even in sleep.[15]

To underline this, with a humorous touch, Freud adds: "I do not know myself what animals dream of. But a proverb, to which my attention was drawn by one of my students, does claim to know. 'What,' asks the proverb, 'do geese dream of?' And it replies: 'Of maize.' The whole theory that dreams are wish fulfillments is contained in these two phrases."[16]

However, what is a wish in a dream is not what is necessarily pleasant or acceptable when awake, because originating as it does in the unconscious, the wish is often of an irrational nature, may be anti-social, and therefore unacceptable to the established moral standards of society.

There is a psychological determinism in dreams. The contents of a dream stem from early infantile experiences, but a particular dream may be evoked by a contemporary event, known as the *day residue*. This means that dreams are a regressive phenomena, but in terms of causality, provide access to unconscious strivings, memories, drives, and regressed experiences. Dreams are a necessary component of psychic life, revealing the true nature of unconscious mental activity.[17]

However, there are distortions in dreams, a form of mental censorship, because there is repression, many feelings being barred from consciousness. Freud illustrates this with the analogy of a political writer who has views that are unacceptable to the established authorities. Accordingly, his attempts to criticize will be suppressed, preferably before they are uttered or printed. This writer must therefore take the censorship into consideration, and if he persists in expressing himself, he will find that it behooves him to moderate his views. In this example, Freud says:

> According to the strength and sensitiveness of the consorship he finds himself compelled either to refrain from certain forms of attack, or to speak in allusions in place of direct references, or he must conceal his objectionable pronouncement beneath some apparently innocent disguise: for instance, he may describe a dispute between two Mandarins in the Middle Kingdom, when the people he really has in mind are officials in his own country. The stricter the censorship, the more far-reaching will be the disguise and the more ingenious too may be the means employed for putting the reader on the scent of the true meaning.[18]

A dream is made up of several components, one being called the *manifest dream*, what may or may not be recalled after waking; the various elements in it called the *manifest dream content*. The other part is the *latent dream content*, which contains the real meaning of the dream, and which can be interpreted via the process of *free association*. The transformation—or disguise—which occurs in the dream, to be sure unconsciously because it occurs in the state of sleep, from the manifest dream to the latent dream, is called the *dream work*. What is so striking about the manifest dream is that it appears to have little relation to logic and rationality.[19]

The dream work itself is based on a process of *condensation and displacement*. Condensation is the abridgment which occurs in the dream image, because the feelings about it are shameful or disagreeable, which is why the representations are brief and laconic. Freud points out that condensation is brought about by *omission*, that "the dream is not a faithful translation or a point-for-point projection of the dream-thoughts, but a highly incomplete and fragmentary version of them."[20]

In relation to the process of condensation, dreams are *overdetermined* in that the dream image is a convergence of many thoughts, feelings, and memories, and that they are personal to the dreamer.

As for the component of *displacement*, which occurs because there is censorship, it is that the essence of the dream is not apparent, and may be disguised by something which is trivial, if not forgotten, in the image of the dream.

The manner in which dream images are represented is highly significant; this process known as *symbolization*. In this process, thoughts in dreams are expressed in symbols, a universal and conceptual primal language. The kinds of symbols that appear in the dream are unique to the particular dreamer, but there are basic universal preoccupations and representations. Freud also points out that symbolism is not peculiar to dreams, and that the use of symbolism antedates psychoanalysis. To give but a few examples of symbolic representations in dreams, parents may appear as a king or a queen, or other exalted figure; a brother or sister as an animal. Water is associated with birth, whereas dying may be represented by the taking of a journey or travelling. Most symbols in dreams are of a sexual nature, and here the symbols are very numerous.[21] The number three is symbolic of the male genitalia, and the penis may be symbolized by a pole, an umbrella, a stick, or by weapons such as knives and guns, and also by pencils and hammers. Female genitalia may be represented by caves, rooms, pockets, and ships; churches and chapels are symbols of a woman.[22]

Lastly, the significance of the psychoanalytic interpretation of dreams has a value that transcends the individual's dream and has the wider application of being a bridge to the cultural realm. Freud notes, about the manifest contents of dreams, that "We very often find pictures and situations recalling familiar themes in fairy tales, legends, and myths. The interpretation of such dreams thus throws a light on the original interests which created these themes, though we must at the same time not forget, of course, the change in meaning by which this material has been affected in the course of time."[23] Citing the legend of the Labyrinth, Freud adds that it "can be recognized as a representation of anal birth: the twisting paths are the bowels and Ariadne's thread is the umbillical cord."[24]

3. The Development of Personality

Psychoanalysis is a part of general psychology, and can fundamentally be described as being a psychology of the unconscious, or a psychology of the depths. Freud's eminent contribution is that he fashioned the concept of the unconscious into a working tool. This concept, which has no anatomical location in the brain, is connected to a constellation of other psychoanalytic theories and methods. As has been noted, the language and interpretation of dreams is based on an understanding of the dynamics of the unconscious. The functioning of the unconscious process, however, is bound up with the conscious process as well, and the crux of mental well-being depends on the balance that exists between these two processes.[25] To illustrate this point, Freud compared the proportions of consciousness to unconsciousness to that of an iceberg. Just as most of the iceberg is hidden from sight, except the tip of it, so most of the unconscious is hidden, and it is the submerged part which is not only the greater portion but the most important and directing one. It is this discovery that was such a blow to man's narcissism. Man could no longer be considered the master of his own mind, and there were unconscious processes over which he exercised little or no control and which were the determining ones in really directing his behavior. And this matter is still the issue of contention for the traditional historians who persist in looking only for the rational, the logical, and the conscious factors in human actions.

It was Freud's interest in the unconscious processes, with its myriad manifestations, and with the causes of neurosis, that led him to consider the individual's early emotional development. The ultimate emotional maturation of an adult, or lack of it, he found to stem from the individual's early relationships. Neurosis in adult life, as well as in childhood, stem from emotional disturbances, and these take on an unconscious component. What is so significant in the theoretical framework that Freud elaborated is that he discerned continuity in mental life, from childhood to adulthood, concluding that the first few years of life are therefore the most important ones. Of predominant influence in this development is the way the parents deal with the child's growing sexual impulses, how they deal with and channel the instinctual conflicts, and in what manner the child is socialized. These will determine his emotional adjustment and his ability to take a positive part in society.[26]

Considering the first few years of life of crucial importance, Freud delineated the development in this period, noting that there were various stages to it, to which he gave the classification of oral, anal, phallic, and oedipal. These stages, which are marked by manifestations of sexual urges, are referred to in their entirety as the psychosexual development. In conjunction with this designation, which represents the psychological and the sexual, and whose unfolding is bound up with the personal drives, Freud postulated the libido theory. This process he explained as being analogous to hunger, because "'libido' as the name of the force (in this case that of the sexual instinct, as in the case of hunger that of the nutritive instinct) by which the instinct manifests itself."[27] In this theory, libido is specifically sexual energy, it is the major source of psychic energy.

The first stage of life in this psychosexual developmental process is the oral one. For the infant, at this time, the mouth is the focal point of its existence. This period, which is approximately the first year and a half of life, is the most critical because the infant is so helpless, so immature, and therefore so dependent on the significant adults, namely the mother or parents. The gratifications of its needs, or the lessening of intense frustration, are at this time primarily oral, as the sucking reflexes are so marked. The mouth, the lips and tongue are sources of pleasure and need, and taken together are an area of the body which is an *erotogenic zone*.[28]

However, satisfying the infant's needs extends beyond the oral cavity, and is dependent on the total care and well-being of the neonate. With the act of being fed, the experiences of warmth, affection, and security are of cardinal importance. The infant is initially totally self-centered, not able to differentiate between itself and the mothering figure, and not concerned with reality, yet having intense needs. Accordingly, the mother's attitude is paramount in this relationship, and unless the infant feels loved, it will not develop into a loving person. If the frustrations and neglect are greater than the satisfactions, then depression will ensue, and, depending on the severity, affect the individual for life. The individual's later personal attitude toward life, whether he is optimistic or pessimistic, will stem from this phase, and will have become unconscious.

To be sure, hereditary characteristics play a role, and affect temperament and constitution, but the mother's attitude toward the child establishes a pattern of interaction which is decisive for future emotional growth and well-being. Therefore, although the mouth is the focal area in the oral stage, there is also a constellation of needs the infant has, which include dependency, immaturity, and a requirement of maternal affection. It is at this time then that the foundations of the individual's personality are laid, and, however they are established, they are profound and lasting.[29]

The second period, which is called the anal phase, is quite different from the oral period, because whereas no demands were placed on the infant in the first one, social demands are introduced in the second. This period, which lasts from approximately eighteen months to three years of age, is marked by attempts to socialize the child, to prepare him to accept the standards of deportment of his environment. What seems mundane is actually a critical matter, for the child develops sphincter control at this time, and the manner his parents use to have the child evacuate his bowels is of utmost significance to the child. To the toddler, his feces are precious, regarded as a gift from him to his parents. However, the kind of resolution there is of the oral period depends on the attitudes of the parents, that is whether they are harsh and critical or tolerant and kindly; the child will react in accordance to the degree of satisfaction established in his relationship with them. If his behavior is met with approval, most likely he will try to please the parents, but if the evacuation of his bowels becomes a source of contention, a battleground, then he will resist or engage in rebellious behavior. Certain character traits can emerge in adulthood which stem from this period because of the manner in which the child learned to channel his aggressive and sadistic impulses, these being stubbornness and frugality if this phase was a contested one, or generosity and positive socialization if it was a benign one. According to Freud, "productivity" on the toilet is the prototype of productivity in adulthood. Although sphincter control is the focal area in what is called the anal period, the nature of the development must be considered in the context of the total relationship of the child to the parent. As Freud succinctly puts it:

> It is here for the first time that they encounter the external world as an inhibiting power, hostile to their desire for pleasure, and have a glimpse of later conflicts both external and internal. An infant must

not produce his excreta at whatever moment he chooses, but when other people decide that he shall. In order to induce him to forgo these sources of pleasure, he is told that everything that has to do with these functions is improper and must be kept secret. This is where he is first obliged to exchange pleasure for social respectability. To begin with, his attitude to his excreta themselves is quite different. He feels no disgust at his faeces, values them as a portion of his own body with which he will not readily part, and makes use of them as his first 'gift', to distinguish people whom he values especially highly.[30]

The third period is the phallic phase, which becomes a precursor of the final form taken by sexual life. It comes at about age two and a half and lasts till approximately three and a half. At this time, distinctions begin to appear between boys and girls, in that for the boys, concern with their genitals take on a preeminent role; hence this phase is named after the phallus. These anatomical differences, Freud says, cause the genders to have different psychic histories. Whereas both sexes explore their own bodies, giving them a primary intellectual interest, both start to realize that one sex does and the other sex does not have a penis. This will cause their paths to diverge. To use Freud's own words, which have become the classical formulation of the divergent development of the sexes, he states:

> The boy enters the Oedipus phase; he begins to manipulate his penis and simultaneously has phantasies of carrying out some sort of activity with it in relation to his mother, till, owing to the combined effect of a threat of castration and the sight of the absence of a penis in females, he experiences the greatest trauma of his life and this introduces the period of latency with all its consequences. The girl, after vainly attempting to do the same as the boy, comes to recognize her lack of a penis or rather the inferiority of her clitoris, with permanent effects on the development of her character; as a result of this first disappointment in rivalry, she often begins by turning away altogether from sexual life.[31]

Without completely giving up the oral and anal wishes from the earlier stages, the child's main impulses now start to be directed toward forming object relations, having recognized that the self is separate from other individuals. At the start of the oedipal period, children of both genders generally have their strongest object relation with their mother. This strong emotional bond means that the mother is more highly cathected than any other person, but with the start of the Oedipal phase this starts to diminish, and as this occurs, the preference for the father increases. However, the daughter's love for her father at this time is less ambiguous than it is for her mother, from whom she has to diminish her emotional attachment. For the boy, the Oedipal period is marked by rivalry with the father because he competes with him for the mother. Freud took this concept from the Greek legend of King Oedipus, who was destined to kill his father and marry his mother. The boy, having incestuous desires toward his mother, fears the more powerful father, a feeling that is then translated, unconsciously, into the fear of castration, as girls apparently seem to be examples of this. The boy eventually gives up this conflict with his father by abandoning his desire for his mother, and with this occurrence fear of castration becomes lessened as concomitantly the boy instead starts to identify with the father. For the girl, the Oedipal situation is a little more complicated. In her case the issue over castration takes the form of unconscious rage at her mother for having permitted her to be born thus, resulting in her having penis envy. She then turns to her father as the principal object of love, because he has the organ she is lacking, but with whom the incestuous wishes will also be frustrated. The oedipal conflict for the woman will be resolved when she ultimately turns to a man, not her father, marries, and has a child.[32]

These phases taken together, which last over roughly the first five years of life, may be characterized as being marked by increasing anxieties and frustrations—though also generally by much learning and satisfactions—and the inability to have sexually the desired objects of love. To be sure, these conflicts are repressed, and amnesia accompanies this period into adult life. Again, there is a resolution inasmuch as there is renunciation and substitutes are found, later in adult life. And there is a resolution to this period when the *genital stage* is achieved, when gratification occurs with someone of the opposite sex who is not a member of the family.

If the resolutions of the various phases are not successful, if the attitude of the parents was harsh and critical, or if there was abandonment, then the basis will have been prepared for later neurosis, psychosis, and a host of other mental disturbances. On the other hand, if the parents were tolerant, kindly, and loving, then the child will have been prepared for adaptation with society. Again, if the resolution of the oedipal phase is successful, the boy will give up his desire for his mother, end the competition he has with the father, and resort to *identification* with him, which means wanting to be a man just like him. The girl will likewise give up her desire for her father and identify with the femaleness of her mother, though an ambiguity in feelings toward her will persist. A common pathology which can result from the way this period is met, if frustration was excessive, and which is a common psychological problem, is that in the case of men there may be tendencies to be passive in their relationship with other men, and for women that they will act and feel competitive with men.[33]

4. The Psychical Apparatus

In still another way, the development of personality can be considered from the process of the mental apparatus, named the structural hypothesis, which consists of the systems *id, ego,* and *superego.* In the mentally healthy person, these systems are largely in harmony with each other, enabling the individual to function well psychically. In the neurotic person, there is a conflict, which is unconscious, between the *ego* and the *id,* the genesis of it stemming from the childhood situation.

To give these agencies, or "psychical provinces" as Freud called them, a brief introductory definition, the *id* may be described as being essentially the instinct, and not concerned with reality; the ego is concerned with reality, is the rational aspect of thought, and mediates between the person and his environment; and the superego is the conscience, the psychic representative of the parents, teachers, and respected social figures.

Although these "provinces" have quite different functions, or conflicting tendencies within the individual, Freud makes the proposition that the id and the superego have one thing in common, namely that "they both represent the influence of the past—the id the influence of heredity, the super-ego the influence, essentially, of what is taken over from other people—whereas the ego is principally determined by the individual's own experiences, that is by accidental and contemporary events."[34]

The id, which Freud calls the "seething cauldron of emotions," concerned with the drives, or the instincts, is the motivating force of all activity and represents the somatic demands on the mind. The id is the reservoir of the wishes and impulses, and strives for discharge, or satisfaction. The newborn infant, for example, is largely dominated by the id, being unconcerned with reality or with the needs of others, but wants its needs and frustrations to be satisfied immediately.

As the infant grows and matures, the ego develops, serving as an adaptive agency. The ego is concerned with reality, and is able to tolerate delays and frustrations. The ego is the executive apparatus in the mind, acting as mediator between the person's biological and psychic needs and the external world. In other words, whereas the id is concerned with the *pleasure principle*, the ego is concerned with the *reality principle*.[35] As the child develops, paradoxically, he is able to learn and to acquire a strong ego only if he experiences and encounters a degree of frustration, which teaches him to temper his unrealistic expectations.

Ultimate emotional maturity, which has the hallmarks of autonomy and independence, depends to a large degree on the psychological environment in which the child was raised, the parents being the first models who conveyed to the child their sense of reality of society.

In regard to the child's completion of the mental development, the superego is the last of the psychic agencies to be acquired, beginning at approximately three years of age, but forming for several more years. At this time too, as the superego is being formed, the Oedipus complex is being resolved. The superego represents the ideals, the standards, the values, and the prohibitions of the parents and the culture, and the child's accepting, or internalizing, them makes it possible for him to eventually take his place in civilized society. To a large extent, the superego, for both sexes, retains primarily the character of the father, of authority, and is considered to be the higher nature of man. The superego, as the heir of the parents, can also be a source of reassurance and comfort, not just punishment and guilt, and to that extent give the individual a positive self-esteem.[36]

The superego, as it develops in childhood, originates in the child's dependence on the responsible adults, from whom he seeks and needs approval, and from whom he tries to avoid punishment. By employing a system of rewards and punishments, parents teach the child to accept their own standards—which may or may not correspond to the accepted standards of society—and in this way mold and direct the child's conscience. Eventually, these standards will be internalized so that the individual, as he grows out of childhood, will not depend on external authority, but will feel personal satisfaction—or guilt—depending on the extent that he follows the standards of the society.

To be sure, there are many exceptions, and many have a poorly formed superego, hence the need for policemen. Furthermore, there is a wide range of behavior, for some individuals have a superego that is too harsh, and even crippling, whereas others have minimal feelings of guilt, disregarding the moral standards of society to the point of violating them and harming others without compunction. The latter is a description of the psychopathic person.

A general formulation of a neurotic conflict, to use the above sets of psychic reaction patterns, is that the conflict takes place between the ego and the id. As for psychosis, that occurs when there is a similar disturbance, but it is between the ego and the external world.[37]

As this brief synopsis of psychoanalytic theory has shown, psychoanalysis offers a radical and different approach to the understanding of man, and, moreover, to understanding the forces of human irrationality. Like other radical intellectual innovations, which are at first resented, today it is much more accepted, and continues to expand. The very opposition—or resistance—can be better understood by using psychoanalytic insights.[38] Freud pointed out the reasons for this as stemming from defenses developed in childhood, because at that time new ideas threatened one's feelings of importance or aroused unconscious feeling of insecurity, which stemmed from feelings of helplessness. Change, even when it is for the better, is not readily accepted.[39]

Psychoanalysis has provided a new dimension to our understanding of man that is more insightful, more extensive, and more humane than former ideas. And indeed, there is now a substantial body of clinical evidence and scholarship which supports the validity of psychoanalytic theories and method of treatments.[40]

5. Philosophy of History

Although Freud did not develop a doctrine which could formally be called a philosophy of history, there is, in the exposition of his psychoanalytic theories, a distinctive and presageful philosophy of history. And Freud expressed the opinion that psychoanalysis "is incapable of creating a *Weltanschauung* of its own. It does not need one; it is a part of science and can adhere to the scientific *Weltanschauung*."[41] Nevertheless, despite Freud's intentions, psychoanalysis decidedly has a point of view. First of all psychoanalysis has a vision of man which is not prescriptive nor moralistic, but seeks to understand him in order to improve the human condition. Psychoanalysis is in the tradition of the thinking of the Eighteenth Century Enlightenment, and by being secular eschews a teleological interpretation of man's role in the world.

Intrinsically, psychoanalysis is itself historical, taking a genetic, or developmental, approach first to the study and understanding of the individual and then of society, as a reading of Freud's works make abundantly clear. Consistent with this approach was Freud's strong personal interest in history, and as his voluminous writings amply demonstrate, he had an excellent knowledge of the past, making frequent well-informed observations and statements on numerous historical personages and events. Underlining this attitude, he once quipped, "only a good for nothing is not interested in the past."[42] Among the many credits that Freud holds, one of them is that he was the first psychohistorian.

Freud's philosophy of history can be gathered from many of his works, but there are some studies that are differentiated by their attention to societal and group developments. There is the estimable *Totem and Taboo*, in which he posits the theory of the primal horde, and *Beyond the Pleasure Principle*, in which he discusses the nature of man's aggressive drives. Freud's philosophy of history is further developed in such later works as *Group Psychology and the Analysis of the Ego*, in which he provides insight into the relationship that exists between a group and its leader. In *The Future of an Illusion*, he examines the role of religion, and he deals with this subject also in *Civilization and its Discontents*, one of his last books, written nearly at the end of his life. *Civilization and its Discontents* is an especially reflective work, a distillation of many of his theories and insights, a piece that may be considered the summation and most specific expression of Freud's philosophy of history. In the works just cited, although the contents differ, there is a common denominator to them—containing a fundamental principle of Freud's philosophy of history—and this is that all societies are aware of human aggression, and therefore they try to curb their aggressive drives.

It follows therefore, that it is precisely because of aggressiveness in people that laws, or curbs, came into being which then enabled us to have civilization. Society recognizes this well, whereby there are so many injunctions against aggressive behavior. This is epitomized, for instance, by the Ten Commandments, reinforced by many religious precepts, and advanced in the ideal "Thou shalt love thy neighbor as thyself." The aim here, as Freud explains in *Civilization and its Discontents*, is to establish control over the individual by developing in him a sense of conscience, so that ultimately his aggressiveness will be self-controlled through feelings of guilt.[43]

Freud personally believed that it was necessary to curb and channel aggression. He illustrated the many ways that societies had of coping with this by studying the area of social psychology. He found that this could be accomplished by uniting a group in love, thereby directing its aggressiveness toward another group. For instance, he gives the examples of the Spaniards and the Portuguese feuding with and ridiculing each other, the English with the Scotch, and the North Germans with the South Germans. He also cites nationalism as fulfilling this purpose, on other occasions the promoting of anti-Semitism, and the persecuting of the bourgeoisie in Communist Russia.[44]

In *Totem and Taboo*, Freud gives his views on the origin and evolution of man, starting from the primitive state and culminating in the establishment of civilization. The story of this development and change is a grim one, for it appears that its achievement came about through violence and murder. The thesis of this work is that in prehistoric times, in a given tribe, or group, there was a powerful male, the father, who was tyrannical, and who would gratify his instinctual impulses by taking all the women in the community for himself. The sons, resenting this, therefore banded together and killed the powerful tyrannical father. But after committing this murder, they felt guilty, which led to the development of conscience, the repression of aggression, and hence made civilization possible. Freud deduced that in all societies human beings have conflicts, that the unconscious processes are universal, and that the prototypic rivalry in the tribal horde between the sons and the father—which is similar to that shown in certain neurotics—is demonstrated in the concept known as the Oedipus complex. There is ambiguity about whether or not Freud meant this postulation to have been a literal one, or a fantasied one. Perhaps it is a psychic reality, an article of faith, rather than an historical reality. However, consistent with unconscious ambivalence, Freud contends that "It is not really a decisive matter whether one has killed one's father or abstained from the deed; one must feel guilty in either case, for guilt is the expression of the conflict of ambivalence, the eternal struggle between Eros and the destructive or death instinct."[45]

In *Totem and Taboo*, Freud has a lengthy discussion on the emotional attitude toward rulers, giving a range of examples from the kings of England to the mikado of Japan. Freud notes that much is expected of rulers, and that they are privileged, but that "alongside of the veneration, and indeed idolization felt towards them, there is in the unconscious an opposing current of intense hostility; that, in fact, as we expected, we are faced by a situation of emotional ambivalence. The distrust which provides one of the unmistakable elements in kingly taboos would thus be another, more direct, expression of the same unconscious hostility."[46] What is so significant about this observation is that the attitudes described here are very similar to the ones that Freud finds are the child's complex of emotions toward his father. These insights led Freud to a conclusion which is paramount in the psychoanalytic approach to the development of civilization, and which indeed is based on renunciation and sublimation, and that is the central issue designated as the Oedipus complex. On this point, Freud is emphatic, and he states:

I should like to insist that its outcome shows that the beginnings of religion, morals, society and art converge in the Oedipus complex. This is in complete agreement with the psychoanalytic finding that the same complex constitutes the nucleus of all neuroses, so far as our present knowledge goes. It seems to me a most surprising discovery that the problems of social psychology, too, should prove soluble on the basis of one single concrete point—man's relation to his father. It is even possible that yet another psychological problem belongs in this same connection. I have often had occasion to point out that emotional ambivalence in the proper sense of the term—that is, the simultaneous existence of love and hate towards the same object—lies at the root of many important cultural institutions.[47]

Freud's psychoanalytic *Weltanschauung*, despite his scientific intentions, did bring him into an adversarial position in regard to the existing ideologies, whether they were political or religious.

Ultimately, Freud did take political positions, even if they were done in a scholarly context. To be sure, Freud took notice of Marxism, demonstrated a grasp of it, but had serious misgivings about it. Psychoanalysis and Marxism differ decidedly in their philosophies of history, but it is instructive to compare these two systems because they both deal with the issue of aggression, though they have different perspectives on it.[48] Karl Marx's view on the causes of aggression, in recognition of its pervasiveness in history, is that it has always existed because it is endemic to the class structure of society. The issue of class struggle is a fundamental tenet of Marxism, but aggression will cease when capitalism is vanquished by socialism, in the course and aftermath of a violent revolution. And aggression stems from the resistance to economic exploitation of one class by another. With this premise, Freud disagreed because he felt that regardless of social systems there will be conflicts, and there will always be an issue about how to control and direct the aggressive instinctual drives of people. Freud makes many perceptive observations on Marx and Marxism, and though giving serious consideration to Marxism, philosophically and psychologically he cannot accept it. However, recognizing that Marxism does have a wide appeal, he comments on the reasons for this, observing that:

The strength of Marxism clearly lies not in its view of history or the prophecies of the future that are based on it, but in its sagacious indication of the decisive influence which the economic circumstances of men have upon their intellectual, ethical and artistic attitudes. A number of connections and implications were thus uncovered, which had previously been almost totally overlooked.[49]

Even though Freud allows this acknowledgment, he disagrees with the essence of Marxism, adding:

But it cannot be assumed that economic motives are the only ones that determine the behaviour of human beings in society. The undoubted fact that different individuals, races and nations behave differently under the same economic conditions is alone enough to show that economic motives are not the sole dominating factors.[50]

This particular observation is noteworthy not just because of its incisive critique of Marxism, but because of what emerges as a dialectic with Marxism, Freud takes what is truly a historical approach to the understanding of different peoples and culture. It is the classical admonition to the historian. Freud's precept stands as a reply to the critics of psychoanalysis who contend that psychoanalysis is not historical, or is ahistorical. Additionally, in his critique of Marxism, by taking psychology into consideration, Freud writes like a psychohistorian, stating that:

It is altogether incomprehensible how psychological factors can be overlooked where what is in question are the reactions of living human beings; for not only were these reactions concerned in establishing the economic conditions, but even under the domination of those conditions men can only bring their original instinctual impulses into play—their self-preservative instinct, their aggressiveness, their need to be loved, their drive towards obtaining pleasure and avoiding unpleasure.[51]

In still another way, which delineates Freud's views on history, and is contrary to Marx's views, is Freud's interpretation on the role of the individual in history. Whereas for Marx the individual person acts essentially in accordance with his class interests and is directed by vast impersonal economic developments, Freud holds that one individual can exert great personal influence and leadership, and by his action on the masses can make a difference in history. On the issue of leadership, and collective at that, Marx at best allows that there is a need for a Communist Party to lead the workers in revolutionary activity. To this, the Freudian reply is that it is erroneous to assume that men act out of material needs when in actuality they act out of psychic needs. Indeed, the great man is necessary in order to bring about progress for the group.[52]

As for the application of Marxism in the Soviet Union, and the course of the Russian Revolution, Freud was both approving and critical. Writing this in the early 1930s, Freud approved of what he felt was an attempt to create a better life, what he calls a "tremendous experiment of producing a new order of this kind is actually being carried out in Russia."[53] Although noting that the Russian Revolution, "—in spite of all its disagreeable details—seems none the less like the message of a better future," Freud does wonder how this "experiment will turn out."[54] And he also adds that the future perhaps "will show that the experiment was undertaken prematurely, that a sweeping alteration of the social order has little prospect of success until new discoveries have increased our control over the forces of Nature and so made easier the satisfaction of our needs."[55] In light of the dissolution of the Soviet Union, Freud's skepticism is prescient indeed.

Freud's most trenchant criticism about the way Marxism was practiced in the Soviet Union, and which by extension was also a criticism of religion, is the following observation:

> Theoretical Marxism, as realized in Russian Bolshevism, has acquired the energy and the self-contained and exclusive character of a *Weltanschauung*, but at the same time an uncanny likeness to what it is fighting against. Though originally a portion of science and built up, in its implementation upon science and technology, it has created a prohibition of thought which is just as ruthless as was that of religion in the past. Any critical examination of Marxist theory is forbidden, doubts of its correctness are punished in the same way as heresy was once punished by the Catholic Church. The writings of Marx have taken the place of the Bible and the Koran as a source of revelation, though they would seem to be no more free from contradictions and obscurities than those other sacred books.[56]

It should be noted that the field of psychoanalysis was unacceptable to the Soviet regime, that it was officially denounced, and was largely banned for being what was considered to be an ideological instrument fostered by the bourgeoisie.[57]

As had been indicated, Freud was critical of religion, but he examined it in an historical manner the same way he did any other expression of human thought. To touch on this as an aside, because it impinges on the present subject, is Freud's view on religion. It will suffice to note how Freud goes to the core of it by raising a philosophical question which is preeminent to religion, and this is the question of what is the purpose of life. Freud advances that this question has never received a satisfactory answer, if it should be answered at all. Nevertheless, he replies that this question can be answered by looking at how people behave, because in their behavior they demonstrate that "They strive after happiness; they want to become happy and to remain so."[58] To Freud, the motivating factors for all human activities are the "two confluent goals of utility and a yield of pleasure."[59]

In sum, by citing what in Freud's own words may be considered to be a précis of his philosophy of history, is his perception that "the events of human history, the interactions between human nature, cultural development and the precipitates of primaeval experiences (the most prominent example of which is religion) are no more than a reflection of the dynamic conflicts between the ego, the id, and the super-ego, which psychoanalysis studies in the individual—are the very same processes repeated upon a wider stage."[60]

That Freud's works are imbued with philosophical concepts and that psychoanalysis may be considered a philosophical system is hardly a coincidence.[61] Already in his youth, when Freud attended the gymnasium in Vienna, he had a keen interest in philosophy. There is an important correspondence that he had with Eduard Silberstein, his good friend, (that is now available in the Freud Archives, located in the Library of Congress) that reveals his penchant for the field.[62] The list of philosophers Freud read and discussed with Silberstein is long indeed, but the most noted ones are Comte, Descartes, Herbart, Hume, Feuerbach, Kant, Mill and Spinoza.[63]

When Freud attended the University of Vienna, even though he was a medical student, he took courses with, and came under the influence of Professor Franz Brentano, a noted philosopher. The philosophers who most influenced Freud, or that he found most inspiring in the sense that they would serve as identificatory models were, in addition to Brentano, Ludwig Feuerbach and Arthur Schopenhauer. With regard to developing psychoanalysis, it appears that Freud was introduced to the concept of the unconscious from his contact with Brentano. Personally, Freud held Brentano in high esteem, both for his brilliance and his iconoclasm.[64]

In a letter of November 8, 1874, to Silberstein, regarding Brentano and philosophy, Freud exclaimed "höre und staune!" (listen and be amazed), about what he is learning.[65] Brentano, Freud described as being "ein prächtiger mensch" (a marvelous human being).[66] In another letter to Silberstein, Freud stated that Brentano was an "idealer mensch"[67] (an ideal human being). Indeed, nineteen years old at the time, Freud was considering becoming a philosopher and took many courses with Brentano, from 1874 to 1876. The course titles were: "Readings of philosophic writings," "logic", and "The Philosophy of Aristotte."[68] Not only did Freud take courses with Brentano, but he eventually met him socially as well, because he had written to Brentano asking him to clarify some philosophical questions he had. Freud observed that Brentano was an independent principled thinker and quite critical of the major philosophers, including Kant. A philosopher Brentano recommended was Comte.[69] Freud was particularly impressed by Brentano, and contemporaries described Brentano as being a charismatic person, with a commanding personality, brilliant and witty.[70] Significantly, Brentano had been a Dominican priest, but he resigned from the priesthood in 1873 because he opposed the promulgation of papal infallibility, adopted in 1870. On another personal note which demonstrated Brentano's own high regard for Freud is his recommendation to Theodor Gomperz, a noted professor of classical philosophy at the University of Vienna and the editor of the collected works of John Stuart Mill, that Freud be the translator of a volume in the series on the work of Mill from English into German. Freud then translated and wrote the twelfth volume in this German language series. Both Brentano and Freud had a high regard for Mill.[71] Brentano's own great work, *Psychology from an Empirical Standpoint* (1874), is seminal in that it served to lay the foundation for phenomenology and Gestalt psychology.[72]

Another philosopher who figures prominently in Freud's correspondence with Silberstein is Ludwig Feuerbach (1804–

1872), a major nineteenth century philosopher who wrote critical works on religion. Not only was Freud influenced by Feuerbach, but so were Karl Marx and Friedrich Engels, indicative of Feuerbach's radicalism. Other intellectuals who were influenced by Feuerbach were Kierkegaard, Nietzsche, Troeltsch, Berdyaev, Heidegger and Sartre.[73] Freud, who knew Feuerbach only from his works, described him to his friend in superlative terms. He wrote to Silberstein that Feuerbach was a philosopher "denn ich unter allen philosopher am höchsten verehre und bewonder"[74] (one who I, more than any other philosopher, revere and admire). Feuerbach's ideas found an echo in Freud's *The Future of an Illusion*, which is an essay by him critiquing religion from a psychoanalytic point of view,[75] and Feuerbach seems to have been a precursor for Freud's ideas in the realm of dream interpretation.[76] Feuerbach also contributed to pointing Freud toward the study of psychology. One of Feuerbach's major works is *Das Wesen des Christentums*[77] (The Essence of Christianity).

In Freud's works, namely the *Standard Edition*, there are numerous references to Arthur Schopenhauer (1788-1860), another noted nineteenth century German philosopher. Freud held Schopenhauer in high regard, as demonstrated by the numerous favorable comments he makes about him. Ernest Jones, too, comments on Freud's approbatory view of Schopenhauer. In a discussion of men Freud considered outstanding, Jones listed them as follows: "Goethe, Kant, Voltaire, Darwin, Schopenhauer, Nietzsche."[78] Not only does this list include Schopenhauer, but this group consists mostly of philosophers. Schopenhauer's renowned work is *Die Welt als Wille und Vorstellung* (The World as Will and Representation), and it is significant here because in that work the author gives sexuality a central position in his philosophy.[79] There are many other similarities between Schopenhauer's philosophy and psychoanalysis, namely, a recognition that people have primitive instinctual and egotistic drives, that they tend to be unconscious, and that these expressions cause conflicts for society.[80] In Freud's "A Difficulty in the Path of Psychoanalysis", he pays tribute to Schopenhauer for being a precursor in developing the concept of the unconscious. Regarding the recognition of mental process, Freud lauds Schopenhauer, noting: "It was not psychoanalysis, however, let us hasten to add, which took this step. There are famous philosophers who may be cited as forerunners—above all the great thinker Schopenhauer, whose unconscious 'will' is equivalent to the mental instincts of psychoanalysis."[81] Freud adds, "It was this same thinker, moreover, who in words of unforgettable impressiveness admonished mankind of the importance, still so greatly under-estimated by it, of its sexual craving."[82]

Although Freud commended Schopenhauer and others for being precursors of psychoanalysis, and that philosophy and literature had shown awareness of the unconscious, he also proclaimed that "Psychoanalysis has seized upon the concept, has taken it seriously and has given it a fresh content."[83] To be sure, it was psychoanalysis that converted the concept into scientific usage. In all, Freud's grounding in philosophy was profound, pervasive, and of paramount importance to him, even if at times he came to exhibit a skepticism toward it. In his mature years, Freud distanced himself from the field of philosophy. Nevertheless, in so many of his works, Freud grapples with philosophical issues. One of his last works, *Civilization and its Discontents*, written at the end of his life, is a summary of his theories, but, as stated above, also a philosophical treatise. In this essay, Freud raises—and addresses—the fundamental philosophical question—what is the purpose of life?[84]

Freud was the heir of many influences, but to study the many philosophers he learned from—and emulated—it should be noted just how much psychoanalysis is indebted to and rests on German nineteenth century philosophy. Pertinently, in 1936 a committee formed to celebrate Freud's eightieth birthday included Thomas Mann, Romain Rolland, Jules Romains, H.G. Wells, Virginia Woolf, and Stefan Zweig. They wrote to Freud congratulating him on his birthday—and honoring him for his discoveries and achievements. In what they considered to be the highest praise, they compared Freud to philosophers. Just as Nietzsche had praised Schopenhauer, so the committee members called Freud "ein Mann mit erzenem Blick" (a man with a penetrating eye).[85]

Notes

1. Ernest Jones, *The Life and Work of Sigmund Freud*, Vol. I, Basic Books, 1955, p. 21.
2. Sigmund Freud, "A Disturbance of Memory on the Acropolis," *Standard Edition*, Vol. 22, The Hogarth Press, 1964, p. 241.
3. Jacques Szaluta, "Freud's Ego Ideals: A Study of Admired Modern Historical Personages," *Journal of the American Psychoanalytic Association*, Vol. 31, 1983, *passim*.
4. Freud, "On Narcissism: An Introduction," *S.E.*, Vol. 14, 1957, p. 94.
5. Jones, *Freud*, Vol. I. p. 29.
6. *Ibid.*, p. 28.
7. *Ibid.*, p. 29.
8. *Ibid.*, p. 45.
9. Frank J. Sulloway, *Freud, Biologist of the Mind*, Basic Books, 1979, p. 28.
10. *Ibid.*, p. 31.
11. *Ibid.*, p. 32.
12. Jones, *Freud*, Vol. I. p. 224.
13. Joseph Breuer and Sigmund Freud, "Studies on Hysteria," *S.E.*, Vol. 2, 1955.
14. Freud, "The Interpretations of Dreams," *S.E.*, Vol. 4, 1953, pp. 96-100.
15. *Ibid.*, pp. 96-121.
16. *Ibid.*, pp. 96-132.
17. *Ibid.*, p. 166.
18. *Ibid.*, p. 142. For an exhaustive examination of Freud's own dreams, as they appear in *The Interpretation of Dreams*, see Alexander Grinstein, *On Sigmund Freud's Dreams*, International Universities Press, 1979.
19. Charles Brenner, *An Elementary Textbook of Psychoanalysis*, Anchor, 1974, pp. 149-151.
20. Freud, "Interpretation of Dreams," *S.E.*, Vol. 4, 1953, p. 281.

21. See for example, Jacques Szaluta, "Freud on Bismarck: Hanns Sachs' Interpretation of a Dream," *American Imago*, Vol. 37, 1980, pp. 215-227.

22. Leon L. Altman, *The Dream in Psychoanalysis*, International Universities Press, 1975 Alexander Grinstein, *Freud's Rules of Dream Interpretation*, International Universities Press, 1983.

23. Freud, "New Introductory Lectures on Psychoanalysis," *S.E.*, Vol. 22, 1964, p. 25.

24. *Ibid.*

25. Reuben Fine, *The Development of Freud's Thought*, Jason Aronson, 1973, pp. 35-38.

26. Hans H. Strupp, *Freud and Modern Psychoanalysis*, Barron's, 1967, pp. 21-26.

27. Freud, "Introductory Lectures on Psychoanalysis," *S.E.*, Vol. 16, 1963, p. 313.

28. *Ibid.*, pp. 313-314.

29. Freud, "Three Essays on Sexuality," *S.E.* Vol. 7, 1953, pp. 179-185.

30. Freud, "Introductory Lectures," *S.E.*, Vol. 16, 1963, p. 315.

31. Freud, "An Outline of Psychoanalysis," *S.E.*, Vol. 23, 1964, p. 155.

32. Freud, "Three Essays," *S.E.*, Vol. 7, 1953, pp. 195, 219-224.

33. *Ibid.*, pp. 197-206; Freud, "'A Child is Being Beaten': A Contribution to the Study of the Origins of Sexual Perversions," *S.E.*, Vol. 17, 1973, pp. 186-204.

34. Freud, "An Outline of Psychoanalysis," *S.E.*, Vol. 23, 1964, p. 147.

35. Freud, "New Introductory Lectures," *S.E.*, Vol. 22, 1964, pp. 73-78.

36. Otto Fenichel, *The Psychoanalytic Theory of Neurosis*, Norton, 1945, pp. 103-109.

37. Freud, "Neurosis and Psychosis," *S.E.*, Vol. 19, 1961, p. 149.

38. Daniel Lagache, *La psychanalyse*, Presses Universitaires de France, 1979, pp. 117-121.

39. For a comprehensive compilation of the many defense mechanisms as well as the definitions of the numerous psychoanalytic terms, see Jean Laplanche and J.B. Pontalis, *Vocabulaire de la Psychanalyse*, Presses Universitaires de France, 1967. The translation into English, by D. Nicholson Smith, with an Introduction by Daniel Lagache is entitled *The Language of Psychoanalysis*, Norton, 1973, and has the added feature of having the terms also listed in German, Spanish, French, Italian, and Portuguese.

40. For an optimistic view on the future of psychoanalysis see Reuben Fine, *The Psychoanalytic Vision*, The Free Press, 1981.

41. Freud, "New Introductory Lectures," *S.E.*, Vol. 22, 1962, p. 181.

42. Suzanne C. Bernfeld, "Freud and Archeology," *American Imago*, Vol. 8, 1951, p. 111.

43. Freud, "Civilization and Its Discontents," *S.E.*, Vol. 21, 1961, pp. 123-124.

44. *Ibid.*, pp. 114-115.

45. *Ibid.*, p. 132.

46. Freud, "Totem and Taboo," *S.E.*, Vol. 13, 1953, p. 49.

47. *Ibid.*, pp. 156-157.

48. Herbert Marcuse, a professor of philosophy who taught at several American universities, tried to reconcile Marxism and Freud's thought in *Eros and Civilization: A Philosophical Inquiry into Freud*, Beacon Press, 1955, and *One-Dimensional Man*, Beacon Press, 1964.

49. Freud, "New Introductory Lectures," *S.E.*, Vol. 22, 1962, p. 178.

50. *Ibid.*

51. *Ibid.*

52. Freud, "Moses and Monotheism," *S.E.*, 1964, Vol. 23, pp. 64-66.

53. Freud, "New Introductory Lectures," Vol. 22, 1962, p. 181.

54. *Ibid.*

55. *Ibid.*

56. *Ibid.*, p. 180. For Freud's feelings toward Moses, a prototypical great man and a figure of paramount importance to him, see Jacques Szaluta, "Freud's Biblical Ego Ideals," *The Psychohistory Review*, Vol. 23, No. 1, Fall 1994, pp. 11-46.

57. For a disputation on ideological grounds, see the account by the Soviet writer V.N. Volosinov, *Freudianism: A Marxist Critique*, trans. by I.R. Titunik, Academic Press, 1976.

58. Freud, "Civilization," *S.E.*, Vol. 21, 1961, p. 76.

59. *Ibid.*, p. 94.

60. Freud, "An Autobiographical Study," *S.E.*, Vol. 20, 1959, p. 72.

61. See, for example the chapter "Psychoanalysis as a Philosophical System" in Reuben Fine, *The Logic of Psychology: A Dynamic Approach*, University Press of America, 1983.

62. The Freud-Silberstein Letters, Container B12, The Sigmund Freud Collection, Library of Congress, Washington, D.C.
63. *Ibid.*
64. Philip Merlan, "Brentano and Freud," *Journal of the History of Ideas*, Vol. 6, 1945, p. 376.
65. The Freud-Silberstein Letters, Container B12, The Sigmund Freud Collection.
66. *Ibid.*
67. *Ibid.*
68. Merlan, "Brentano and Freud—A Sequel," *Journal of the History of Ideas*, Vol. 10, 1949.
69. Walter Boehlich, ed. *The Letters of Sigmund Freud to Eduard Silberstein, 1871-1881*, trans. by A.J. Pomerans, Cambridge, 1990, p. 129.
70. William J. Mc Grath, *Freud's Discovery of Psychoanalysis: The Politics of Hysteria*, Cornell University Press, 1986, p. 112.
71. Merlan, "Brentano and Freud," *Journal of the History of Ideas*, Vol. 6, 1945, pp. 375-376.
72. Paul C. Vitz, *Sigmund Freud's Christian Unconscious*, Guilford Press, 1988, pp. 50-52.
73. Robert R. Holt, "Freud's Adolescent Reading: Some Possible Effects on His Work," in *Freud: Appraisals and Reappraisals*, Vol. 3, ed. Paul E. Stepansky, The Analytic Press, 1988, p. 180.
74. The Freud-Silberstein Letters, Container B12, The Sigmund Freud Collection.
75. Marx W. Wartofsky, *Feuerbach*, Cambridge University Press, 1977, p. 448.
76. Mc Grath, *Freud's Discovery*, pp. 106-107.
77. Ludwig Feuerbach, *Das Wesen des Christentums*, Vol. 5, Akademie-Verlag 1973.
78. Ernest Jones, *The Life and Work of Sigmund Freud*, Vol. 2, Basic Books, 1956, p. 415.
79. Arthur Schopenhauer, *Die Welt als Wille und Vorstellung*, Vol. 3, Brockhaus, 1891.
80. W. Bischler, "Schopenhauer and Freud: A Comparison," in *Sigmund Freud: Critical Assessments*, ed. L. Spurling, Vol. 1, *Freud and the Origins of Psychoanalysis*, Routledge, 1989, pp. 186-187.

81. Freud, "A Difficulty in the Path of Psychoanalysis" *S.E.*, Vol. 17, 1955, p. 143.

82. *Ibid.*, p. 144.

83. Freud, "Some Elementary Lessons in Psycho-Analysis," *S.E.*, Vol. 23, 1973, p. 286.

84. Freud, "Civilization and its Discontents," *S.E.*, Vol. 21, 1973, pp. 75–76.

85. Das Commité fur die Glückwunsch-Addresse an Prof. Dr. Sigmund Freud (The Committee for the Birthday Address to Freud), Series E, Carton 4, The Sigmund Freud Collection, Library of Congress, Washington, D.C.

Chapter 3

Psychohistory: For and Against

1. The Critics

In order to better understand and define psychohistory it is essential to present and examine the contending positions and the contrasting interpretations in this field. Such a presentation and discussion will put psychohistory in better relief. Psychohistory is a revolutionary break with the traditional study of the past, but this approach is contested, opposed for myriad reasons. These objections must be considered, and in doing so they will aid in comprehending this new field. The nature of the controversy has already been touched on in the introductory chapter of this book; in this chapter the issues, theories, and methods that are juxtaposed in the consequential intellectual discourse will be further elucidated. The criterion for selecting the works to be discussed illustratively in both parts of this chapter is that they are primarily of a theoretical nature. The critics will be considered first.

Just as psychohistory now has certain names almost synonymously identified with its practice, on the other side of the controversy there are historians whose names are associated with the stand against it. The historian most notable in the opposition, and who was cited earlier, is Jacques Barzun. His book, *Clio and the Doctors: Psycho-History, Quanto-History, and History*, has become the classic adversarial statement against the new approaches of writing history (which includes quanto-history, as the title shows). Taking an historical perspective, Barzun, in his introduction, holds the view that "psycho-history and its congeners form the latest wave in the succession of waves that began with the writing of history itself," and that they reflect the contemporary "decline" of a true sense of history.[1] Accordingly, these newest manifestations in the writing of history are pseudo-historical, and are not to be considered "progressive." Instead, because there are swings in the historical pendulum, the new phase may, according to Barzun, just as accurately be considered to be reactionary.

What are Barzun's objections? First of all, psycho-history, in his view, departs from what history is all about because of its use of technical language, which is really jargon. In this respect, this "specialism", causes psychohistory to fail, being unable to "sustain its claim", and because "the substance of history is transmitted into sublimated mental states."[2] As he says "psychologizing with the aid of history"[3] is not history anymore than a psychiatric case report is history.

To be sure, in presenting his critique, Barzun describes what in his opinion is good history writing, which gives his book the additional feature of being an historiographical essay. On the question of method, which is the search for the diagnostic and which is bound to fail, and which is talked about but not demonstrated, nor properly described, Barzun states that "dynamic or depth psychology boils down to the vocabulary that has filtered out of successive teachings and hypotheses."[4] Not only that, he also warns that there are a variety of psychologies available, in addition to the Freudian one, which itself is splintered, so that the making of a selection among them is in itself a problem. In effect, since it is not possible to establish a precise standard, despite all the talk about method that occurs in psychohistory, it just does not exist.

On the critical issue of evidence and its uses, and the kinds of conclusions that psychohistorians deduce from it, Barzun finds that they are gravely lacking. What passes for evidence is nothing more than the use of language, and it is used for purposes of "self-deception". Barzun uses examples to bear out his position from Walter Langer's book, *The Mind of Hitler*. Barzun shows how psychohistorians use what he calls "weasel words", and quoting from Langer, he italicizes them to emphasize his contentions. The following are the examples (referring to Hitler) that Barzun quotes: "The fact that as a child he *must have* discovered his parents during intercourse. An examination of *the data* makes this conclusion *almost inescapable* [the data are some remarks not even hinting at such an event], and from *our knowledge* of his father's character and past history, it is *not at all improbable. It would seem* that his feelings on this occasion were very mixed."[5] Such practices, Barzun submits, are "of the most treacherous kind,"[6] for to the psychohistorian conjecture turns into fact.

Barzun recognizes that psychohistorical theory as such does not require such misdeeds, and that many psychohistorians are trained historians and have demonstrated their competence. However, what is so questionable is the applying of clinical evidence from another field for explaining bygone events. And in the sources available to historians, such as diaries, letters, and other documents, dream material—important in psychoanalysis—is rarely available. Based on the requirements for psychoanalytic treatment, the record available to the historian is "meager", making such practices the cause for poor historical products. Whereas other historians, regardless of whether they are biased or not, whether intellectually honest or not, can be challenged to produce their sources for all to see, the psychohistorians cannot be pinned down as such. Because of the way psychohistorians use evidence, and if only they have access to what Barzun considers to be "signs," or "metaphors," or "projections," which give them "undiscussable insights", then, he asserts, the psychohistorian "has stepped off the common ground of evidence."[7]

Barzun takes issue with the notion of being able to turn history into a science, and he debunks the psychohistorians belief that he understands motives in historical situations because he knows how to detect the unconscious. Using Napoleon as a case in point to understand why he was able to be an effective leader, Barzun affirms that a scientific knowledge of the amount of food Napoleon consumed, or the size of his brain, is not of interest to us. Rather, his training at Brienne would be pertinent, and how he appraised men and handled opponents, and how he directed his armies. But, as Barzun adds, "to change levels and explore portions of his being in which he resembled thousands of his contemporaries—liability to disease, imputed neurosis, bad temper, sexual tastes—would not be to understand *him*, though items under those headings might provide picturesque trimmings to a portrait."[8] To dwell on such matters, he contends, would make Napoleon "disappear under a mass of trivialities giving the impression that he was the most commonplace of men."[9]

What Barzun favors, because it is possible and desirable, is that the writing of history stay "within the realm of common sense" because "its judgments, attitudes and language are those of common sense."[10] This approach should be the philosophic basis. Barzun also postulates what he feels should be the personal qualities of the historian. Ideally, he should have a love of fact and truth, be worldly and independent-minded, and be able to assess evidence sagaciously. That, he says, "comes from knowing men and affairs, which in turn comes from experience: the best historians tend to be men acquainted with public life and over forty years old."[11]

Barzun's conclusion is that psychohistory (and quanto-history) still does not supersede the traditional way of studying history, and that psychohistory is neither history nor science. For him, the standards of judging history, after all, have not changed.

The year of the publication of Barzun's book, another traditional historian of note, Gertrude Himmelfarb, with her article "The 'New History,'" joined the debate. In presenting her position on history, Himmelfarb objected to the growing designation of being "traditional," because that designation, in her opinion, was talking on a pejorative connotation in the face of what she called the "new history."[12] Her complaint was that the formerly narrative approach to history was now ceding to the analytic. As she observed, the customary questions that historians have asked, such as 'what happened?' and 'How did it happen?' are being replaced with the question 'why did it happen?'[13] Concurring with Barzun, whom she applauds, she notes that the psychohistorian's commitment to psychoanalysis "precludes a commitment to history as historians have always understood it."[14] As she interprets it, "Psychohistory derives its 'facts' not from history but from psychoanalysis, and deduces its theories not from this or that instance but from a view of human nature that transcends history."[15] In her opinion, psychohistorians eschew the basic criterion of historical evidence, which is that of accessibility to all historians. She strongly adds: "it violates the basic tenet of historical method: that the historian be alert to the negative instances that would refute his thesis and to alternative explanations that would make his own more tenuous. The psycho-historian, convinced of the absolute rightness of his own theory, is also convinced that his is the 'deepest' explanation of any event, that any other explanation falls short of the truth."[16]

With exasperation, she vents her personal reactions to psychohistory, and in the instance of her criticism of Erikson's *Young Man Luther*, Himmelfarb exclaims: "The boldness of Erikson's thesis is matched by a methodological audacity that leaves the conventional historian breathless."[17] In her attempt to detach psychohistory from history she underlines her position by claiming that psychohistory gets its validity not from history, but from psychoanalysis. Still another objection, which is commonly raised, is that psychohistorians use a method that was devised for use by psychoanalysts on a living patient, on a person (or a group) that is not available when it comes to studying past situations. Because of what appears to Himmelfarb to be an arbitrary imposition and imputation on people in the past, she cannot accept psychohistory. In other words, psychohistorians, not observing the rules of the historical craft, are not historians. As she emphatically declares, psychohistorians, "not only the worst but also the best of them—repeatedly fail to observe these elementary rules of evidence."[18] In a somewhat confounded tone, perplexed by psychohistorians' flouting of conventions, she compares psychohistorians to ideologues and theologians, who employ intangible canons of evidence, and who find "truths not accessible to the ordinary man."[19] Finally, Himmelfarb dismisses psychohistorians from the profession, finding that the "psychohistorian, however brilliant as a psycoanalyst, cannot be held responsible as a historian because he has transcended the realm of history."[20]

The most extensive and the most furious attack on psychohistory to date is the book by David E. Stannard, *Shrinking History: On Freud and the Failure of Psychohistory*, published in 1980. The very title and subtitle announce the partisanship of the author, a practice that is rare among academic historians; the title is also pejorative, if not contemptuous, as the words "Shrinking History" have the intention of evoking thoughts of witch doctors, mysticism, and quackery. This work is a veritable cannonade against psychohistory, the comments on the dust-jacket immediately informing the reader of the nature of the contents and enlisting appropriate critics for the task. One reviewer calls Stannard's book "deadly" and the "death knell for psychohistory," and another declaims that the book is "demolishing its pretensions" and that "this should be the death blow" for psychohistory.[21] Indeed, the tone, theme, and contents are belligerent.

What is especially distinctive about this work, unlike the others just discussed, is that Stannard is not just interested in refuting psychohistory, but in going after its foundation—psychoanalysis. Stannard's thesis is that psychohistorians advance explanations and draw conclusions even though they lack evidence for their claims, drawing as they do on a theory that is lacking in credibility. Stannard compares psychohistorians to those who invoke divine intervention as an explanation for what occurs in the affairs of men. This should not be done, both lacking evidence or such claims.

With an array of studies and figures, Stannard tries to prove that psychoanalysis is not scientific, and that psychoanalysts are less than honest about how they judge how patients progress. Not only that, but psychoanalysis does not demonstrate a higher rate of cure than other therapies, or for that matter no therapy at all. In a curious denial and paradoxical recommendation, he claims that it is not his intention "to dissuade those in need from seeking professional advice, nor to suggest that such people would do just as well to talk with a witch doctor or a college student or a psychiatric patient about their problems, although in individual cases, it seems, that *may* be good advice,"[22] He also adds, parenthetically, "There is little doubt that in many cultures witch doctors are more successful than any Western psychotherapist might be."[23] Stannard even has Freud himself doubting the value of psychoanalysis, for he quotes him as saying that he didn't think that psychoanalytic cures could compete with those of Lourdes, since more people believe in miracles than in the existence of the unconscious.[24]

Stannard charges that psychoanalysis is scientifically pretentious. The very essence of psychoanalysis, with its concept of the unconscious, is unacceptable. Constructing what in

Stannard's opinion is a logical progression, he argues that psychoanalytic theory is unfounded and "must collapse," and "with the collapse of psychoanalytic theory goes the essential underpinning of psychohistorical explanation."[25] To achieve this goal Stannard debunks one of the most celebrated cases in the field of psychoanalysis, the case of "Little Hans," entitled by Freud *Analysis of a Phobia in a Five Year Old Boy*. Although the work in this case contributed to advancing significant theoretical concepts, such as the understanding of phobias, the Oedipus Complex, anxiety, and many others, Stannard contends that Freud did not have the proper evidence for the conclusions he made. The reasons for believing this, as Stannard points out, was that what Freud learned about the five year old Hans was limited because the information came from the father, not the boy, and the boy had developed an antipathy toward his father. As for the cure which Freud claims he effected, the boy could have been helped by behavioristic techniques too, and most likely, in time he would just have outgrown the phobia, as other children outgrow theirs.[26]

Stannard goes so far as to compare psychohistory to astrology, for like astrology, there is a purposeful semantic vagueness about it. In such cases, the theories cannot be tested or refuted. Referring to the concept of anal-erotic traits to exemplify this contention, Stannard maintains that it is applied so broadly that it fails to explain anything. Many historical figures are considered to be anal, as are entire cultures, the West being so described and the East likewise. In Stannard's own words, "the anal-erotic hypothesis is logically and analytically useless. The concept is in principle irrefutable. Because in theory it is all inclusive, can accommodate any set of facts supplied, and potentially explains everything, in truth it is powerless to effectively explain anything."[27]

Stannard hammers away at all the fundamental theoretical concepts of psychoanalysis, repudiating the Oedipal concept, the pleasure principle, the tripartite division of the mind into id, ego, and superego, and many others, dismissing them all on the basis that they cannot be observed or investigated. And if the final defense of psychoanalysis is its solipsism, that a person's empirical experiences are really irrelevant, because what counts is what is subjectively believed, felt, and repressed, then psychoanalysis completely fails to live up to what are considered to be objective standards of verifications. The thrust of his argument is that "The implications of this position for psychoanalysis are troubling enough, but for *psychohistory* they are nothing short of devastating."[28]

Although Stannard's target is psychohistory, most of his book is taken up with contradicting psychoanalysis. But in doing so, it is to make psychohistory appear to be untenable. As for his specific objection to psychohistory, Stannard finds that it is irresponsible and ahistorical. In time, he believes, psychohistory will survive only *"as artifact,"* and some day people will view the field as having been a misguided attempt at establishing a false science.[29] Psychohistorians, basing their work on psychoanalysis, have not produced good history. Stannard, who does show that he is closely familiar with the psychohistoral literature and psychohistorians, in conformance with his stance, considers their work of little value, with the exception of Erikson's. About him he says, "Among psychohistorians only Erik Erikson has produced work that, despite its evident limitations, might be deserving of such praise . . ."[30]

If there is a value to psychohistory, he is willing to concede, then it is that it has "jarred the profession of history" and "forced that profession to look a bit more carefully at its standards and purposes, and it has insisted that deeper analyses of traditional historical data are both possible and necessary."[31] Stannard adds that psychohistory, which in its essence is reductionistic and trivial, must be rejected because it "does not work and cannot work."[32] Stannard ends his book trumpeting that: "The time has come to face the fact that, behind all its rhetorical posturing, the psychoanalytic approach to history is—irremediably—one of logical perversity, scientific unsoundness, and cultural naiveté. The time has come, in short, to move on."[33]

Although Salo W. Baron, the dean of Jewish historians for approximately a half a century, and the author of the magisterial eighteen volume study *A Social and Religious History of the Jews*, among his many other works, is placed in this "con" section, he is hardly a conventional opponent of psychohistory. Rather, he is classified here only because of his criticism of Freud's own attempt at doing psychohistory, namely his work on Moses. Baron's critical review of Freud's *Moses and Monotheism*, first published in 1939, and subsequently reprinted in other volumes, including the popular anthology *Psychoanalysis and History* by Bruce Mazlish, has become a classic criticism of Freud's interpretation of Moses.[34] This review by Baron has also drawn adverse comments from Ernest Jones in his biography of Freud.[35] Additionally, what is unique about Baron, in the present context, is that he had personal contacts with Freud, having attended the lectures Freud presented at the Vienna University Medical School. With regard to these lectures, Baron felt that he "had been privileged to attend them."[36] It is also pertinent to note that Dr. Max Schur, Freud's personal physician and author of the acclaimed biography *Freud: Living and Dying*, published in 1972, was also Baron's doctor when he lived in Vienna.[37] Speaking of Freud, Baron said that "Despite my deep admiration for the Master", he could not accept his theories because of the "basic weaknesses of the factual material upon which he had built his construction."[38]

Appositively, in addition to Baron's celebrated review, in his *The Contemporary Relevance of History: A Study in Approaches and Methods*, he includes a significant chapter on psychohistory, along with a critical bibliography on the subject.[39] In this work, Baron makes many favorable comments about the psychohistorical approach to history for he recognizes that where certain leading historical personalities have left ample biographical material behind, they are "fit objects for the quest to uncover certain less obvious aspects of their emotional life".[40] Concerning Moses, however, Baron is critical of the assertions Freud made, and because of the dubious quality of the sources upon which these rested, he euphemistically remarked that this "did not endear him to historians."[41] What is of paramount importance to historians then, Baron says, is their sources, and their reliability, which must be carefully examined.[42] Freud, according to Baron, was arbitrary in the way he used sources, and the sources themselves were not reliable. Freud, he points out, depended on biblical scholarship on Moses written before World War I, and these works were not regarded favorably in their own time.[43] Freud wrote *Moses and Monotheism* largely before 1912, but it was not published until 1938. By that time, the "majority of biblical scholars" had rejected the works Freud had based his work on.[44] And, Baron adds, "Today the views are even more superannuated."[45]

Baron contends that Freud himself had many reservations about his interpretation of Moses being an Egyptian. As evidence of Freud's ambivalence about this study is Baron's noting that Freud initially had planned to use the subtitle "An Historical Novel" for it.[46] Perhaps, Baron says, this doubt contributed to Freud's postponing the publication from 1912 to 1938. In effect, what Freud did was to fit the facts to the theory, thereby manipulating history for his personal needs. Baron is emphatically critical of such practices, and he goes so far as to make a comparison of such practices to what Nazi and Soviet writers did when writing their history. Baron, however, is more accepting of Freud's work on Leonardo da Vinci and Woodrow Wilson because the sources available to him were more reliable. Furthermore, Baron recognizes that in some instances, as in the case of da Vinci, Freud posed good questions, thereby adding new insights into this exceptional painter-scientist.[47]

Even though Baron is critical of Freud's interpretations, he also recognizes that existing conventional methods of evaluating and understanding the character and motivations of even living persons are far from being accurate, as demonstrated by the conflicting views that exist of many political leaders. In substance, Baron regards the value of employing psychoanalysis in the study of history as another explanation, but it should not be a replacement for history.[48]

There are many more critics of psychohistory, but they cannot all be discussed here.[49] However, the major objections to psychohistory have been presented, and the numerous other critics generally continue to elaborate on the issues and points unfolded here. In sum, the opponents maintain that psychohistory is not history, that what is advanced as evidence in psychohistorical studies cannot be verified, that it is reductionistic, and that it is even based on a theory that is questionable, or at any rate not applicable outside a therapeutic situation.

Rather than giving a critique of the above charges—and misrepresentations—at this point in the text, the objections will be addressed in the section that follows. The advocates of psychohistory, in making their case for it, will provide the replies to the opponents. Furthermore, as the stands of the supporters of psychohistory are presented, the reasons for their advocacy of the field will serve as rebuttals and critique. In the conclusion of this chapter, an evaluation of the contending positions will be made.

2. The Case for Psychohistory

As has been shown, psychohistory has many critics; however, the advocates of psychohistory have been growing in numbers and influence, despite the initially near universal staunch opposition to the field. Commensurate with the growth in numbers, there is now also a large psychohistorical literature which can be drawn upon to explain the field. And in terms of the debate, more is being written by the exponents than by the critics, the production of psychohistorical publications becoming veritably profuse. But this was not always so.

The declaration of birth of psychohistory in academia may be dated from the time that William L. Langer gave his ringing presidential address on December 29, 1957 at the annual conference of the American Historical Association. As the president of the American Historical Association, and therefore one of the deans of history, his speech, challengingly entitled "The Next Assignment," at one of the world's most prestigious conclaves of historians, was a clarion call for a new approach to the study of the past. Langer's very eminence, based on distinguished and respected scholarship, and enhanced by his professorship at Harvard University, assured some attention and consideration of the advocacy of the "assignment" he recommended, even though this was hardly an orthodox one. This particular presidential address marks a critical demarcation in the growth of psychohistory, and is so frequently cited in the psychohistorical literature that it is a touchstone in the field.

Langer's pioneering address, to be sure, is impressive, for it also shows a breadth of knowledge, exhaustive documentation, familiarity with several academic disciplines and historical periods, and research in several languages, such as French, German, Italian, and, of course, English. The thesis of this address is simply that if historians are to deepen their historical understanding, then they must learn to employ psychoanalysis, including its subsequent developments and variations.[50]

Langer's exposition of what he advises to be the new approach becomes an advocacy and cogent argument for psychohistory. Unabashedly lauding Freud for his achievements, and noting the work of the many psychoanalysts who have since him added to our knowledge of human development, Langer proclaims that psychoanalysis has become an indispensable theory for the study of personality. Furthermore, he rhetorically raises a question of central importance to the historian by asking, "How can it be that the historian, who must be as much or more concerned with human beings and their motivation than with impersonal forces and causation, has failed to make use of these findings?"[51] Then, being candidly provocative, he added: "Viewed in the light of modern depth psychology, the homespun, commonsense psychological interpretations of past historians, even some of the greatest, seem woefully inadequate, not to say naive. Clearly the time has come for us to reckon with a doctrine that strikes so close to the heart of our own discipline."[52]

It should be noted that when Langer delivered this address it was at the annual banquet of the conference, and that on just this occasion he spoke before hundreds of historians. Another psychohistorian, Frank E. Manuel reports that the audience was "ill-prepared for the bombshell that fell into their midst" on that evening, and that as Langer spoke "There were visible stirrings among members of the audience that a behavioral scientist of any school would have identified as consternation."[53]

Indeed, with barbed words, he accused historians of maintaining an "iron curtain" for the profession by their exclusion of what they fearfully perceived to be unorthodox doctrines. Mindful of their views, he tackled their objections to psychohistory. To the typical complaint of those historians who feel that not enough data may be available on an individual on which to make interpretations, Langer retorts that this may be said for any subject that a historian studies. Not only that, but in the case of prominent historical figures, there is often an abundance of documentary material. On the subject of studying an individual, he caustically admonished: "We historians must, if we are to retain our self-respect, believe that we can do better with the available evidence than the untrained popular biographer to whom we have so largely abandoned the field."[54]

Audaciously arguing the conservatism of historians, Langer accused them of having an attitude which prevented them from "opening new horizons as our cousins in the natural sciences are constantly doing."[55] In what is an exhortation, he warned: "If progress is to be made, we must have new ideas, new points of view, and new techniques. We must be ready, from time to time, to take flyers into the unknown, even though some of them may prove wide off the mark."[56]

Langer also urged further exploration in the study of groups, the expressions of the "collective mentality" as shown in mass movements. But this area too is dependent on understanding individual psychology. Langer then turned to a discussion of the period known as the Black Death in the fourteenth century, similar epidemics at other times, and how they affected populations. He also touched on popular reactions to these epidemics, ranging as they did from general demoralization, sexual immorality, a rise in criminality, mass feelings of terror, anxiety and depression, a search for scapegoats, to fears of retribution from a wrathful God. What is so pertinent is that Langer advances a psychoanalytic interpretation of these phenomena, submitting that "All men, as individuals, carry within themselves a burden of unconscious guilt and a fear of retribution which apparently go back to the curbing and repression of sexual and aggressive drives in childhood and the emergence of death wishes directed against the parents. This sense of sin, which is fundamental to all religion, is naturally enhanced by the impact of vast unaccountable and uncontrollable forces threatening the existence of each and every one."[57]

In the context of his discussion on groups and the individual, Langer also mentions Luther. But what is germane is that Langer ties in Luther's personal emotional conflicts with those of others in his time. Langer's address, which was delivered shortly before the publication of Erikson's book on Luther, shows some remarkable concurrence in interpretation with Erikson's. To illustrate this with one important example, the issue of Luther's popular acceptance, Langer believes that "It is inconceivable that he should have evoked so great a popular response unless he had succeeded in expressing the underlying, unconscious sentiments of large numbers of people and in providing them with an acceptable solution to their religious problems."[58]

Langer, who in this speech had said that if he were a younger man he himself would take the direction he was advocating, urged his fellow historians "to leave none of these possibilities unexplored".[59] He said that it was of vital concern for our understanding of the past for the profession not to neglect the irrational manifestations in human development. His last sentence is prophetic: "We may, for all we know, be on the threshold of a new era when the historian will have to think in ever larger, perhaps even in cosmic, terms."[60]

Despite the inspirational tone of Langer's address, and the ingenious logic he employed, a mass of historians did not immediately rise to heed his summons. Nevertheless, in the years which followed, the "next assignment" developed a host of supporters to advance and effectuate psychohistory.

There was, in the 1950's, another lonely voice, that of Richard L. Schoenwald's, also a professional historian who advocated the use of psychoanalysis in history. At this time, Schoenwald was on the periphery of the profession, as his article, "Historians and the Challenge of Freud," (as well as others at this time) was not published in a major historical journal. Indeed, in this article, which is written in a light popular style, his main aim is to bring attention to Freud's ideas. Written before psychohistory was baptized by that name, Schoenwald deals here mostly with Freud's background, his career development, the sources now available on him, and tries to show that Freud's thought should not be felt to be forbidding. This brief article is not psychohistorical as such, but it is a modest attempt at pointing in that direction, as when Schoenwald states that Freud has created "an instrument whose workings might be suggestive for the historian."[61] He adds and concludes with the promise that if historians were to pay careful attention to Freud they would be well rewarded.

In an essay published in the 1970s, Schoenwald makes valuable theoretical observations on the nature of psychohistory. To be sure, though firmly in the psychohistorical camp, he takes the position of trying to understand the reasons for the lack of acceptance of psychohistory by traditional historians. First, in terms of supporting the field, he agrees with the general emphasis on unconscious motivations shown in psychohistorical studies, but he also wants attention to be shown to the adaptive aspects of behavior, the ego functions, and how these then connect with society. This is an additional area that, Schoenwald points out, Erikson has pioneered in doing. What concerns Schoenwald (but this article was published in 1973) is that there is still a lack of standards for psychohistory, and he complains that there are only a few, isolated, self-taught psychohistorians. It is indicative of the state of psychohistory in the early 1970s that he could appraise it in such lamentable terms as there is "no place generally agreed upon to go for training, no system of training generally agreed upon, no cohesive body of scholars who know and support each other, no journal, and no means for promoting collective morale and offsetting the attenuation of intellectual range and audacity which result from dismaying professional indifference and bitter professional opposition."[62] By the 1990s these problems had been to a large extent rectified, inasmuch as there are now several psychohistorical journals and frequent conferences for psychohistorians (in a footnote, Schoenwald acknowledged the recent genesis of two such journals).[63]

As for Schoenwald's cognizance on the lack of acceptance of the field, he offers the opinion that on the one hand historians find it hard to reconcile psychoanalysis with the study of treaties, trade balances, or the price of bread, or to thereby understand groups and nations—topics which have been at the center of historical studies—but on the other hand, he is concerned about the lack of outstanding psychohistorians who would set an example for others to follow. He notes that all too often those who have advanced psychohistory were not originally professionally trained as historians. Recognizing that much good work has been done, he nevertheless ends on a tentative note, feeling that for psychohistory "the promise yet remains."[64]

Still another eminent historian, H. Stuart Hughes has been a leading early proponent of the field, advancing that there is a necessity for the rapprochement between psychoanalysis and history, the interdisciplinary aspect being the new terrain for historians. Appositively, he asks, "why have historians and analysts taken so long to see what they have in common?"[65] Hughes then proceeds to give a well reasoned explanation, contending that although both psychoanalysts and historians sustain criticisms from colleagues in other fields, because it is claimed that their respective fields are not scientific enough, they should not be so diffident. Undeterred by the attack that psychohistorical explanations cannot be verified, Hughes, using assertive language, argues that on the contrary, the seemingly "lack of conventional scientific grounding constitutes its peculiar strength."[66] In a pithy sentence, Hughes proclaims: "Psychoanalysis *is* history—or possibly biography."[67] After all, both the historian and the analyst have the same goal, which is to "liberate man from the burden of the past by helping him to understand that past."[68]

Hughes emphatically urges historians to avail themselves of psychoanalysis because the historian is, like the analyst, concerned with the fundamental issue of human motivation, and psychoanalysis has the benefit of providing "a fund of understanding richer than that afforded by any other disciplines."[69] Unequivocally, Hughes states that psychoanalysis is especially congenial for the study of history because:

> its rules of evidence and of relevance are permissive in the extreme, and it is alert to the symptomatic importance of the apparently trivial; what a less imaginative method might dismiss out of hand, the analyst (or the historian) may well put at the center of his interpretation. In this sense, history in its turn is psychoanalysis: in their study to motive the two share the conviction that everything is both relevant and random, incoherent and ordered, in the all-inclusive context of a human existence.[70]

To the charge that psychohistorians are indifferent to historical evidence, to data, an article by William Saffady, "Manuscripts and Psychohistory" is a particularly compelling reply.[71] Furthermore, the special merit of this article is that it shows that psychohistorians are even more sensitive to, and more interested in, all kinds of records than are the traditional historians. The author, an archivist and psychohistorian, is concerned with the collecting and the availability of all kinds of materials, especially as the nature of psychohistorical research poses distinct challenges and problems. In this respect, where there is a wealth of sources useful to the psychohistorian, there is the question of what is of paramount value to him. In fact—and in a word—everything.

In Saffady's appraisal, although revelatory personal records are rare, such as information that would be available to an analyst in a classical psychoanalytic therapeutic situation—dreams, free associations, childhood memories, fantasies, and many other personal productions—there are sources available, often in abundance, that provide information for the study of individuals and of society. These records are manuscript materials, from collections of personal papers, verbatim and nontextual records, and memorabilia, which, as Saffady recognizes, "psychohistorians have made most effective use of familiar manuscript materials containing information dismissed by more conventional researchers as unimportant."[72] Also, autobiographies, diaries and letters have been useful for the insights they provide into child-rearing practices, family life, and group studies.

Essentially, the psychohistorian, using the same sources as other historians, uses them more profitably. Moreover, the psychohistorian is interested in records that others are indifferent to, such as photos, diaries (for indications of personal feelings), letters (for the dynamics of interpersonal relationships), drafts, the marginalia in manuscripts, handwriting (and the changes that occur in it), sketches and doodles, etchings, drawings, paintings, physicians' reports, oral voice recordings (which also indicate emotional attitudes), evidence of hobbies, clothing preferences, and there are still many other items that could be added to this list. Indeed, psychohistorians are not casual about sources and records, and to the alert psychohistorical researcher any shred of evidence may be significant.[73]

To continue in this vein, the charge of indifference to documentation should really be leveled at the traditional historians, for, as Saffady also shows, the psychohistorian is concerned with materials that the others are oblivious to, or even denigrate. As Saffady proposes, attention should be given to "documents that reveal the emotional climate of the times, psychiatric hospital records, and sources reflective of child-rearing practices, as well as attitudes toward overcoming the problems associated with the acquisition of the professional files of physicians and lawyers, two potentially great sources of valuable information."[74] Ironically, because psychohistoral investigators are interested in understanding people "warts and all," there is the issue of the propriety in revealing personal information, and in tandem with that, the question of just how much material can be released to psychohistorians by manuscript curators.[75]

A prolific psychohistorian, who has published in the field on both sides of the Atlantic, is Rudolph Binion, originally trained as a traditional political historian. Binion, whose psychohistorical writings, as he says, are not of "the common cut," has written *Soundings: Psychohistorical and Psycholiterary*, which features essays on both the theory and the practice of psychohistory.[76] The essays contained in this volume were conceived and written over a span of twenty years and are cameo studies on diverse aspects in twentieth century European historical and intellectual events. This book has the unique quality of inviting the reader to "feel" along with the author how he approaches, examines, and evaluates his subjects. Writing in a personal and candid manner, Binion enlists the empathy of the reader and directs him in the "Doing of Psychohistory," which is one of the chapter titles in the book. Binion, in defining psychohistory, recommends this mode because it leads to "Understanding history through motives and motives through history,"[77] specifying that it is psyche that causes history.

Binion's advice to the neophyte psychohistorian is to begin his work by selecting a biographical subject. He does not claim that this should be a hard and fast rule, but should be regarded as a recommendation because our conceptualizations on the individual psyche are at this time more advanced than that on groups (the particular essay under consideration was written in 1977). On the issue of evidence, which to Binion is of paramount importance, he warns that in order to learn to understand someone well inwardly, the documentary sources extent must be mastered. To achieve the desired results, Binion counsels that "it takes an intellectual and emotional stunt both strenuous and delicate. The researcher must empathize and analyze at once."[78] For example, if he is working on Napoleon,

He must imagine himself Napoleon setting sail from Alexandria and ask himself: 'What am I doing unconsciously in setting sail from Alexandria?' His empathy must be perfect to yield Napoleon's answer, yet only partial for him to catch the answer when it comes. That is, he must make believe in earnest and still know that he is making believe. This comes to an artificial, controlled ego-split.[79]

In another salient statement, he asks rhetorically how one can know when he has the right answer. His reply is that:

Right answers come piecemeal, each piece a breakthrough with a compelling rush of unsuspected associations. Psychohistorical analysis proceeds about like dream analysis on a grand scale except that the associations thrown up involve new material facts that then check out. This is retrodiction. It dispels any and all self-doubt on the researcher's part.[80]

Binion, however, disagrees somewhat with the general direction that psychohistory has been taking, as he feels that the field "is infested with a would-be professionalism oriented toward clinical models. Such models of individual personality disserve it because of their tangential relevance."[81]

To be sure, despite this last criticism and his advice on the preference and practicality of studying an individual, Binion is not only a strong exponent of psychohistory, but he specifies that when psychohistory succeeds with understanding collective causality, then it will be in a decidedly strong position. He closes on a challenging and hopeful note, holding the opinion that for psychohistory "with a whole uncharted realm of human reality before it, it is also more exciting than ever before."[82]

One of the most comprehensive books on the methodological and theoretical issues in psychohistory is Saul Friedländer's *History and Psychoanalysis: An Inquiry into the Possibilities and Limits of Psychohistory*, which was originally published in French in 1975 (the translation into English appeared in 1977).[83] Although Friedländer published this book well before Stannard published his, Friedländer's book can stand as a rebuttal to Stannard's, but only the highlights of *History and Psychoanalysis* will be mentioned here.

Because the very essence of psychoanalysis is historical, having the factors of "Time," "development" and "memory" in a primary role, Friedländer formulates that it is a discipline that is identical with history, allowing the two fields to be integrated.[84] Similar to the historian's approach, the analyst gets to know an analysand by getting to know his past—his history. As a significant case in point, Friedländer reminds the reader that Freud, as the founder of psychoanalysis, personally was extremely interested in the past, impressed by the weight of it, both for the individual patient and for society in general. In accordance with his formulation, Friedländer deduces that psychoanalysis is the theory of choice for the historian because it is "concerned with extremely complex aspects of human motivation that are likely to interest the historian, and that it is a structurally coherent theory, whatever its conceptual shortcoming may be."[85]

Friedländer also is concerned with the issue of verification, of adequate documentation, which he considers one of the problem areas of psychohistory, or as he states in the subtitle to his book, the limitations. Citing Erickson as an example, whose works he generally approves of, he nevertheless winces at some of the inferences that Erickson makes in creating Luther's Gestalt. Friedlander cautions that in the creation of a psychobiography "One can define an unconscious structure, both in its typical and its specific characteristics, *but its genesis is sometimes inaccessible to historical study,*"[86] [author's italics]. This, he reasons, is because childhood events are difficult to reconstruct and there is usually insufficient documentation for that period. Friendländer also thinks that Freud's theories do not go far enough to be able to understand the psychic processes of later life, but notes that in this area Erickson has advanced beyond Freud, and that Carl Jung has gone even beyond both of them. This complimentary expression on Jung is surprising, for it is rare for a Freudian historian to suggest that Jung's work can be helpful. Friedländer has this inclusion as a recommendation to the historian to be eclectic, and accordingly, Jung and others could possibly help to resolve historical problems.

Friedländer raises the question of the possible effects of a personal analysis on the historian himself, pointing out that it could create a dilemma for him. On the one hand, a personal analysis is advisable, but on the other, it could dispose the historian to a new bias. This, he feels, could occur because psychoanalysis is a process that is emotionally so personally and intensely involving. Ideally, however, a successful analysis should resolve the issue of transference "toward the analyst *and toward psychoanalysis as well*"[87] [his italics], and should enable the historian to maintain his critical abilities in the face of his work.

For all his doubts and reservations, Friedländer concludes that psychoanalysis is still "the most complete explicative paradigm we have of human behavior,"[88] and that the psychohistorical approach has enabled historians to both shed new light on traditional problems and make possible the study of new problems. Altogether, psychohistory contributes "to the integration of various historical methods into a global approach tending toward a total history."[89]

Still another distinctive work that is a call to the profession and germane to this part of the debate is Peter Gay's *Freud for Historians*.[90] Published in 1985, this work may be ranked as perhaps the most extensive study, being of book length, whose main purpose is the signal advocacy of psychohistory. And the title leaves no doubt about the author's position. Since this work came from the eminent Peter Gay, easily one of the most distinguished historians in the United States, a professor with an endowed chair at Yale University, such a tome would seem to be welcomed by all psychohistorians. Even though Gay wrote a substantive defense on the uses of psychoanalysis in history, this work has hardly been celebrated by some historians and was in some instances attacked by them. In recognition of *Freud for Historians*, the *Psychohistory Review* devoted part of an issue for a symposium on it, and the discussion over this volume was lively indeed.[91] Whatever the merits of the criticisms might be, it appears that the publication of a vigorous defense of psychohistory in 1985 was relatively late. The psychohistorical beachhead was established in the 1960's and 1970's, when to be a psychohistorian was considered to be notoriously unorthodox by the historical profession. By the 1980's psychohistory had become better established, or at least the theoretical justification, even if its practice was accepted less than enthusiastically in college and university history departments. Still, Gay's book should be regarded as a fresh synthesis of many of the previous positions, and justifications regarding psychohistory, buttressed by the clinical literature from the field of psychoanalysis.

In *Freud for Historians*, Gay takes the most common objections made by historians to the application of psychoanalysis to history and attempts to refute them. Many of the objections typically trotted out, even if meant solemnly, are made to sound amusing by Gay. The common objections are that the dead cannot be analyzed, and individual groups, classes and nations cannot be placed on the couch and analyzed. Gay retorts, with irony, that not only the dead cannot be analyzed, but neither can the living.[93]

In any case, the opposing argument goes, the traditional criteria or pillars of the craft used by historians to study the past, that of good scholarship, based on solid data and good common sense, are so well established that historians hardly need to employ questionable Freudian theories. Furthermore, they argue, psychoanalysis is intrinsically unhistorical because it does not recognize change in human nature over time, which is a tenet fundamental to traditional history. To cite just one more charge against psychoanalysis, it is that what Freud did, at best, was to deal with people's problems which were limited to those of *fin-de-siècle* Vienna.[94] Therefore, Freud's work hardly has an application to the twentieth century and to other epochs and situations.

Gay then takes on the task of addressing these charges, and at the same time catalogues some of the deplorable anti-intellectualism displayed by the opponents. First, Gay maintains, as have others, that historians have always been psychologists, but they were amateur psychologists. And, whether they recognize this or not, historians have long held a variety of theories, or personal notions, concerning human nature. However, this common sense psychological approach operated without formal acknowledgement.[95] But now, with the introduction of psychoanalysis in the last several decades, the historical profession has demonstrated an "ill-concealed anxiety", skepticism and downright opposition.[96] On the other hand, Gay is complimentary of those psychohistorians who employ psychoanalysis, observing that it has become "the psychology of choice for a brash, isolated, but irrepressible minority."[97] After surveying the contentions of the opposition, Gay believes that psychoanalysis has nevertheless remained marginal to the profession, and the "imperviousness" is even more notable outside of the United States, namely among historians in Britain, France, Germany, and Italy.[98] In a pithy and witty sentence, Gay remarks that "In short, psychohistory is highly visible, but mainly as a target."[99]

What differentiates this study is that Gay not only rebuts the detractors in the historical profession, but he also turns his attention to the psychoanalysts who are skeptical toward historians for attempting to do psychohistory. Many psychoanalysts seem to question the validity of the "objective" data that is so elemental for historians and are doubtful of "applied psychoanalysis," or psychohistory.[100] Gay says, about this equivocal attitude, that "The psychoanalytic historian must be prepared to face skepticism from Freud's followers almost as much as from his denigrators."[101] In the chapter "Reason, Reality, Psychoanalysis and the Historian," Gay details the differences between these two fields. He depicts them in a manner that is apodictic and risible. Tensions exist, Gay says, that stem from the fact that "Psychoanalysis broods on landscapes of fancied rapes and mental murders, of uncontrolled fantasies and florid symptoms of dreams, distortions, and delusions."[102]

In describing the cardinal principle of psychoanalytic treatment, which is for the analysand to speak freely, to say whatever comes to his mind—known as free association—Gay wittily notes that Freud's recommendation could cause consternation because "The fundamental rules reads like a deliberate and provocative insult to civility. The patient is supposed to report not merely all the trivialities and obscenities that sober human beings normally screen out from their speech, and often from their thoughts, but also the most absurd, the least consequential, of his mental meanderings."[103] Gay's presentation highlights how the two approaches are at odds, each side regarding the other with a degree of disdain. Although Gay pays extensive attention to the respective approaches, which provides the reader with ample demonstrations of how they should compliment each other, he is less than sanguine about this impasse, for he says that "The incompatibility between the psychoanalyst's and the historian's worlds appears to be so blatant that any call for reconciliation must sound Utopian."[104]

After a discussion of psychoanalytic concepts and examples of "social psychopathology—giving collective irrationality—Gay shows that George Lefebvre, who pioneered in the study of group behavior of the French peasantry during the French Revolution of 1789, would have been better served if he had applied psychoanalytic theories to his subject. Speaking of Lefebvre, Gay makes an observation that has a general application and that is: "The Freudian dispensation would have eased his perplexities, for it disposes over dynamic, many-layered explanations of mental products that are far more adequate to their composite and puzzling nature than the grand simplicities that most historians have felt compelled to accept as satisfactory."[105]

Finally, in advancing his case for why historians should use Freud, but at the same time arguing that psychoanalysts should also benefit from historical developments, Gay states ". . . just as historians can, under the impress of psychoanalysis, enlarge and enrich their sense of historical reality so psychoanalysts, attentive to what historians have discovered about past events, can enlarge and enrich their sense of psychological reality."[106]

To round out this section of the discussion, William M. Runyan's essay "Alternatives to Psychoanalytic Psychobiography" is useful for the additional issues he raises in this debate. Although the purpose of Runyan's essay is to explore alternative approaches to the field, his particular presentation of the issues involved, nevertheless, reinforce the case for the psychoanalytic approach. For example, whereas psychoanalytic theory places a primacy on childhood developments, Runyan notes that there may be a paucity of evidence for that period of the figure studied. Although this is a common criticism, Runyan argues that on the matter of reconstituting a subject's life, Freud himself, in his work on Leonardo da Vinci, and Erikson, in his biography of Luther, made reconstructions of these persons without having adequate evidence.[107] With regard to such interpretations, Runyan cites Phyllis Greenacre, a leading authority in psychoanalysis, who maintains that reconstruction is feasible when later adult developments are considered and if the practitioner is psychoanalytically informed. Once certain patterns of behavior, characteristics, and problems are known, then, Greenacre contends, "the experienced psychoanalyst knows just as definitely as the internist observing later sequelae of tuberculosis . . . that the deformity is the result of specific acts upon the growing organism."[108] For the traditional historian, Runyan cautions, such practices are objectionable. But, even if these caveats are meant to illustrate what is to be avoided, Runyan's disputations that follow become substantiations for psychohistory.

On the other hand, Runyan contends that even where the evidence is lacking to answer certain questions about some figures "this in no way impairs the possibility of developing psychological interpretations of the many aspects of behavior and experience of historical individuals for which there is adequate evidence."[109] Runyan then proceeds to enumerate the evidential advantages that the psychobiographer has over the psychotherapist. Even if the psychohistorian does not have the material available in the treatment situation, such as free association, dreams, and transference issues, the psychobiographer generally has the advantage of possessing information on the subject's entire life. Unlike the historical figure, who we may assume had a full life, the patient's life is not over and is probably relatively young at the time of treatment. Furthermore, the psychobiographer is not limited to the information the analysand provides, but usually has access to a vast array of sources and documents.[110] Also, Runyan draws to the historian's attention the factor that if a subject was a literary, or creative person, he may have left a "wealth of creative material, perhaps expressing inner psychological states and conflicts, that may, with caution, be drawn in interpretation of the subject's personality."[111] In this vein, Runyan says that the subject may have left material which could be substitutes or free association, such as drawings, as President Theodore Roosevelt did.[112] A last and most important point that is unique, is that the historical information is publically available to all, to be critically studied. In sum, Runyan says "the psychobiographer often has access to information not available to the psychotherapist, such as information about the person's whole life span, from associates of the individual, and from the analysis of expressive or creative activities."[113]

After a critical examination and balancing of the various approaches, Runyan comes down on the side of psychohistory, recognizing its merits even if it is at times qualified. Decidedly, he concludes: "Personally, this search for alternatives has led me to have increased respect for the utility of psychoanalytic theory in psychobiography. While some aspects of psychoanalytic theory, such as a belief in the primary causal importance of early psychosexual experience, should probably be modified or abandoned, other aspects of the theory, such as the concept of unconscious motives and conflicts, or the operation of defense mechanisms, may prove of fundamental utility for psychobiographer. Psychoanalytic theory also has the heuristic value of leading investigators to explore a range of hypotheses that might not otherwise have occurred to them"[114]

This chapter has reviewed a variety of opinions on psychohistory—the pros and the cons. As has been shown, the critics reject psychohistory because they feel that it is not history, while those who favor the field counter with the claim that psychohistory is actually a superior and better informed history.

On the paramount issue of documentation, on the availability and use of data, whereas the critics contend that there is not enough information available on which psychohistorians make their interpretations, the supporters reply that they too are aware of the problem, but that for many events and personages there is even an abundance of sources. Certainly, this question could be raised about any historical problem that is considered. How much is enough? Indeed, it can be demonstrated that psychohistorians are more concerned with and sensitive to data—in its infinite variety—than are the traditional historians. Furthermore, by taking a psychohistorical approach the data can be used to yield information, meanings, and interpretations that the traditional historians will not see or will neglect. The principles of validation apply to the psychohistorians as well as they do to others, guided, as they should be, by the usual test for documentation.

To be sure, all historians face epistomological problems, all starting off with a blank page as they seek to reconstruct the events that occured in the past. Ultimately, however, the industry, the ability, and the perspicacity of the individual historian determine the merit of his end product. Although some opponents of psychohistory do not condemn psychoanalysis, as such, even psychoanalysis is faced with a similar problem, a problem of universal import to the creator of a literary work in any field. All seek to achieve what Leopold von Ranke enunciated in the dictum "Wie es eigentlich gewesen ist." For example, the psychoanalyst Donald P. Spence, in his book *Narrative Truth and Historical Truth: Meaning and Interpretation in Psychoanalysis* notes that analysts face this issue too because patients do not necessarily want to be revealing about themselves, try to dissimulate, and have unconscious blocks. And analyst themselves have biases, have countertransference reactions to the patient, and that these dispositions affect the reports they make on their patients. Instead of arriving at the ideal of the "historical truth," at accuracy, of what really happened, the analyst really achieves "narrative truth," a reconstruction of experiences that are subjectively reported.[115] And the reasons for this, as with the reporting of other accounts, are that a patient has to convey in words the complex of experiences of his past, such as dreams, memories, images, and fantasies. Even eyewitness testimony can be unconsciously distorted.

This kind of self-criticism, which can also be found in the writings of Freud as well as of other psychoanalysts, does not negate the value of psychoanalysis. On the contrary, it shows that many are aware of the problems faced by the practice of psychoanalysis. And the best critics of psychohistory, the most astute and sophisticated critics, are the psychohistorians themselves, as was shown by their critique of the field. Although all historians search for "facts," facts ultimately have to be interpreted, and to replicate that past is difficult for anyone. But the great merit of psychohistory is that it allows for a holistic approach to the study of the individual and society.

As for the profession of psychohistory, there is no monolithic control or direction of the field, meaning that there is no ideological orthodoxy to it. As has been noted, although there are certain common denominators that the practitioners hold, there are also differences in emphasis and changes that have occurred over the years.[116] Briefly put, there has been a general shift from the concentration on depth psychology, with its stress on pathological and unconscious motivations, to the more widely inclusive ego-psychology, which gives greater attention to the adaptive abilities of the individual. Hence, many psychohistorians stress the need for an expanded conceptual framework to deal with the range of human personality and its interrelationship with environmental situations. Still, what is the essential core, and most psychohistorians agree, is the primacy that psychoanalysis holds for the study of the past.[117]

In this great debate between the two contending sides each holds to a philosophy that is diametrically opposed to the other. The above presentation of their respective views has demonstrated that the differences between them are intellectually irreconcilable, that compromise is not possible.

Notes

1. Jacques Barzun, *Clio and the Doctors: Psycho-History, Quanto-History, and History*, University of Chicago Press, 1974, p. 10, p. 3.
2. *Ibid.*, p. 17.
3. *Ibid.*
4. *Ibid.*, p. 33.
5. *Ibid.*, p. 45.
6. *Ibid.*
7. *Ibid.*, p. 49.
8. *Ibid.*, p. 64.
9. *Ibid.*
10. *Ibid.*, p. 102.
11. *Ibid.*, p. 114
12. Gertrude Himmelfarb, "The 'New History,'" *Commentary*, Vol. 59, January 1975, p. 73.
13. *Ibid.*, p. 72.
14. *Ibid.*, p. 73.
15. *Ibid.*
16. *Ibid.*
17. *Ibid.*, p. 74.
18. *Ibid.*, p. 76.
19. *Ibid.*
20. *Ibid.*
21. David E. Stannard, *Shrinking History: On Freud and the Failure of Psychohistory*, Oxford University Press, 1980.
22. *Ibid.*, p. 49.
23. *Ibid.*
24. *Ibid.*, p. 48.
25. *Ibid.*, p. 58.

26. *Ibid.*, p. 59–62.
27. *Ibid.*, p. 69.
28. *Ibid.*, p. 115.
29. *Ibid.*, p. 152.
30. *Ibid.*, p. 155.
31. *Ibid.*
32. *Ibid.*, p. 156.
33. *Ibid.* Peter Loewenberg refutes Stannard's work, calling him closed-minded. See his book review, "Expanding History. Shrinking History: On Freud and the Failure of Psychohistory," *Partisan Review*, Vol. 51, No. 1, 1984, pp. 133–137.
34. Salo W. Baron, "Book Review of Moses and Monotheism," in Bruce Mazlish, ed. and with Introduction, *Psychoanalysis and History*, pp. 50–55.
35. Cited by Salo W. Baron, *The Contemporary Relevance of History: A Study in Approaches and Methods*, Columbia University Press, 1986, p. 125. For Jones' objection, see Ernest Jones, *The Life and Works of Sigmund Freud*, Basic Books, 1957, Vol. III, p. 370
36. Baron, *Contemporary Relevance of History*, p. 53.
37. *Ibid.*, p. 125.
38. *Ibid.*, p. 53.
39. *Ibid.*, see especially pp. 123–128.
40. *Ibid.*, p. 52.
41. *Ibid.*, p. 53.
42. *Ibid.*
43. *Ibid.*
44. *Ibid.*
45. *Ibid.*
46. *Ibid.*
47. *Ibid.*, pp. 56–55.
48. *Ibid.*, p. 58.
49. For a critical, but moderate, opinion on Freud's influence on history, (the article being a review of the book on Woodrow Wilson by Freud and William C. Bullitt) see the stand by Barbara W. Tuchman "Can

History Use Freud? The Case of Woodrow Wilson," *The Atlantic Monthly*, Vol. 219, February 1967, pp. 39-44. For a debate on psychohistory in France, see *Bulletin de la Societé d'Histoire Moderne*, Sixteenth series, No. 6, 1980, pp. 12-15. For a comparison between traditional history and psychoanalysis, and a state of the art of the field in France, Germany and the United States, see the German language article by Hans-Ulrich Wehler, "Zum Verhältnis von Geschichtswissenschaft und Psychoanalyse," *Historische Zeitschrift*, Vol. 208, 1969, pp. 529-554.

50. William L. Langer, "The Next Assignment," *Psychoanalysis and History*, ed. Bruce Mazlish, Grosset and Dunlap, 1971, pp. 87-107.

51. *Ibid.*, p. 90.

52. *Ibid.*

53. Frank E. Manuel, "The Use and Abuse of Psychology in History," *Daedalus*, Vol. 100, Winter 1971, p. 205.

54. Langer in *Psychoanalysis and History*, p. 92.

55. *Ibid.*, p. 88.

56. *Ibid.*

57. *Ibid.*, p. 102.

58. *Ibid.*, p. 105.

59. *Ibid.*, p. 106.

60. *Ibid.*, p. 107.

61. Richard L. Schoenwald, "Historians and the Challenge of Freud," *Western Humanities Review*, Vol. X, 1956, p. 108.

62. Richard L. Schoenwald, "Using Psychology in History: A Review Essay," *Historical Methods Newsletter*, Vol. 7, 1973, p. 12.

63. For an essay on the state of the art of psychohistory in the late 1970s, see Richard L. Schoenwald, "The Psychological Study of History," in *International Handbook of Historical Studies: Contemporary Research and Theory*, eds. G.G. Iggers and H.T. Parker, Greenwood Press, 1979, pp. 71-85.

64. *Ibid.*, p. 18.

65. H. Stuart Hughes, *History as Art and Science*, Harper and Row, 1964, p. 42.

66. *Ibid.*, p. 47.

67. *Ibid.*

68. *Ibid.*
69. *Ibid.*, p. 48
70. *Ibid.*
71. William Saffady, "Manuscripts and Psychohistory," *The American Archivist*, Vol. 37. 1974.
72. *Ibid.*, p. 554.
73. *Ibid.*, pp. 555-559.
74. *Ibid.*, p. 563.
75. *Ibid.*, p. 564.
76. Rudolph Binion, *Soundings: Psychohistorical and Psycholiterary*, Psychohistory Press, 1981.
77. *Ibid.*, p. 117.
78. *Ibid.*, p. 118.
79. *Ibid.*
80. *Ibid.*, p. 120.
81. *Ibid.*, p. 125.
82. *Ibid.*
83. Saul Friedländer, *History and Psychoanalysis: An Inquiry* into the Possibilities and Limits of Psychohistory, Trans. by Susan Suleiman, Holmes and Meier, 1978.
84. *Ibid.*, p. 11.
85. *Ibid.*, p. 12.
86. *Ibid.*, p. 48.
87. *Ibid.*, p. 124.
88. *Ibid.*, p. 16.
89. *Ibid.*, p. 122.
90. Peter Gay, *Freud for Historians*, Oxford University Press, 1985. Among the most notable works in psychohistory is Gay's multivolume *The Bourgeois Experience: Victoria to Freud*, W. W. Norton, 1984-1995.
91. See "Symposium: Gay on Freud," *The Psychohistory Review*, Vol. 5, No. 1, Fall, 1986, pp. 81-104. Richard Schoenwald, one of the critics, disagrees with Gay's view that psychoanalysis should be an "auxiliary" to history. Instead, Schoenwald argues, that the past should be stud-

Psychohistory: For and Against

ied psychologically. Schoenwald regards Gay's book as being a "booklength editorial" that will not serve to "convert" many historians, in "Comment by Richard Schoenwald," pp. 84-89. Eli Zaretsky, who is also critical of Gay's book, says that Gay makes a case for Freud that need not be argued, that historians need to learn from Freud. At the same time, Zaretsky also says that Gay "vastly underestimates the significance of Freud" because he did more than advance our understanding of personality. Rather, like Plato's philosophy, Freud's psychoanalysis has served to reorganize "human knowledge and thought," in "Comment by Eli Zaretsky," pp. 89-94.

92. See especially chapter 4, Gay, *Freud for Historians*, pp. 116-143.

93. *Ibid.*

94. *Ibid.*, p. 79.

95. *Ibid.*, p. 4.

96. *Ibid.*, p. 7.

97. *Ibid.*

98. *Ibid.*, p. 16.

100. *Ibid.*, p. xv.

101. *Ibid.*

102. *Ibid.*, p. 116.

103. *Ibid.*, p. 118.

104. *Ibid.*

105. *Ibid.*, pp. 142-143.

106. *Ibid.*, p. 143.

107. William M. Runyan, "Alternatives to Psychoanalytic Psychobiography," in *Psychology and Historical Interpretation*, Oxford University Press, 1988, p. 221.

108. *Ibid.*, p. 222.

109. *Ibid.*, p. 221.

110. *Ibid.*, pp. 221-222.

111. *Ibid.*, p. 222.

112. *Ibid.*

113. *Ibid.*

114. *Ibid.*, p. 238.

115. Donald P. Spence, *Narrative Truth and Historical Truth: Meaning and Interpretation in Psychoanalysis*, Norton, 1982, pp. 279-296.

116. See for example the article by Bruce Mazlish, "Reflections on the State of Psychohistory," *The Psychohistory Review*, Vol. 5, March 1977, pp. 2-11.

117. A strong stand for the uses of psychoanalysis and for psychohistory is taken by Jean-Maurice Bizière, "'Before and After'. Essai de psychohistoire," *Revue d'histoire moderne et contemporaine*, Vol. XXVII, April-June 1980, pp. 177-207.

Chapter 4

Erik H. Erikson: Contributions to the Development of Psychohistory

1. The Concept of Identity

When Erik H. Erikson died, at the age of ninety-one, on May 12, 1994, the *New York Times* published a nearly full page obituary on him the following day. This was not the first time that the *New York Times* had so eminently recognized him. Indeed, such extensive coverage in the media is exceptional for an intellectual figure, but the article is cited here as a measure of Erikson's success.

The obituary traced the beginnings of his career as a children's therapist, which began with his analysis by Anna Freud in Vienna and his collaboration with her in founding a psychoanalytically oriented school for children. At the same time, in 1927, he met Sigmund Freud, with whom he socialized. In 1930, he married Joan Serson, a dancer and artist, and just three years later, the year Hitler came to power, he left Vienna to settle in the United States. There, his reputation as a child analyst grew, and he taught at several universities. While teaching at the University of California in the 1950s, he had a brush with McCarthyism. Rather than sign a loyalty oath declaring that he was not a Communist, he resigned his position. He opposed the oath, on the grounds that it was a violation of the First Amendment, and he became a "cause célèbre."[1] He then joined the staff of the Austin Riggs Center in Stockbridge, Massachusetts, and continued to publish prolifically. In the 1960s, he taught at Harvard and the Massachusetts Institute of Technology, retiring in 1970. In 1987, in affiliation with Cambridge Hospital, which is part of the

Harvard Medical School, the Erik Erikson Center for scholars and clinicians was founded, and in homage named after him.[2]

Only a few months before his death, in the fall of 1993, the *Psychohistory Review* published another special issue on Erikson.[3] A previous one had been published in 1976. The many articles in the 1993 issue continued the dialogue on his work and contributions, but now there was a shift in the approach to Erikson. In the mid-seventies, the critique was of his work, whereas now the emphasis had shifted to a closer look at the personality of Erikson, and, accordingly, how his personal life had a bearing on, and was reflected in, his work.

Again, the fact that the *Psychohistory Review*, the premier psychohistorical journal, should devote two entire issues to Erikson, less than twenty years apart, is exceptional, and attests the importance of Erikson's work. What is relevant now, as is discussed more fully below, is that in the 1993 issue, four significant articles take four different yet congruous developmental approaches to Erikson. One by Howard I. Kushner, argues that Erikson had his own "unresolved issues", which affected his work in a dissatisfying way.[4] Another, by Louise E. Hoffman, contends that his early work on Hitler, which led to his study of other world leaders, reflected his youthful interest in art.[5] A third, by Peter Heller, finds that Erikson's "painterly way of seeing things,"[6] as applied to his work on Luther, is subjective and historically erroneous. The fourth, however, by David C. Anderson, is sympathetic to Erikson, strongly disagrees with his critics, and regards him as a daring and inestimable explorer—a modern Leif Ericson.[7]

What is so germane in surveying the work of Erikson and the issues in the debate regarding the merits of his contributions in these pages it its bearing on the very issues confronting the field of psychohistory. Erikson's work is prodigious and it covers a multitude of subjects, interests, and disciplines, and these topics are the threads of psychohistory. They include the various theoretical approaches which have developed in the field of psychoanalysis and how they affect the study of history. They are also the important issues of our day, namely, gender, race, and cultural diversity.

Six years before his death, on June 14, 1988, the *New York Times* published still another major article on Erikson. This extensive article covered most of the front page of the Science

Section, part C, and the major part of still another page. It included a prominent photograph nearly 6 by 7 inches of Erikson (as did the *New York Times* in 5/13/1994) and his wife Joan, and also had an insert of this photograph and a capsule summary of the article to alert the reader on the very front page of Section A. What is noteworthy about this article is the fact that his work was initially ignored, especially in academic circles. Now he was being prominently celebrated for his contributions to the understanding of man in the leading American newspaper.[8]

Again, just the essential points regarding Erikson's latest addition to his theories, as discussed in the *New York Times*, will be cited. The article pointed out that Erikson, approaching 87 years of age, had profoundly affected the psychological views of human development, and had again broken new ground by adding to his earlier formulations on the life cycle, the latest one now being on old age. The essence of the latest work on the stages of life is Erikson's elaboration on the significance of wisdom and old age. The point that he makes is that the achievement of wisdom in old age is the fruit of an emotionally successful life. In the final stages of life, as there is growing physical disintegration of the body, "the struggle is between a sense of one's own integrity and a feeling of defeat,"[9] or despair. If the former stages have been negotiated successfully, then the individual achieves a sense of "completeness, of personal wholeness that is strong enough to offset the downward psychological pull of the inevitable physical disintegration."[10]

Erik Homburger Erikson, feted in the *New York Times* as a psychoanalyst, is also the preeminent psychohistorian of our time. He has been a pioneer and leader in the application of psychoanalysis to history, and may be considered the founding father of popular psychohistory in the sense that he brought attention to it and promoted its acceptance in the years following the Second World War. Moreover, the popularity of his works has extended beyond academic circles. Not only has Erikson been prolific, but in acknowledgment of his notable achievements and ensuing prominence, he has himself become the subject of an extensive biographical and critical literature, and many conferences have been held in his honor.[11]

Although his first publications received little attention, especially by historians, by the 1960s his work was well recognized and he was highly acclaimed. But in recent years the validity of his concepts have come in for serious questioning and criticism by other psychohistorians. Nevertheless, whether hailed or criticized, Erikson stands out as a significant scholar in the field of psychohistory; his works have been a landmark for the field. It was he who was in the forefront in achieving for psychohistory a large measure of its acceptance and success.

In 1957, Erikson's *Young Man Luther* was published. Ignored at first, it eventually became a best-seller, and was commended as a paradigm for writing psychohistory. His other works also received wide attention, particularly *Childhood and Society*, published in 1950; *Insight and Responsibility* 1964; *Gandhi's Truth*, 1969 and *Life History and the Historical Moment*, 1975. In his eighties, he wrote with Joan M. Erikson and Helen Q. Kivnick *Vital Involvement in Old Age*, 1986. He also wrote numerous articles, of which "The Dream Specimen of Psychoanalysis," published in 1954 by the *Journal of the American Psychoanalytic Association*, is one of the most important contributions to the understanding of dreams since the publication of Freud's *The Interpretation of Dreams*, and a moving and eloquent tribute to Freud.

Among Erikson's unique achievements, was becoming a distinguished professor at Harvard University, despite no advanced degree. As for his personal background, Erikson was born in Germany in 1902, his parents apparently were Danish, though there are some questions about this. His parents separated, before he was born, and his mother left for Germany. There she met the pediatrician, Dr. Homburger, whom she married. The young Erik was then given his stepfather's name, and spent his childhood and adolescence in Germany where he was educated in a *Gymnasium*. After graduation, instead of going to a university, he travelled throughout Europe with the intention of becoming an artist.[12] In his twenties he was attracted to psychoanalysis, joining the circle of Freud's early supporters. He studied with Freud's daughter Anna, and like her he also had no medical training. It should be noted that Anna Freud, who achieved distinction in the field of psychoanalysis and its uses for children's therapy, did not possess the usual academic credentials. Erikson also met and worked with other leading psychoanalysts in Vienna, including Heinz Hartmann and August Aichhorn. Like Anna Freud, Erikson too was interested in the new area of child psychoanalysis, going on to become a psychoanalyst specializing in the treatment of children.

Building on psychoanalytic theory, Erikson accented and formulated the development of personality and identity in relation to gender and social roles. His view of human growth is that each person passes through a series of major crises as he goes through life, or, as he calls it, the life cycle. Personal identity, meaning the feelings about one's abilities, self-confidence, sense of direction and harmony with one's environment, is a recurring and essential theme in his work. In particular, his concept of *identity crisis* is central to his theoretical constructs.[13] For instance, as Erikson explains, the root of young Martin Luther's problems is lack of self-confidence and direction, and a feeling of alienation from his society. This was fundamentally an issue of identity.

Departing to some extent from classical psychoanalytic theory, Erikson emphasizes the persons inter-actions with his social and personal setting, with his culture, and, accordingly, how at each stage in the life cycle there is a critical confrontation between the individual and his environment. How the critical crises, or the particular developmental tasks that are pertinent, are overcome depend on the maturity of the individual as he approaches each stage. Those which Erikson finds occurring in early childhood largely correspond to Freud's formulations of the oral, anal, and phallic stages. In Erikson's seminal work, *Childhood and Society*, first published in 1950, he posits and defines what he calls the "Eight Ages of Man," which he considers to be the life cycle of man and for which he provides an epigenetic chart of development. This methodological formulation is Erikson's conceptual schema for studying a person's life history. As *Childhood and Society* became central to Erikson's work, and will be referred to below—and because many critics cite it—its formulations need to be amplified.

These "ages", also termed, "stages," will now be described. The first of these stages has the rubric "Basic Trust vs. Basic

Mistrust," and applies to the period of infancy. If, at that time, the infant's needs are met in a regular, dependable, and warm manner by the maternal figure, then a positive orientation will occur and the child will have a *basic trust* in people. If this does not occur, then it will lead to depressive and schizoid states, and to the defense mechanism of projection. This mechanism attributes personal inner hostile feelings to others, thereby endowing "significant people with the evil which actually is in us."[14] As for the positive defense of introjection, "outer goodness" becomes "an inner certainty."[15] What is of theoretical significance is that Erikson ties this development to that of man's institutions, as they relate to his attitudes toward religions. As Erikson explains, "Trust born of care is, in fact, the touchstone of the *actuality* of a given religion. All religions have in common the periodical childlike surrender to a Provider or providers who dispense earthly fortune as well as spiritual health."[16]

The second state is called "Autonomy vs. Shame and Doubt." In this period of infancy and early childhood the nature of parental discipline and attitudes will lead the child to either develop self-confidence and self-control, or to having feelings of low self esteem and doubt. He must therefore be encouraged and supported in his initiatives for independence and protected "against the potential anarchy of his as yet untrained sense of discrimination"[17] so as to protect him from experiencing *shame and doubt*. If this does not occur, then the child will become obsessive, developing a precocious conscience, which leads to neurosis, and will have an effect on the way he deals with his environment. Acquiring a proper sense of proportion about himself and the world will help to maintain for society the principles of law and order. If the child was protected from developing the crippling feelings of undue doubt and shame, then "the sense of autonomy fostered in the child and modified as life progresses serves (and is served by) the preservation in economic and political life of a sense of justice."[18]

The third stage is one of "Initiative vs. Guilt," applying to the period of pre-school, from about three to five years of age. The developmental task for the child at this stage is to develop a sense of purpose and direction, but this occurrence depends on the degree of encouragement the parents give to the child. If the child's difficulties at this time are magnified and exacerbated, then he will lack confidence and will have feelings of inferiority, guilt, and anxiety. Characteristically, children at this stage will have fantasies, on the one hand of being a giant or a tiger, but on the other hand of being quite fearful. In accord with Freud, Erikson notes that this is the stage of the "castration complex." This stage, with implications for the next one, then "sets the direction toward the possible and the tangible which permits the dreams of early childhood to be attached to the goals of an active adult life."[19] And with his usual consideration for the social and psychological, Erikson notes that "Social institutions, therefore, offer children of this age an *economic ethos*, in the form of ideal adults recognizable by their uniforms and their functions, and fascinating enough to replace, the heroes of picture book and fairy tale."[20]

The fourth age, from beginning school age to puberty, is one of "Industry vs. Inferiority," and sets the stage for the "entrance into life." The child, in going to school, enters a "culture all by itself, with its own goals and limits, its achievements and disappointment."[21] In this respect, the "fundamentals of technology" are learned, a kind of education which takes place in all cultures, regardless of the level of its sophistication. What is critical for the child at this decisive stage is that he achieve a sense of adequacy, a sense of industry, otherwise he "may become the conformist and thoughtless slave of his technology and of those who are in a position to exploit it."[22]

The fifth age, that of "Identity vs. Role Confusion" is the stage that is the most renowned. It comes in late adolescence or early adulthood, and may be characterized by the possibility of an *identity crisis*, which means that there may be confusion for the youth about his role, resulting in undesirable antisocial attitudes and a generational conflict. This is of import because it can include a rejection of parental and cultural values along with doubts about one's sexual identity. As Erikson says about this consequential stage, "The adolescent mind is essentially a mind of the *moratorium*, a psychosocial stage between childhood and adulthood, and between the morality learned by the child, and the ethics to be developed by the adult. It is an ideological mind--and, indeed, it is the ideological outlook of a society that speaks most clearly to the adolescent who is eager to be affirmed by his peers, and is ready to be confirmed by rituals, creeds, and programs which at the same time define what is evil, uncanny, and inimical."[23] He also adds these words of caution: "In order not to become cynically or apathetically lost, young people must somehow be able to convince themselves that those who succeed in their anticipated adult world thereby shoulder the obligation of being the best."[24]

In the sixth stage, "Intimacy vs. Isolation," there should be a resolution of the identity crisis for the young adult, and it should lead to the establishment of intimate bonds of love and friendship, and the development of positive values and strong standards of ethics. The opposite of this development results in isolation and hostility. Erikson repeats Freud's view that the mark of a normal person is his ability to love and to work: "Lieben und arbeiten."[25] To attain this goal successfully is not just an individual matter, nor is it solely sexual, for its achievement comes when "It is integral to a culture's style of sexual selection, cooperation, and competition."[26]

With the seventh age, of "Generativity vs. Stagnation," at the period of middle age, it is necessary to work up to one's potential and provide guidance for the next generation. This ability, that is generativity, "is an essential stage on the psychosexual as well as on the psychosocial schedule," and when it does not take place leads to regression," often with a permanent sense of stagnation and personal impoverishment."[27] It may even lead to invalidism, physical or psychological, or excessive self-concern.

In the final age of the life cycle, this stage will be characterized by "Ego Integrity vs. Despair." Coming after age sixty, the individual who has adapted himself to the triumphs as well as to the disappointments in his life, and who can look back on his life and accept its meaning, will have achieved *ego integrity*. He who has not achieved this experiences and suffers from fragmentation, fear of death, and despair. Moreover, as it is now too late to start another life, there is disgust, to hide the despair. Erikson captures this feeling in an observation made by Edmond Rostand: "mille petits dégouts de soi, dont le total ne fait pas un remords, mais un gêne obscure."[28] Erikson stipulates the requirements and criteria for the good life as follows:

"In order to approach or experience integrity, the individual must know how to be a follower of image bearers in religion and in politics, in the economic order and in technology, in aristocratic living and in the arts and sciences. Ego integrity, therefore, implies an emotional integration which permits participation by followership as well as acceptance of the responsibility of leadership."[29]

And in his conclusion, which rounds out the life cycle, Erikson states that there is a connection between infantile trust and adult integrity because "healthy children will not fear life if their elders have integrity enough not to fear death."[30]

Again, to these eight stages, Erikson has now added a ninth phase, as cited earlier.[31] Erikson's methodological concept of epigenesis has generated controversy among psychohistorians. Many find it a viable formulation and others reject it as too mechanical. Nevertheless, this framework has been a valuable contribution to the study of the life history of every personality, and hence of psychohistory.

Childhood and Society is a richly rewarding and thought-provoking book. Erikson ranges over a wide variety of topics, from the theory of infantile sexuality to modes of child rearing among American Indians. He contrasts the Sioux and the Yurok, discusses American and German identity, and the evolution of identity, which is the underlying theme connecting the varied essays.

2. *Young Man Luther*

In line with Erikson's interest in childhood, crises in adolescence and early adulthood, he turned to studying Martin Luther as a young man. Moreover, Erikson's book, *Young Man Luther: A Study in Psychoanalysis and History*, is a landmark in the field of psychohistory. In this work, Erikson elaborates an interpretation of Luther's personality and patterns of behavior based on his ideas of the epigenesis of the life cycle. He emphasizes the stages of individual autonomy, identity crisis, and generational conflict and how they applied to Luther. Furthermore, Luther is particularly significant in that he is one of the preeminent revolutionaries of all time, the creator of an ideology and hence exceedingly controversial, and a person whose actions had manifold consequences for Germany and the world.

What is so arresting and noteworthy of study about Luther is not just his defiance of the Pope, as such acts were not novel, but the nature of his protest and the electrifyingly widespread acceptance of his stand, which led to the great schism in Christendom. To look at this development psychohistorically raises the two following questions: what motivated this young man and what were the reasons for his success? In this work, as Erikson applies his schema of the life cycle, he examines the interplay of the individual in the context of the historical situation, but in this case that of the great man in history. Erikson declares that it is not his intention to treat Luther like a patient, diagnosing him by the use of so many clinical terms, but to study Luther's life history in relation to the historical process. The value of this approach to Luther, according to Erikson, is "to lift his individual patienthood to the level of a universal one and to try to solve for all what he could not solve himself."[32] Yet a close reading of *Young Man Luther* by a psychoanalytically informed person will show that even if psychoanalytic language is infrequently explicitly employed, the main constructs of psychoanalytic theory may be discerned. Actually, Erikson is both a follower of Freud and a creative innovator in the uses of psychoanalysis, advancing that Freud's contributions can most meaningfully be used as a *technique of observation*, rather than as a formula about personality development.

In accordance with a psychoanalytic orientation, Erikson places emphasis on Luther's youth, his relationship with his father and mother, and later, how the feelings he had toward his parents were displaced on to the Pope, God, and the church. The Pope and God are traditional father images, while the church can represent the mother. Let us consider the main features of Luther's background and personal life. He was born in 1483 and entered the University of Erfurt at the age of seventeen. A few years later, during a trip home from Law School, he was caught outdoors in a thunderstorm, during which lightning struck close to him. This incident has become celebrated in the annals on Luther, for while being terrified, he prayed to St. Anne and vowed that if he lived he would enter a monastery. True to his promise, he entered an Augustinian monastery in 1505, significantly, an order which was academically highly regarded, for young Martin had been a brilliant student and he seemed to be destined for a succesful career in law—the career which his father wanted for him. However, this change in career was vehemently opposed by his father, Hans Luder.[33] The dominant personality and influence during Luther's formative years was his father, a harsh man who acted at times excessively punitively toward his son. Luther's mother is also discussed by Erikson, but to a lesser extent, and this is because less is known about her than about the father. Although she provided him with a good amount of maternal care in his early years, thereby allowing him to acquire "basic trust," she beat him too, and once very severely for a trivial transgression.[34] The essence of the dynamics of the relationship between parent and child is elucidated by Erikson in the following manner:

> The interpretation is plausible that Martin was driven early out of the trust stage, out from under his mother's skirts, by a jealously ambitious father who tried to make him precociously independent from women, and sober and reliable in his work. Hans succeeded, but not without storing in the boy violent doubts of the father's justification and sincerity; a lifelong shame over the persisting gap between his own precocious conscience and his actual inner state; and deep nostalgia for a situation of infantile trust.[35]

Martin's defiance of his father caused him much psychic conflict, and soon after he became a priest it apparently led to his having a crisis chronicled as "The Fit in the Choir," which is also the title of a chapter entirely devoted to this episode in *Young Man Luther*. In this incident, which occurred in the monastery during a service in which there was a citing of Christ curing a man possessed by a "dumb spirit" (Mark 9:17), and the reading of this section included an address to Christ made by a father in the statement "And one of the multitude answered and said, "Master, I have brought unto thee my son, which hath a dumb spirit,"[36] Luther became convulsed. Losing control of himself, or consciousness, he fell to the ground, raving, appeared "possessed", and in rage shouted either in German or in Latin, "Ich bin's nit! Ich bin's nit!" ("It isn't me!") or "Non sum, non sum!" ("I am not!").[37] Erikson suggests that as his father felt disappointed in Martin, and attributed his decision to being "possessed" by the Devil rather than to being inspired by God, Martin having this fit meant that he was both rebuking and affirming his father. The fit revealed his personal struggle, proved his father's point, but it was also an act of defiance. And eventually, to be sure, he was not able to accommodate himself to the Church.[38]

That Luther was a tormented person is well documented. While he was a priest he was beset with personal doubts which were transformed into religious doubts. For the twelve year period from the age of twenty-one, which marked his decision to become a priest, until the age of thirty-three, when he nailed the ninety-five theses to the church door in Wittenberg, this act being the momentous turning point in his life, his career in the Church was a distinguished one. It included receiving a doctor of theology degree and teaching at the University of Wittenberg. His superiors in the Church recognized that he was intellectually gifted, and they encouraged him. However, as Martin came to question aspects of theology and Church practices, demonstrating unconventional thinking, he came to be considered eccentric, radical, and challenging. Luther was an exceptional man, speaking out forcefully and intelligently against corruption in the Church.[39] Whereas others were aware of this too, and accepted the situation with resignation or indifference, Luther made it an issue. From being considered serious, pious, and original at first, he came to be regarded as a troublemaker. In fact, he became too scrupulous, even compulsive in his behavior, as when he would go to confession and confess for hours and then ask for further special appointment. In time, he became alienated and increasingly self-preoccupied, despite having attained responsible administrative and teaching positions.[40] Erikson, who in his investigations seeks to understand the qualities which distinguish the outstanding individual, in his speculations about great men in general and on Luther in particular, advances insights which may have a general application. He finds that:

> I could not conceive of a young great man in the years before he becomes a great young man without assuming that inwardly he harbors a quite inarticulate stubbornness, secret furious inviolacy, a gathering of impressions for eventual use within some as yet dormant new configuration of thought—that he is tenaciously waiting it out for a day of vengeance when the semideliberate straggler will suddenly be

found at the helm, and he who took so much will reveal the whole extent of his potential mastery.[41]

In 1517, Luther posted his historic ninety-five theses on the door of the castle church in Wittemberg. The Reformation had begun. This act impelled Luther to ever increasing defiance of the established religious authorities. The posting of the theses had been done in the traditionally accepted way for beginning a discussion on a particular theological issue or question, but this is not how it came to be interpreted. The translation of the theses from Latin into German, and hence their wide dissemination, ignited popular indignation, revealing the latent depths of resentment that existed against certain prevailing practices of the Catholic Church. Gathering momentum, in time, not only did Luther criticize the corruption in the church, but he also attacked and rejected the Pope's authority. To Luther, the Pope did not have the right to be the ultimate interpreter of Scripture. Instead, Luther advocated the revolutionary doctrine of the priesthood of all believers. And in accord with the growing nationalism, which he helped to arouse, in 1520 he wrote his *Address to the Christian Nobility of the German Nation*.[42] He appealed to the German princes to advance the Reformation and to stop Rome's financial exploitation of Germany. In another key theological divergence, in contrast to Catholicism's emphasis on good works as well as faith as being necessary to achieve salvation, Luther propounded the doctrine of justification by faith. In his interpretation of the Scriptures, God was loving. And though humans were sinful, Luther believed that faith alone was sufficient for the gift of salvation. Repudiating still another Catholic tradition, that of celibacy of the clergy, Luther married a woman who had been a nun. He had six children with her, and he named his first-born son Hans, after his father.[43]

Luther's rebellion became an example that had far reaching consequences, sparking many religious and social movements. In respect to this, there is a curious paradox about Luther as a revolutionary. Alongside his advocacy of free conscience, he fostered a conservative modality of unconditional subservience to civil authority. For instance, when the peasants revolted against serfdom, inspired by Luther and looking to him for leadership, he condemned their action in the most vitriolic terms. He wrote a pamphlet in 1525, the title of which gives an unequivocal indication of his attitude toward them: *Against the Robbing and Murdering Hordes of Peasants*. In it he wrote, "A rebel is not worth answering with arguments, for he does not accept them. The answer for such mouths is a fist that brings blood from the nose."[44] Previous to writing this tract, and consistent with his political views, he had admonished that "no insurrection is ever right no matter what the cause . . . my sympathies are and always will be with those against whom insurrection is made."[45] In the quelling of the rebellion of 1525 which became known as the Peasants' War, to cite the statistic that Erikson accepts, 130,000 peasants were massacred by soldiers.[46] Indeed, this is a staggering figure, and Luther bears a share of the responsibility for it.

Erikson was well aware that Luther was a controversial person, not just for splitting Christendom, but because of the draconian measures he advocated, and which were implemented for suppressing civil disobedience. He was intolerant of other religious groups, such as the Anabaptists whom he attacked for interpreting his ideas too radically. He also turned against the Jews for now refusing to convert to Protestantism. This reactionary record caused him a loss of popular support, and contributed to splitting the Protestant movement.

This record raises the question why Luther was so inconsistent. In regard to this controversy, Luther's behavior suggests that he was acting toward those who would not accept his beliefs in the same way his father had acted toward him when he disagreed, and this behavior stemmed from a vehement ambivalence toward his father. Although Erikson does not use this term, he relates Luther's reactionary stands and pronouncements to his early conflicts with his father, some of which have been pointed out. This dichotomy in Luther originated in his being driven out too soon of the "trust stage" by his father, and Erikson explains that in his mature years, Luther found a "theological solution." His conflicts found an accommodation in a "spiritual return to a faith which is there before all doubt, combined with a political submission to those who by necessity must wield the sword of secular law—seems to fit perfectly his personal needs for compromise."[47]

Nevertheless, Erikson has a high opinion of Luther, finding that:

> Luther was the herald of the age which was in the making and is—or was—still our age: the age of literacy and enlightenment, of constitutional representation, and of the freely chosen contract; the age of the printed word which at least tried to say what it meant and to mean what it said, and provided identity through its very effort.[48]

And finally, in what is the highest praise, Erikson compares Luther to Freud because they both made invaluable contributions to man's thought. In a sublime and discerning summation of their influence, which necessitates quoting the paragraph in its entirety, Erikson declares:

> Both men endeavored to increase the margin of man's inner freedom by introspective means applied to the very center of his conflicts; and this to the end of increased individuality, sanity, and service to men. Luther, at the beginning of ruthless mercantilism in Church and commerce, counterpoised praying men to the philosophy and practice of meritorious works. Subsequently, his justification by faith was absorbed into the patterns of mercantilism, and eventually turned into a justification of commercialism by faith. Freud, at the beginning of unrestricted industrialization, offered another method of introspection, psychoanalysis. With it, he obviously warned against the mechanical socialization of men into effective but neurotic robots. It is equally obvious that his work is about to be used in furtherance of that which he warned against: the glorification of 'adjustment.' Thus both Doctor Luther and Doctor Freud, called great by their respective ages, have been and are apt to be resisted not only by their enemies, but also by friends who subscribe to their ideas but lack what Kierkegaard called a certain strenuousness of mental and moral effort.[49]

After publishing *Young Man Luther*, Erikson continued his prolific output. Besides writing psychohistorical studies of a primarily narrative nature he has also been a theoretician, dealing with and elaborating on the methodology of this interdisciplinary field. Here too, Erikson has made signal contributions, and has had a wide influence on many scholars, in addition to those in the field of history.[50]

Some of Erikson's theoretical contributions have already been noted, such as his "Nine Ages of Man" which postulate how a person's life unfolds. However, what Erikson advocates is not a formula but a technique of observation. To do this, he cautions, is a two fold task: one is to look at the shapers of history as full individuals, the other is for the researcher to look at himself introspectively. To elaborate on this point, Erikson feels that introspection is a necessary component of the methodology, an aspect he calls "disciplined subjectivity."[51] In his book, *Insight and Responsibility*, although addressing himself primarily to clinicians, when he wrote that "the psychotherapist must include in his field of observation a *specific self-awareness* in the very act of perceiving his patient's actions and reactions,"[52] this advice was also intended for historians. He further discusses this approach in his essay "On the Nature of Psycho-Historical Evidence: In Search of Gandhi," specifically stating that the historian, like the clinician "must serve the curious process by which selected portions of the past impose themselves on our renewed awareness and claim continued actuality in our contemporary commitments."[53] Charles B. Strozier, in an article on Erikson, interprets this as meaning that "the psychohistorian likewise searches his own unconscious feelings toward individual lives and collective events in the past to understand the relationship between otherwise confusing or superficially irrelevant data."[54]

In sum, Erikson, who came to psychohistory with training and experience as a psychoanalyst, has made wide ranging contributions to understanding the spectrum of human development. Accordingly, his work has dealt with the issues of methodology, developmental theories, studies on childhood and adolescence, women and their development, the meaning of play and ritual, religion, and, of course, formulations on psychohistory—and this listing is far from being all inclusive.

3. Assessments of Erikson

Yet, side by side with the immense recognition and standard homage accorded to Erikson's work, there is also a literature that is quite critical of it. And it is psychohistorians themselves who express serious objections to Erikson's theories and interpretations, and make trenchant and penetrating criticisms of his work. Those who disagree also cover the range of issues that Erikson deals with, and those critics who will be selected now to provide examples moreover happen to be the acknowledged leaders in the field. In 1976, the *Psychohistory Review* published an entire issue devoted to Erikson, and some of the following comments will indicate the nature of the criticisms. To cite but a few highlights from this issue as examples, let us begin with the issue of "disciplined subjectivity" and its ramifications. Although Strozier, who is mentioned above, is quite sympathetic and open to Erikson's work, he wonders if some of his recommendations can be implemented. In his assessment, Strozier believes that the promoting of self-awareness is a meritorious goal but that since it cannot really be defined, because the criteria are lacking, it cannot be achieved.[55] Another critic, John J. Fitzpatrick, who also approves of Erikson's work but has serious reservations about it, notes that in the epigenetic theory there is a grave methodological problem because there is "*no* acceptable method of verifying the theory."[56]

Still another prolific psychohistorian who has studied Erikson's work, Richard L. Schoenwald, criticizes Erikson for his particular style of writing, for the way he expresses himself. Addressing himself to psychohistorians, Schoenwald forthrightly declares that:

> We psychohistorians ought to face squarely the fact that Erikson has never been easy to read, and face, too, the possibility that he has been extensively misread and then sundered into more or less usable bits and pieces. Many of us suspect or agree that a certain opaqueness and diffuseness in conceptualization and in prose, present virtually from the start, have grown worse, and after all, we would calculate, aging commonly means a weakening of some powers.[57]

The last example in presenting a variety of criticisms, whose article was published in the journal *Social Policy*, is also the most mordant. Joel Kovel, who is a psychiatrist as well as a psychohistorian goes so far as to state that "for all its obvious merit there is something deeply wrong with Erikson's psychohistory."[58] Furthermore, Kovel even finds Erikson to be misleading. Admitting that Erikson appears to be "judicious," and "balanced," Kovel admonishes that the overall effect of Erikson's writing is puzzling. To use Kovel's own withering words: "Try to remember what he has said and a cloud tends to form. After a while it begins to oppress. The prose now appears glossy, pompous, sententious, moralizing. We are being harangued, albeit with style. The ultimate effect is obscurantist, repressive, politically stagnant."[59]

Then, taking aim at the cardinal concept of Eriksonian theory, Kovel denigratingly labels it an "identity salad," explaining that in its composition "any ingredient can be made to blend with the taste of the whole."[60] To continue, in a censuring interpretation which goes to the heart of Erikson's formulations, Kovel declaims:

> Meanwhile we get too much regaled with the cheap perfume of identity, as handy an all-purpose concept as ever existed for covering up a lack of critical conception. Now we see identity linked to parallel developments in culture ('an all-inclusive human identity must be part of the anticipation of a universal technology'); now we learn of it apodictically ('For in all parts of the world, the struggle now is for the anticipatory development of more inclusive identities—note Erikson's italics, a much used way to inflate a sagging idea'); indeed, whenever we come across some element of history with psychological qualities, Erikson reaches into his satchel, hauls out an identity term, and pins it on. If it didn't muddle explanation so, we might begin to regard identity as a new kind of punctuation.[61]

As referred to earlier, the special issue of the *Psychohistory Review* published in 1993, offered still another critique of Erikson's work, but now it was being done when Erikson was ninety years of age. In the introduction to this issue, Lawrence J. Friedman, the guest editor, made some pertinent comments on Erikson's influence, but now from the perspective of the 1990's. He noted that while Erikson still had many defenders, and that the "stridency" so apparent in the 1976 issue had diminished, all contributors to the 1993 issue saw shortcomings in his work, but the extent varied.[62] The striking shift, Friedman noted, is that now there was a special emphasis on Erikson the person and how his "life impacted the texts."[63] As to the reason why Erikson has been so popular and so studied, Friedman, paraphrasing Erikson's words and applying them to him, was of the opinion that "a historically innovative leader is largely the product of the intersection between his efforts to resolve pressing issues in his own life and the circumstances and concerns of those around him."[64]

The lead article in this issue, by Howard I. Kushner, "Taking Erikson's Identity Seriously: Psychoanalyzing the Psychohistorian," by being ironical in the title, establishes the tone of the contents of the article.[65] Not only is Kushner's article the most critical and far-ranging of all the selections, in this issue, it goes to the core of the significant issues in the Eriksonian *corpus* and as they apply to the methodological dimension of psychohistory. Kushner, a psychohistorian, takes Erikson to task for his formulation of the "identity issues" and for the way he employs ego psychology. The promise of the uses of ego psychology for the psychohistorian was that there would be less emphasis on the pathological aspects of an individual or of society but would include historical and cultural factors in explaining behavior. Kushner argues that Erikson's formulation of the "identity crisis" is "elusive", that he employs ego psychology erroneously, that in fact the main historical figures he has studied have been quite pathological, namely Luther, Gandhi, and Hitler.[66] For example, when it comes to studying Gandhi, Erikson waffles. On the one hand, Kushner says that Erikson claims that he does not want to "reduce Gandhi to his symptoms," but on the other hand, supposedly eschewing a pathological analysis, describes Gandhi "as an obsessive compulsive who projected his own fears of dirt, sexuality, and internal disorder on his family, his followers, and his nation."[67] Then Erikson contends that Gandhi was not ill. With Luther too, Erikson both recognized and minimized his pathology. Kushner quotes Erikson that Luther's life "approached what today we might call a borderline psychotic state in a young man with prolonged adolescence and reawakened infantile conflicts."[68] Again, Erikson's interpretation of ego psychology is misleading, when in fact, he investigates historical characters who are particularly pathological. With these examples, touched on quite briefly here, Kushner takes on those historians who have advanced and employed Erikson's formulations. Those psychohistorians who have depended on Erikson have tended to produce studies that are psychologically reductionistic. Kushner singles out several psychohistorians who in recommending Erikson, have pointed other psychohistorians in the wrong direction. For instance, Fred Weinstein and Gerald N. Platt (who will be discussed in Chapter 5) warned historians not to "overestimate" pathological behavior at "the expense of reality factors" compounded their error by their "prescription" of an even "heavier dose of Erikson."[69]

To cite just one more psychohistorian, pertinent for his choice of subject matter, Robert G.L. Waite studied Hitler in the light of Erikson's identity crisis, and came close to conclusions about Hitler based on very little evidence—for example that Hitler was a sexual pervert.[70] Kushner notes too that there are historians who have studied Hitler, without even the use of psychology, who have recognized that Hitler was pathological. The many historians who have availed themselves of the Eriksonian paradigm have done themselves a disservice.[71]

If the above criticisms seem sharp, they are just the foundation for even more telling blows aimed at the Eriksonian theoretical edifice. Kushner picks up on several of Erikson's recommendations for psychohistorians, which are to have empathy for the subject, for Erikson's identification with Luther, for his uses of his stages of development in studying Luther, and for his own resolution of his childhood "identity crisis," and finds that Erikson hardly achieved his dictums.[72]

Principally, Kushner notes that Erikson, for all his admonitions, did not resolve his own identity issues, overlooked significant evidence on Luther, and used psychoanalytic theories in a faulty way. Erikson, in his autobiographical statements, wanted his readers to believe that he too had once had a conflict with his identity, but that he had resolved it. Erikson's resolutions are hardly a model, says Kushner, because the question of his paternity troubled him, and he dissembled on his emotional reparations.[73] Born and raised in Germany, whereas his mother was born in Denmark, he seems not to have known his natural father. His mother married Dr. Theodor Homburger, a German-Jewish pediatrician, and Erikson was raised in the Jewish faith. Erikson has not been clear about the origins of his mother, who apparently was Jewish.[74] The point is that Erikson seemed pre-occupied by what he felt were unresolved questions in his background, and which was compounded by the rise of anti-Semitism in Germany. Not surprisingly, he left Germany for the United States in 1933, the year Hitler came to power. What Kushner finds curious, and the question that he raises, is why would Erikson incessantly refer to himself as a Dane?[75] Even where the question of national origin was irrelevant, as in some of his academic writings in the United States, he would volunteer that he was a Dane. But who and what was his father? Was he a Dane and a Lutheran?[76] While this is not clear, it seems that he was rejecting his parents who had raised him. Kushner, detective-like, finds that of 13 other contributors to Erikson's collection of essays, *The Challenge of Youth*, published in 1963, only Erikson listed his national origin.[77] Kushner is hardly concerned with Erikson's ethnic background, but he makes an issue of it, arguing that it is "a matter of public concern," because of "the extent that it provides insight into his psychohistory."[78] And Erikson's simulation does not accord "in light of his often stated explanation that one's identity is derived from cultural experience rather than from biological accident."[79]

Taking sharp aim at Erikson's pivotal construct, Kushner says, "Perhaps part of the reason that Erikson's identity concept seems ultimately so fuzzy is that he has evaded that meaning of his cultural roots in formation of his own identity. Erikson has described such a conflict in others as the heart of an unresolved identity crisis."[80] And, he adds, "identity crisis may have proved so powerful and yet so elusive for Erikson because it described the central problem of his own life."[81]

As mentioned above, Erikson engaged in many activities and had many interests, and he addressed himself not just to matters of the past, but also to contemporary issues. Sometimes his beliefs and positions involved him in controversy, as for instance with feminists, who criticized his traditionalist views of women. At other times he responded to the political controversies of the day. The 1960s and early 1970s in the United States were marked by social turmoil and Afro-American radicalism. In 1971 Erikson met with one such radical leader, Huey P. Newton, of the Black Panther Party, with whom he had a series of conversations, and which were then published under the title, *In Search of Common Ground.*[82]

Although these meetings were relevant for the psycho-historical approach to black radicalism and Erikson's involvement served to illuminate these issues, this matter is touched on here because Kushner has noted this exchange as being another instance of Erikson's particular use of ego psychology, but now in regard to the Afro-American situation. Again, Kushner notes, Erikson's position and interpretation "reveals both the contradictions and the personal nature of the identity—crisis formulation."[83] Kushner notes that Erikson apparently unconsciously reveals his feelings of ambiguity about his parents' background, as when he interjects on Newton's explanation of becoming a radical activist with: "But why? That's the point. There must have been something in your background, *in your choice of parents*, (Kushner's emphasis) in the place you grew up, which made you independent."[84] And, whereas

Erikson posits that "an authentic identity can only emerge from the acceptance of one's cultural experience," Kushner states that Erikson contradicts himself because his identity is "informed by a fantasized biological essentialism, while it attempts to remain hitched to the winds of cultural fashion."[85]

But if Kushner takes Erikson to task for his ambiguous recommendation to the Black Panther leader Newton, his criticism of Erikson's work on Luther is far more serious and censorious. Kushner says that Erikson's recreation of Luther rests on a "startling omission,"[86] and this is the death of several of Luther's siblings and his and his mother's reaction to these occurrences. Kushner both criticizes Erikson's disregard of evidence and challenges his use of ego psychology as an interpretative tool. Kushner emphatically writes that "it is baffling, at first that he would dismiss such severe early object loss as unimportant to Martin's later behavior."[87] What Erikson should have considered according to Kushner, is an object relations approach, which grapples with childhood pre-verbal events and conditions, and which would be so germane to enhancing our understanding of Luther. And, it appears, Luther displayed the psychological manifestations of not having resolved the mourning process stemming from the loss of his siblings. Kushner then sees a parallel, and applies the words Erikson used to interpret Luther on Erikson. He quotes: "In Luther a partially unsuccessful and fragmentary solution of the identity crisis in youth aggravated the crisis of his manhood."[88]

Kushner characterizes Erikson as a person pre-occupied with his biological paternity, which affected his personal identity, and since he didn't know his natural father he mourned him all his life. Thus, Kushner says "Erikson's evasion of the *meaning* of his own early object loss makes it impossible for him to recognize Luther's."[89] The substance of Kushner's critique is that by re-inventing his origins, Erikson promoted "biological essentialism" over "cultural experience."[90] This, says Kushner, has served to cast doubt on the value of Erikson's theoretical constructs, which really "serve to remind us of the idiosyncratic nature of his psychohistory."[91]

The second article in the 1993 special issue by David C. Anderson, "Beyond Rumor and Reductionism: A Textual Dialogue with Erik H. Erikson," takes a more sympathetic approach to Erikson and his work.[92] Again, the personalities that Erikson has studied take center stage: Luther, Hitler and Gandhi, to whom Jesus is added. What is so arresting, again, is that in the course of his critique, Andersen takes issue with the many critics of Erikson, as well as his supporters. Indeed, Andersen serves to illustrate that Erikson drew much personal and academic attention. Andersen ranges over many issues, noting Erikson's impact on so many fields. A special value of this article is that Andersen highlights Erikson's perspective on female psychology.[93] Aside from the controversy over gender issues, Erikson's work on this question further demonstrates the breadth of his interests.

Citing the feminist critic Carol Gilligan, Andersen noted that she disagreed with Erikson's model of the developmental experience of women. It will suffice to note that Gilligan, who also felt that there was some merit to Erikson's work on gender differences, is paraphrased by Andersen as placing Erikson "somewhere between being proto-feminist and a tragically sexist old man."[94]

What Gilligan objects to is Erikson's emphasis on the mother as primarily a nurturing figure, who ideally enables her child to surmount the obstacles of the various early stages of life, beginning with the establishing of "basic trust" in the child. By extension, it may be inferred, that great men, who are of such concern to Erikson, need nurturing mothers.[95] However, in the Eriksonian schema, the father plays a pivotal role too.

Andersen's article also calls attention to Erikson's interest in theology. He praises the Dutch scholar Hetty Zock for writing a fine work on Erikson and considering him "as a major representative of modern theological thought."[96] In this regard, Andersen notes, Erikson published a work in 1981 on Jesus of Nazareth, entitled *The Galilean Sayings and the Sense of "I,"* in which he saw a link between Freud's psychoanalytic insights and Jesus' acts.[97] To cite only one comparison, just as Freud employed aspects of a patient's transference therapeutically, so did Jesus, who used faith to stop a woman from hemorrhaging.[98] Andersen recognizes that Erikson was often unclear in his writings, and that his scholarship was not rigorous, but that he was really interested in positing parables. He notes that it "made very little differences to him whether his point was illustrated by fact or legend as long as the point could be made."[99] And in a pithy sentence, Andersen says: "Erikson left us better stories than theories."[100] Andersen says many positive things about Erikson, considering him to be a man concerned with the problems of modernity, that he was critical and optimistic, creative in the way he interpreted leading historical figures with his psychological insights and who "charmed and inspired a generation of students and readers from diverse fields of study who launched their own creative journeys."[101]

The last two articles which will be cited briefly in the present context also consider certain of Erikson's works as an outgrowth of his personal experiences. Louise E. Hoffman in "Erikson on Hitler: The Origins of Hitler's Imagery and German Youth," makes some very suggestive observations on Erikson's interest in Hitler.[102] Her intentions are to trace Erikson's work on Hitler, and to "suggest ways in which its own epigenetic process affected its form and impact."[103] She finds that Erikson and Hitler were "outsiders," were interested in art, disliked formal education, and spent time in their youth wandering. To be sure, Hoffman emphatically states that Erikson is not like Hitler, but that these parallels in their lives may have contributed to Erikson's interest in Hitler.[104]

It is from Erikson's initial work on Hitler that he ventured into psychohistory. And since it is with a sense of foreboding that he left Germany, he had strong personal reasons for wanting to understand Nazism. His work, in this regard, was further stimulated, as detailed by Hoffman, by the interest that United States governmental intelligence agencies had in the psychology of Hitler and his movement, bringing Erikson's work to their attention.[105]

Peter Heller opens his article "Erikson on Luther" by stating that "Erikson was my first, beloved, most inspiring and most humane teacher in the humanities."[106] He adds, however, that now after 60 years, once more his student, he is going "to render him belated and ambiguous homage."[107] Heller, also takes aim at Erikson's *Young Man Luther* and says that he took liberties in the way he depicted Luther, which, like several of Erikson's many other books, for all their merits, is "a veritable repository of theory, portraiture, wisdom, and phantasy, is an instance of this pleasing and tantalizing mixture."[108] Heller too, criticizes Erikson's studies, which while being innovative in their interdisciplinary dimension are undertaken without adequate knowledge of the disciplines of the various fields. But Heller's main objection of Erikson, which he says determines how he works, the subjects he chooses, who he considers to be great men, is that the personal "mediatory modes are relatable to Erikson's own 'identity',"[109] which he acquired from his own childhood. In less than flattering terms, Heller says that this caused Erikson to develop a "conciliatory readiness for amiable compromise, his humane and endearing opportunism, and his refusal to be decisive,"[110] and which temperamentally was so different from his acknowledged teachers, Sigmund and Anna Freud.[111]

It has been commonplace for psychohistorians to pay homage to Erikson and recognize the influence he has had on their work. These acknowledgements border on the routine, and to make a listing of those who have been influenced by Erikson, even if only partial, would read like a *Who's Who* among psychohistorians. A few psychohistorians are cited below to illustrate Erikson's influence and the various paths they have taken. Most of those selected below have been singled out by Kushner in his article on Erikson and criticized for taking an Eriksonian line, but they happen to be among the most prolific psychohistorians. Although they are criticized for having employed a faulty model, the intention of citing them is that those psychohistorians who have depended on Erikson have expressed their appreciation for him and were stimulated to make contributions in psychohistory.

To begin with, Mazlish, though not cited by Kushner, but a leader in the field, has been explicit in paying tribute to Erikson. In *The Leader, the Led, and the Psyche: Essays in Psychohistory*, published in 1990,[112] Mazlish explicitly acknowledges Erikson's influence. He writes, "As I moved toward work in psychohistory, as part of my general interest in history and its methodology, Erik H. Erikson was a major inspiration illuminating both psychoanalytic theory and its application to historical materials."[113] As the very title of this book indicates, the relationship between leader and led that Mazlish pursues is the kind of subject that Erikson himself repeatedly explored.

Another psychohistorian who was also influenced by Erikson, but taken to task for it by Kushner is John Demos. Demos, whose works have focused on the family, child rearing, and adolescence, is pronounced in his appreciation of Erikson. In *A Little Commonwealth: Family Life in Plymouth Colony*, Demos frames his work in Erikson's well known paradigms, stating that "My overall model of individual development is the one presented in the work of Erikson—what he has called the 'eight ages of man.'"[114] He then explains his reason for doing so by noting that "this scheme tries to bring together important aspects of growth and conflict in the biological, the psychic, and the cultural settings. Each of the different stages relates to some particular issue, some fundamental 'psychosocial' task and its resolution both in the individual personal and in society as a whole."[115] Demos affirms his debt to Erikson in his other works that followed, such as *Past, Present, and Personal: The Family and the Life Course in American History* and in *Entertaining Satan: Witchcraft and the Culture of Early New England*.[116]

Two other prolific psychohistorians, Robert J. Lifton and Kenneth Keniston, who were instrumental in establishing the "Wellfleet Gatherings," in Massachusetts, which Erikson attended, as well as other psychohistorians, and which led to the publications of their essays by the members of this group in *Explorations in Psychohistory: The Wellfleet Papers*, edited by Lifton, with Eric Olson,[117] also had high praise for Erikson. Lifton, in the preface, says of Erikson "I had embraced his work, which I saw as opening up a highly significant intellectual dimension while most of psychoanalysis seemed stagnant."[118] And speaking of Keniston's role, Lifton says, "Keniston and I shared not only an immersion in Erikson's work, and a combination of involvement with and criticism of the psychoanalytic tradition, but also a strong interest in the compelling interplay of youth and history."[119] Lifton has written on a wide range of subjects, with special attention to catastrophic events and human survival as in *Death in Life: Survivors of Hiroshima, Revolutionary Immortality: Mao Tse-Tung and the Chinese Cultural Revolution, Living and Dying* (with Eric Olson) and more recently, *The Nazi Doctors: Medical Killing and the Psychology of Genocide*.[120] Keniston has two essays in the *Wellfleet Papers*, one

"Psychological Development and Historical Change" deals with the life cycle in various cultures, and the other "Revolution or Counterrevolution" examines the young people's counterculture of the 1960's.[121] Among his books, *The Young Radicals* and *Youth and Dissent* also have an Eriksonian tone.[122] Indeed, the above mentioned psychohistorians hold Erikson in high esteem, and are a response to the critics of Erikson.

Many deductions can be drawn from the vast scholarship on Erikson, as assessed above. Over the many years of Erikson's professional productivity, the lauditory reactions have been tempered by critical disparagement. Yet, an investigation of Erikson, his work and influence establishes that there obviously has been an enormous interest in him and his achievement. In sheer volume of print, based on the number of his own publications and what has been written on him and his works, Erikson stands out as the pre-eminent intellectual figure in psychoanalysis and in the humanities to have lived in the second half of the twentieth century.

The above varying assessment of Erikson by so many psychohistorians raises many questions not only about his work, but the reasons for his immense influence. Although such an investigation would be appropriate for another volume, the question is how to explain such enthusiasm for his ideas, side by side, with such disapproval? What makes this controversy even more interesting is that historians, who by training if not by temperament are critical minded, would so embrace Erikson's models. Furthermore, all the individuals discussed above have a common denominator in that they are all psychohistorians. Ultimately, the presenting of this wide assessment was to demonstrate the vast extent of Erikson's influence.

As has been noted, Erikson's work has generated an intellectual partisanship. For some, his work stands as a model, but by others, it is severely criticized. Both sides, with many nuances in between, have valid arguments, but all recognize that Erikson has made valuable contributions. Perhaps Erikson's greatest contribution is that he has stimulated so much questioning, so much controversy, and so much research, and that he has thereby created a dialectical process which has been fruitful for the advancement of a fuller and more perceptive understanding of people and society.[123] Not to obviate the validity of the criticisms, Erikson nevertheless remains popular, respected, and widely read. In so much of his writings there is a distinctive characteristic of insightfulness, of observations that have textured meanings, and of thought provoking qualities.

Notes

1. *New York Times*, May 13, 1994.
2. *Ibid.*
3. "Special Issue: Erik H. Erikson," *The Psychohistory Review*, Vol. 22, No. 1, Fall 1993.
4. Howard I. Kushner "Taking Erikson's Identity Seriously: Psychoanalyzing the Psychohistorian," *The Psychohistory Review*, Vol. 22, No. 1, Fall 1993, pp. 7-27.
5. Louise Hoffman, "Erikson on Hitler: The Origins of 'Hitler's Imagery and German Youth'," *The Psychohistory Review*, Vol. 22, No. 1, Fall 1993, pp. 69-86.
6. Peter Heller, "Erikson on Luther," *The Psychohistory Review*, Vol. 22, No. 1, Fall 1993, p. 88.
7. David C. Andersen, "Beyond Rumor and Reductionism: A Textual Dialogue with Erik H. Erikson," *The Psychohistory Review*, Vol. 22, No. 1, Fall 1993, p. 88.
8. *New York Times*, June 14, 1988.
9. *Ibid.*
10. *Ibid.*
11. Robert Coles, *Erik H. Erikson: The Growth of His Work*, Little, Brown, 1970. "Special Issue on Erik H. Erikson," *The Psychohistory Review*, Vol. V, No. III, December 1976. Mel Albin, editor, *New Directions in Psychohistory, The Adelphi University Papers in Honor of Erik H. Erikson*, Lexington Books, 1980. The National Psychological Association for Psychoanalysis, "Erik H. Erikson and Otto Rank: Clinical and Cultural Implications For Today," *Symposium*, November 20, 1982, New York City.
12. Coles, *Erikson*, pp. 12-14.
13. Erik H. Erikson, *Childhood and Society*, Norton, 1963, *passim*. For Erikson's intellectual debt to Freud, and a comparison of their views, see Patrick H. Hutton, "The Psychohistory of Erik Erikson from the Perspective of Collective Mentalities," *The Psychohistory Review*, Vol. 12, No. 1, 1983, pp. 18-25.
14. Erikson, *Childhood*, p. 249.
15. *Ibid.*, pp. 248-249.

16. *Ibid.*, p. 250.
17. *Ibid.*, p. 252.
18. *Ibid.*, p. 254.
19. *Ibid.*, p. 258.
20. *Ibid.*
21. *Ibid.*, p. 259.
22. *Ibid.*, p. 261.
23. *Ibid.*, pp. 262-263.
24. *Ibid.*, p. 263.
25. *Ibid.*, p. 265.
26. *Ibid.*, p. 266.
27. *Ibid.*, p. 267.
28. *Ibid.*, p. 269.
29. *Ibid.*
30. *Ibid.*
31. Erik H. Erikson, Joan M. Erikson, and Helen Q. Kivnick, *Vital Involvement in Old Age*, Norton, 1986. Erikson wrote this work in collaboration with his wife, and Helen Q. Kivnick, a psychologist who did research on aged people. The authors explain that this book represents their "joint reflections" on old age. As indicated in the title, they feel that "vital involvements" are necessary at each stage of life, but what makes the 9th or concluding stage of life pertinent for study is that people now are living longer than in past eras, pp. 13-14.
32. Erik H. Erikson, *Young Man Luther: A Study in Psychoanalysis and History*, Norton, 1962, p. 67.
33. *Ibid.*, p. 26.
34. *Ibid.*, p. 67.
35. *Ibid.*, pp. 255-256.
36. *Ibid.*, p. 23.
37. *Ibid.*
38. *Ibid.*, pp. 36-40.
39. *Ibid.*, pp. 226-229.
40. *Ibid.*, pp. 166-169.

41. *Ibid.*, p. 83.
42. *Ibid.*, p. 229.
43. *Ibid.*, pp. 234-237.
44. *Ibid.*, p. 236.
45. *Ibid.*, p. 235.
46. *Ibid.*, p. 236.
47. *Ibid.*, p. 256.
48. *Ibid.*, p. 224.
49. *Ibid.*, p. 252. For an interpretation of Luther's father's personality which differs from Erikson's see the article by a scholar of the Reformation, Lewis W. Spitz, "Psycho-history and History: The Case of Young Man Luther," *Soundings*, Vol. 56, 1973, pp. 182-209.
50. For a discussion of his influence, see Paul Roazen *Erik H. Erikson. The Power and Limits of a Vision*, The Free Press, 1976.
51. Erik H. Erikson, *Insight and Responsibility*, Norton, 1964, p. 53.
52. *Ibid.*
53. Erik H. Erikson, "On the Nature of Psycho-historical Evidence: In Search of Gandhi," *Daedalus*, Vol. 97, no. 3, 1968, p. 695. See also, by Erikson, *Gandhi's Truth: On the Origins of Militant Nonviolence*, Norton, 1969.
54. Charles B. Strozier, "Disciplined Subjectivity and the Psychohistorian: A Critical Look at the Work of Erik H. Erikson," *The Psychohistory Review*, Vol. V, no. III, 1976, p. 29.
55. *Ibid.*, pp. 30-31.
56. John J. Fitzpatrick, "Some Problematic Features of Erik H. Erikson's Psychohistory," *The Psychohistory Review*, Vol. V, no. III, 1976, p. 22.
57. Richard L. Schoenwald, "The Problem of Erikson," *The Psychohistory Review*, Vol. VI, no. 1, 1977, p. 79.
58. Joel Kovel, "Erik Erikson's Psychohistory," *Social Policy*, Vol. 4, 1974, p. 60.
59. *Ibid.*
60. *Ibid.*, p. 63.
61. *Ibid.*, p. 62.
62. Friedman, "Introduction," *The Psychohistory Review*, Vol. 22, 1993, pp. 1-3.

63. *Ibid.*, p. 4.

64. *Ibid.*, p. 6.

65. Kushner, "Taking Erikson's Identity Seriously," *The Psychohistory Review*, Vol. 22, 1993, p. 7.

66. *Ibid.*, p. 9.

67. *Ibid.*, p. 11.

68. *Ibid.*, p. 10.

69. *Ibid.*, p. 8.

70. *Ibid.*, p. 13.

71. *Ibid.*, pp. 8-16.

72. *Ibid.*, pp. 19-23.

73. *Ibid.*, p. 20.

74. *Ibid.* Kushner points out that this issue was first discussed by Marshall Berman in the *New York Times Book Review*, March 30, 1975.

75. Kushner, "Taking Erikson's Identity Seriously," *The Psychohistory Review*, Vol. 22, 1993, p. 20.

76. *Ibid.*

77. *Ibid.* To be sure, in the section of the book entitled "Notes on Contributors," which provides capsule biographical information on the authors, only Erikson is identified by national origin. See, *The Challenge of Youth*, ed. by E.H. Erikson, Anchor Books, 1965, pp. 338-340.

78. Kushner, "Taking Erikson's Identity Seriously," *The Psychohistory Review*, Vol. 22, 1993, pp. 20-21.

79. *Ibid.*, p. 21.

80. *Ibid.*

81. *Ibid.*

82. Kai T. Erikson, ed., *In Search of Common Ground*, W.W. Norton, 1973.

83. Kushner, "Taking Erikson's Identity Seriously," *The Psychohistory Review*, Vol. 22, 1993, p. 21.

84. *Ibid.*

85. *Ibid.*, p. 22.

86. *Ibid.*, p. 23.

87. *Ibid.*, p. 24.

88. *Ibid.*, p. 26.
89. *Ibid.*
90. *Ibid.*, p. 27.
91. *Ibid.*
92. David C. Andersen, "Beyond Rumor and Reductionism: A Textual Dialogue with Erik H. Erikson, *The Psychohistory Review*, Vol. 22, 1993.
93. *Ibid.*, p. 36.
94. *Ibid.*
95. *Ibid.*, p. 48.
96. *Ibid.*, p. 35.
97. *Ibid.*, p. 50.
98. *Ibid.*, p. 51.
99. *Ibid.*, p. 59.
100. *Ibid.*
101. *Ibid.*, p. 63.
102. Hoffman, "Erikson on Hitler," *The Psychohistory Review*, Vol. 22, 1993, p. 69.
103. *Ibid.*, p. 70
104. *Ibid.*, p. 71.
105. *Ibid.*, pp. 72–81.
106. Heller, "Erikson on Luther," *The Psychohistory Review*, Vol. 22, 1993, p. 87.
107. *Ibid.*
108. *Ibid.*, p. 88.
109. *Ibid.*
110. *Ibid.*
111. *Ibid.*
112. Bruce Mazlish, *The Leader, The Led, and The Psyche: Essays in Psychohistory*, University Press of New England, 1990.
113. *Ibid.*, p. v.
114. John Demos, *A Little Commonwealth: Family Life in Plymouth Colony*, Oxford University Press, 1970, p. 129.

115. *Ibid.*

116. John Demos, *Entertaining Satan: Witchcraft and the Culture of Early New England*, Oxford University Press, 1982 and *Past, Present, and Personal: The Family and the Life Course in American History*, Oxford University Press, 1986.

117. Robert J. Lifton and Eric Olson, eds., *Explorations in Psychohistory: The Wellfleet Papers*, Simon and Schuster, 1974.

118. *Ibid.*, p. 11.

119. *Ibid.*, p. 12.

120. Robert J. Lifton, *Death in Life: Survivors of Hiroshima*, Random House, 1968; *Revolutionary Immortality: Mao Tse-Tung and the Chinese Cultural Revolution*, Vintage Books, 1968; *Living and Dying*, Prager, 1974; *The Nazi Doctors: Medical Killing and the Psychology of Genocide*, Basic Books, 1986.

121. Kenneth Keniston, "Psychological Development and Historical Change," pp. 149-164, and "Revolution of Counterrevolution?" pp. 288-323, in *Explorations in Psychohistory*, 1974.

122. See Kenneth Keniston, *The Young Radicals*, Harcourt, Brace & World, 1968; *Youth and Dissent*, Harcourt Brace Jovanovich, 1971.

123. For a comprehensive listing of works by Erikson, but only up to 1976, indeed an impressive compendium, see Robert Coles and John J. Fitzpatrick "The Writings of Erik H. Erikson," *The Psychohistory Review*, Vol. 5, no. III, 1976, pp. 42-46. For an extensive appraisal of Erikson's work, in which he is regarded as an heir of Freud, even if Erikson made revisions in Freud's Theories, see Philip Pomper's chapter "Erikson" in his *The Structure of Mind in History: Five Major Figures in Psychohistory*, Columbia University Press, 1985, pp. 81-114.

Chapter 5

Psychoanalytic Theory: Post Freudian Developments

1. Ego Psychology

Since the Second World War, to use it as an approximate divider, there has been a shift and growth in the variety of psychodynamic models employed by psychoanalysts and psychohistorians. Concomitantly, there has been a rich accretion in the theoretical dimensions, one of these significant developments being the change in emphasis from id psychology to ego psychology. What this has meant for psychohistorians is a change from emphasis on the inner drives of the individual to the individual's relationship with society, with a group, and the influences these situations have on the human personality. Another important model elaborated since World War II is that of object relations theory, which emphasizes the nature of emotional attachments between two people, and is based on the kinds of identifications made in the first year of life. In the dissemination of psychoanalysis, because it is a science, there has been an acceptance, exchange, and dialogue that is international in scope, but, as will be shown, there have also been responses to psychoanalysis which are influenced by national and historical conditions.

The most influential theoretician and practitioner since the death of Freud was Erikson. He made significant contributions to what has become known as ego psychology. But Erikson, and others who followed, built on the foundation made by Freud. Freud pointed the way with such studies as *Totem and Taboo* and *Moses and Monotheism*. In *Group Psychology and the*

Analysis of the Ego, Freud examined the interraction between the individual and his environment in groups such as the army and the church. He found that both institutions bore similarities to the family.[1] As the development of Freud's work and thought show, his theories on id psychology were more methodically formulated than were those on ego psychology, in part because they were made earlier in his career.[2] Yet, many of the subsequent theoretical developments, which were made in the 1930s and in the immediate decades following his death in 1939 were achieved by individuals who had personally worked with Freud. One was Heinz Hartmann.

Heinz Hartmann is considered to be the greatest theoretician in the field of psychoanalysis since the death of Freud, whose student he had been. Born in Austria, Hartmann emigrated to the United States in the 1930s. His *Ego Psychology and the Problem of Adaptation* was published in 1939, and is distinguished for advancing ego psychology. His reformulation earned him the epithet "father of ego psychology." Hartmann's substantive contribution lies in showing how normal adaptation to the social environment occurs. Accordingly, Hartmann was interested in the functions of the ego, how it develops, and how normal development differs from pathological development.

One of his main and initial points is the concept of adaptation, which he regards as "primarily a reciprocal relationship between the organism and its environment."[3] For man, the "crucial adaption"[4] is to the social structure, and he is expected to work at improving it. In this sense, adaptation, or leading a relatively healthy life, depends upon the individual modifying himself and his environment.

Hartmann also postulates the existence of an inborn ego apparatus. He says, "Not every adaptation to the environment, or every maturation process, is a conflict," referring to developments "*outside of conflict*" [Hartmann's italics] such as thinking, language, recall-phenomena, productivity, and motor development.[5] These are known as the apparatuses of primary autonomy, meaning that the ego develops by itself, independently of the id and the drives. A third theoretical assumption is that of the "conflict-free sphere." According to this assumption, adaptation does not have to be marked by mental conflict, or trauma. In this view, Hartmann moved psychoanalysis into the realm of the study of normal behavioral development, as well as the pathological.[6] In this context, Hartmann introduced the concept of an "average expectable" environment for the child, which stresses the importance of early maternal influence on the infant, and their reciprocal interaction.[7]

Hartmann's reformulation of psychoanalytic theory has increased attention on external reality, thereby expanding psychoanalysis to include a general psychology of human behavior. Ego psychology has thus provided "the meeting ground for psychoanalysis, experimental psychology, and social science in general."[8] Hartmann's work is profound, and it represents a major contribution. In evaluating Hartmann's work, the eminent psychoanalytic writer Reuben Fine pointed out that "what Hartmann really did was to clear up an ambiguity in Freud's own thinking. At some times Freud wrote as if instincts were the only motivating forces in human beings, whereas at other times he explicitly recognized the 'ego instincts' or what today would be called the autonomous cognitive factors."[9]

Approximately two decades later, Fred Weinstein, a historian, and Gerald M. Platt, a sociologist, in collaboration, contributed to the advancement of psychohistorical theory. They elaborated on the work of Freud, Erikson, Hartmann, and others. They have been further influenced by the sociologist Talcott Parsons. The range of the various theoretical works they draw upon is remarkable in that it demonstrates how much psychohistorical theory has grown since Freud's seminal discoveries.

In their first book, *The Wish To Be Free: Society, Psyche, and Value Change*, Weinstein and Platt integrate the concepts of ego psychology with those of object relations, which Talcott Parsons had previously blended with sociological thought. They apply these to the nature of change and social processes in history. This interface of theories and disciplines are continued and expanded in *Psychoanalytic Sociology: An Essay on the Interpretation of Historical Data and the Phenomena of Collective Behavior*. They argue that personality does not cease to develop at any particular time, whether at the time of the resolution of the Oedipal conflict, or in adolescence, which is marked by identity crises, (the traditionally accepted psychoanalytic positions) but can change at later times, depending on societal circumstances. They also say that personal identity and behavior are conditioned by many environmental processes, beyond the influences of the family.[10] And they reject the view that the family is the key to social institutions because there are many widely shared symbolic processes that are not confined to the family. What is of paramount influence then, and what determines in large measure people's learning, behavior, and direction, is society. Richard L. Schoenwald evaluates *Psychoanalytic Sociology*, as "the largest advance in thinking about psychohistory since the work of Erikson and opens the way to a future which seems abundant in promise."[11]

Two years after the publication of *Psychoanalytic Sociology*, Weinstein and Platt issued a warning to psychohistorians. In "The Coming Crisis in Psychohistory," they asserted that psychohistory was still quite limited because of the theoretical limitations of psychoanalysis in dealing with groups and movements. they also criticized psychoanalytic theory, on the grounds of its assumption that people react to social realities on an essentially unconscious level, or in terms of their drives. Rather, they said, people react to, and deal with, problems and issues as they affect them in a realistic, conscious manner. Moreover, such fundamental psychoanalytic ideas as identification, internalization, and related processes "suggest that character traits and motivations are or can become independent of drives. The classic position, derived from emphasis or instinctual conflicts originating in fantasy, points in the opposite direction."[12] The problem, as they see it, is that historians cannot explain all developments in society by the use of drive theory. As they declare: "The ontogenetic–familial orientation may be decisive of *therapy*, but the parallels between therapy and history are limited and risky at best. The problems of the historian and the problems of the clinician are distinct."[13]

What Weinstein and Platt propose is to integrate the social and psychic realities of history, because, as in the case of revolutionaries, it is not possible to separate them from the social order from which they come, and because they are not independent of their circumstances. Due to the theoretical inadequacies of psychoanalysis, despite the work of Erikson and Hartmann and the other ego psychologists, group phenomena cannot be properly studied, hence the excessive production of biographical works by psychohistorians. Weinstein and Platt contend that these issues pose a contradiction for psychohistory, and they assert that it is imperative that there be a reversal of the classic drives reality paradigm. In other words, not "drives-ego" but "ego-drives" are most significant because "Social conflict occurs when *the integrative bases for action in society are disrupted by change*" [Weinstein and Platt's italics].[14] Following their constructive criticism, they offer a new direction for psychohistory. Since each historical event is unique, they point out, psychohistorians should not approach their subjects of study with predetermined theoretical constructs in mind. Instead, they advise them to "approach data with a sense of the processual nature of human interaction with the environment rather than in terms of predispositional categories."[15] Primary attention should be given to the manner that people interact with their environment, and this should be done in conjunction with the theoretical formulations of ego psychology, object relations, and object loss.[16]

In the last publication by Weinstein that will be cited here, "The Transference Model in Psychohistory: A Critique," he takes to task Freud's concept of transference. This concept is fundamental to understanding the nature of therapy; transference is the sum total of feelings and experiences that an analysand brings to the therapeutic situation. Freud contended that one's transferences affected all areas of emotional life. And psychohistorians have generally accepted this interpretation of the transference as having a validity and applicability to their own work. Weinstein rejects this parallel because he believes that psychoanalytic therapy takes place in a situation that is unique, which is established and maintained in order to facilitate the expression of intra-psychic conflicts and to thereby deal with them therapeutically. Weinstein further qualifies the nature of the therapeutic situation, characterizing it as an artificial situation, like no other, specially requisite for being able to work out pathological symptoms and manifestations. Disagreeing with the way psychohistorians use the transference model, Weinstein points to a lacuna in psychohistorical theory. He expresses the view that "The realistic ego capacity which Freud identified as active in therapy and in everyday social action has never been studied intensively, nor have the major implications been drawn out and especially not in terms of routine activities in the everyday world."[17] To briefly mention but one solution that Weinstein offers to redress the incorrect emphasis, he recommends that this could be ameliorated "by taking more seriously the actor's [historical figure] own interpretation of events and the reasons they give for their diverse responses to these events."[18]

The essence of Weinstein's and Platt's work is that if psychohistory is to be a viable methodology for understanding the past it must jettison the presuppositions that pertain to psychoanalysis. What historians do is not similar to what therapists do; their approaches and their work are not congruent.

Whereas Weinstein calls into question the application of psychoanalytic clinical practice to history, Peter Loewenberg in "Psychoanalytic Models of History: Freud and After" contends, on the contrary, that insights can be gained from the therapeutic situation and that certain clinical models are appropriate for elucidating historical issues.[19] Loewenberg, who accepts the recent advances in psychoanalytic theory, innovatively employs a tool used in clinical practice—countertransference. Tracing the shifts from libidinal drive theory to the more current ego psychological and objects relations constructs, Loewenberg draws attention to the application of countertransference in psychoanalytic therapy. This concept should also be recognized and employed heuristically by the historian.[20]

Just as a psychotherapist has subjective feelings for his or her patient, and should be cognizant of them, so too should the historian be consciously aware of his reactions to this subject or material. In this essay, Loewenberg demonstrates the utilization of these feelings and reactions and effectively applies them to several historical figures, namely Richard Nixon, Adolf Hitler, and Leon Blum. Although the issue of transference is presented here as a theoretical one, it should be noted that Loewenberg has had clinical training in psychoanalysis, whereas Weinstein contends that such training is hardly necessary in order to be a psychohistorian.[21]

In a critique of Fawn Brodie's *Richard Nixon: The Shaping of His Character*, in which Loewenberg recommends ego psychology, he proposes that it is not enough to explain why Nixon lied, or that he was a perennial liar. Noting that Brodie applied an instinctual drive model of psychohistory to Nixon, Loewenberg finds that such an approach has limitations, despite its strengths and persuasiveness. Brodie's thesis is that lying was characteristic of Nixon, that his victories could be attributed to lying effectively, which she traces to the particular nature of his relationships with his parents. Loewenberg questions this thesis because he feels that it does not sufficiently take into account Nixon's ego strengths. One of Nixon's ego strengths was his ability to cope with a reality filled with stress and defeat. He was able to adapt to new and unforeseen situations and could assess the future realistically. At times he could distinguish facts from his own wishes, but he also failed to discern the real world.[22]

In advocating ego psychology, Loewenberg emphasizes that the historian should carefully examine Nixon's adaptive capabilities and see where he functioned effectively and realistically. Loewenberg sums up his recommendation for the ego psychological model with a strong endorsement and a challenging question "This model and method are supremely historical because they are pre-eminently time specific, always posing the question: why now?"[23]

The psychohistorical question then is not just why Nixon was a liar, but also why the Watergate scandal occurred. After all, Nixon was a seasoned lawyer and politician and had achieved the pinnacle of political success in spite of adversity. With the Watergate scandal, the judgments Nixon made—his reality testing—failed and he faced impeachment by the Congress. Again, the issue is why this occurred "*at that time,* (Italics the author's) but not all his prevaricating life."[24]

The same ego psychological model and questions can be applied to Hitler as well. That Hitler was destructive needs no elucidation, and that he was a failure in school and early adulthood has been substantially documented. What is more perplexing is why Hitler became so successful, acquiring power in 1933 and then having a long string of diplomatic successes, until World War II. Here again, Loewenberg points out that Hitler demonstrated great skill in convincing fellow party members to support him and in winning a mass following. He was able to manipulate the Catholic Church, the army generals, the industrialists, the youth, and the workers. In his foreign policy from 1933 to 1940, his many "successes," which included violating international treaties with impunity, dwarfed Bismarck's achievements. But after 1940, his string of successes came to an end, and his capable intrigues failed him. The denouement began in 1940, when the defeated British army retreated to Dunkirk, and Hitler allowed its army to escape back to England. Then, following a series of procrastinations, he failed to invade and conquer England, and instead declared war on the Soviet Union, and finally declared war on the United States in 1941. After a series of major miscalculations, the catastrophe Hitler had caused culminated in disaster for the German army at Stalingrad, and a monumental retreat on all international fronts followed. Loewenberg, who surveys the historiography on Hitler and notes a variety of interpretations, again raises the question of Hitler's abilities, and why he had begun to fail after he too had reached a pinnacle of success.[25]

The other major issue under consideration by Loewenberg is the utilization of countertransference. Citing the work of Harold Searles, a psychoanalyst, Loewenberg explains the significance and import of countertransference. Countertransference is defined as the "feeling states in the therapist," which is the personal and emotional response of the therapist to the patient.[26] This self-awareness is consequential because it helps the therapist to understand and treat the patient more effectively. Like the therapist, the historian has subjective feelings, which may be critical, antagonistic, or sympathetic, and which he brings to the study of his subject. Specifically, these feelings, which may be conscious or unconscious, and cover the range of emotions, are anger, anxiety, hostility, joy, sadness, and, obviously, many other emotional expressions.[27]

Loewenberg gives examples, having detected this aspect of how several historians have apparently unconsciously revealed their "countertransferences" in their studies. Two brief examples will suffice, one where the biographer reproaches his subject, and the other where the historian demonstrates insightful empathy. Joel Colton, who wrote the biography *Leon Blum: Humanist in Politics*, is clearly sympathetic to his subject, but he reveals a degree of impatience, or annoyance, with Blum.[28] Colton upbraids Blum for having allowed himself to be captured and imprisoned in France and eventually in Germany for five years. Colton argues that Blum should have fled to England, as deGaulle did in 1940. Not only would Blum have saved himself much suffering, but he would have given greater stature to the Free French movement in France and abroad, and would have diminished the standing of the Vichy regime for the American and British governments. Colton considers Blum's decision not to leave France in 1940, because he said that he did not want to desert his country, as a rationalization, which played into the hands of his enemies. So many others had departed, and were thereby more effective for their cause, Colton insists.[29]

To this, Loewenberg replies: "The historian Colton is visibly arguing impatiently with his subject. It is as if he is saying 'Can you not see how you are guiltily playing into the hands of your enemies who will destroy you!'"[30] Loewenberg, continuing in this course makes an important recommendation to historians who study Blum, and which has a general application to all researchers: "And it is a cue to his successor historians to look very closely at the conflictual motives, especially the irrational and unconscious ones, in the conduct of Leon Blum, not only after the Armistice, but also on issues of action and passivity, guilt and aggression, initiative and reality testing, in his political decision making."[31]

In another example, Loewenberg cites the historian Kenneth Stampp for being able to use his countertransference feelings in order to understand why the South not only lost the Civil War, but was able to reintegrate easily into the Union. In his work, *The Imperiled Union: Essays on the Civil War*, Stampp examines the usual factors used to explain why a country wins or loses a war.[32] These are the physical elements such as manpower, economy, technological resources, and the behavioral ones such as civilian morale and capabilities of the armed forces. However, as Loewenberg notes, Stampp also looks at the unconscious reasons for not only why the South was defeated, but why it accepted defeat so readily. Stampp ascertains that the Confederacy lost the war because it did not have a firm commitment to its cause, because Southerners were not really convinced that slavery was righteous, hence their defensive rhetoric.[33] This doubt was affirmed as the war came to an end and as its resistance collapsed. Significantly, unlike other countries who have been occupied, no guerilla movement developed in the South, to fight against great odds as did the Algerians against France and the Vietnamese against the United States until they triumphed. After the war was over, the South acquiescently rejoined the union and slavery was abolished. By applying an ego psychological model, as Loewenberg says, Stampp was able to explain why so many Southerners had conflicted feelings about their cause and why they unconsciously welcomed their defeat. Indeed, Loewenberg has high praise for Stampp's interpretation, and he sums up, stating that: "What is elegant in this insight is that the historian is using his countertransference and his informed empathic listening to the discourse of history in order to supply the data of interpretation. He is interpreting a visible defense. In his general interpretation, Stampp is, of course, applying without citation the dynamics of unconscious ambivalence and guilt that Freud first elaborated in the historically and clinically so useful discussions of 'Those Wrecked by Success' in his 1916 paper 'Some Character Types Met With in Psychoanalytic Work'."[34]

The above presentation has been a sketch of the main theoretical developments, and they are those which have occurred largely in the United States. Many other contributors could not be included, but the indication is clear that psychoanalysis and psychohistory are in a state of intellectual ferment and in prodigious expansion in the United States. In making this observation, it must be noted that there is a constant interchange of ideas on an international level as well. Achievements which occur in one country serve to influence developments elsewhere. It is recognized that the United State has become the center for these developments. This result was achieved in conjunction with an international exchange of ideas. It will suffice to add that what promoted the United States to acquire its preeminence in psychohistory and related fields is due to its traditions of intellectual freedom and acceptance of change, and that these features attracted the numerous analysts who left central Europe in the 1930s. Formerly, psychoanalysts had been heavily concentrated in Austria and Germany. Another country that benefited from this emigration was Great Britain: the reasons for its attraction being similar to those of the United States. This takes us now to survey the theoretical developments in Great Britain.

2. The British School

Psychoanalysis made significant forward strides in Great Britain beginning in the 1930s. Today it is established in Britain as one of the main centers of the field. Some of the developments which took place there have earned the proponents the designation "British School." Although this kind of national appelation is exceptional in psychoanalysis, it reflects the extensive and novel developments which occurred there. In England as elsewhere, however, the developments were by no means uniform, and differences in theory led to rifts among classical analysts.

An event which acted as a fillip for psychoanalysis in England was the fact that Sigmund Freud settled there in 1938. He was warmly welcomed there after his flight from the Nazi invasion of Austria. After his death, his daughter Anna, who had also moved to England and who had by this time become an eminent psychoanalyst in her own right, carried on the classical tradition established by her father. Still another commanding person in the field, who had been one of Freud's early collaborators, was the physician Ernest Jones. He eventually became the dean of British psychoanalysis, a role he maintained until his death in 1958. A prolific writer, he pioneered in the applications of psychoanalytic theory to the understanding of literature. In the 1950s he published a monumental three volume biography of Freud. It is a masterpiece that ranks with the greatest biographical works.[35]

Anna Freud made many contributions to psychoanalytic thought and was also a leader in its application to the treatment of children. Although Anna Freud is discussed here in connection with the "British School," it is because much of her work was accomplished in England, and not because she belonged to this school. In fact, her theoretical orientation is at odds with that of the other leading child analyst Melanie Klein, a founder of the British School. Anna Freud's theoretical orientation is similar to that of Heinz Hartmann's.

Several of Anna Freud's books have become essential for their contribution to the study of children and for their theoretical advancement of psychoanalysis in general. In addition, Anna Freud founded and directed the world renowned

Hampstead Child Therapy Clinic. Hampstead served as both a treatment center for children and as an institution for the training of analysts. Focusing on child analysis, Anna Freud wrote *The Psychoanalytic Treatment of Children* and *Psychoanalysis for Teachers and Parents*, both published in the 1920s. In these two works she delved into the mental and emotional life of children, contributing to the understanding of their fears and wishes, their obsessions and phobias. She supported and amplified her views by providing new data on the early developmental stages of childhood first posited by her father. These studies elucidate how children learn to cope with the significant figures in their lives, their parents, siblings, and friends.[36]

Anna Freud continued to make valuable theoretical contributions during World War II by studying the effects of dislocation and bombing on young children. In *War and Children*, written in collaboration with Dorothy T. Burlingham, Anna Freud showed that the sight of destruction and death as such were not as traumatic to children as believed, contrary to the prevailing attitudes that adults held about how children react to such scenes. Rather, they found that it was far more traumatic for young children to be separated from their mothers.[37]

Anna Freud's *The Ego and the Mechanisms of Defense*, published in 1936, ranks with the most important psychoanalytic books ever written, made a major theoretical contribution. She systematized and elaborated the defense mechanism, and demonstrated that the ego chooses from a wide array of defense mechanisms, in addition to repression. Repression, rather than being a dissociation from consciousness, is redefined by Anna Freud as an unconscious act of the ego in the face of an anxiety-provoking situation.

As she notes, psychoanalysis is more than just a psychology of the unconscious, for the ego, "as the seat of observation,"[38] must also be considered. Making a key point, which serves to advance theory and practice, Anna Freud explains that: "From the beginning analysis, as a therapeutic method, was concerned with the ego and its aberrations: the investigation of the id and of its mode of operation was always only a means to an end. And the end was invariably the same: the correction of these abnormalities and the restoration of the ego to its integrity."[39] Besides repression, she describes and clarifies the mechanisms of regression, reaction formation, isolation, doing and undoing, projection, introjection, turning against the self, reversal, and sublimation.

In the second part of the book, which deals with examples of how to avoid psychic pain and degrees of personal danger, Anna Freud elaborates on such defenses as denial (in fantasy and in word and act), restriction of the ego, identification with the aggressor, and altruistic surrender.[40]

The theories and methods advanced by Anna Freud were consonant with those applied in adult therapy, and in the case of children, depended on the development of the child's verbal abilities. However, there were other analysts who wanted to push the inquiry of childhood development back into the pre-verbal period.

In what grew out of reconsideration of classical Freudian theory, with its stress on instincts or id phenomena, the "British School" emerged, and its theoretical orientation was subsumed under the rubric "object relations school." This development occurred in Britain in the 1930s and 1940s, its most prominent exponents being Melanie Klein, W. Ronald Fairbairn, Harry Guntrip, and Donald W. Winnicott.

Melanie Klein, a pioneer in the investigation of infantile mechanisms of projection and introjection, conceived theories which, although they gained wide acceptance in Britain, clashed with the views of Anna Freud on the subject of child analysis. It is this schism which gave rise to the contending schools.

The main features of Klein's work is her emphasis on the psychic processes which occurred in the pre-oedipal period, and her hypothesis about childhood development in the first year of life. Originally living and working in Hungary, her novel principles and techniques brought her work international attention. In 1925, Ernest Jones invited her to present her work in England, where she settled. Among her innovations in clinical techniques were the analysis of the free-associative play of very young children. Her theory diverged from the classical in that she felt that superego developments occur even during the first two years of life, and that the important drives in this early period are the aggressive ones. Also, in the early development of the infant, there is a phenomenon which she calls splitting. The process of splitting stems from the infant's separation of the mother into a good and bad object, meaning that she alternates between being a gratifying and a frustrating figure. This mental polarity decreases at the time of weaning, when the infant recognizes the mother as one person. The quality of relationships in adult life is therefore dependent on the kinds of object relations developed earlier. Klein's views of object relations are at the core of her theoretical and clinical formulations.[41]

As for the schism mentioned earlier, it will suffice to note that Anna Freud objected to Klein's views on the grounds that it was not possible to go back to preverbal experiences and that Klein disregarded the significance of transference.

Klein, as the progenitor of a school, has received much attention and been the subject of numerous biographies. An exhaustive and sympathetic biography of Klein is by Phyllis Grosskurth, *Melanie Klein: Her World and Her Work*, published in 1986.[42] Typical of innovators, Klein encountered much controversy, but in her case, a degree of notoriety. To be sure, she was invited to come to Britain, and her membership in its society bolstered its prestige. As one British analyst said, the British society "suffered a good deal from inferiority feelings"[43] in regard to societies in Vienna, Berlin, and Budapest. Grosskurth considers that Klein was a woman who was vilified for striking out on her own.[44] Nevertheless, Klein had many supporters, including Ernest Jones, and she trained with two noted analysts, who were close to Freud, Sandor Ferenczi and Karl Abraham. Born in Vienna (1882–1960) she married at the age of seventeen, and had three children. Klein's personal life has received particular attention because critics charged that her theoretical positions were so at variance with her domestic life. Klein, who gives such centrality to the infant-mother relation, was herself an indifferent, if not neglectful mother toward her children.[45] In her clinical work, she caused an uproar when it was discovered that a paper she presented on a child at a psychoanalytic meeting, supposedly a patient, turned out to be her own son. Grosskurth sensitively portrays Klein as a woman who experienced much psychic pain and had frequent bouts of depression. In fact, Grosskurth says, Klein's paper, "A Contribution to the Psychogenesis of Manic-Depressive States," "seems to have been written in a state of manic depression during the summer of 1934."[46]

In her reformulations, Klein, in emphasizing the role of the mother in the pre-oedipal period, minimized the role of the father. Not that Freud disregarded the role of the mother, as in the significant oral period for the infant, but Klein's work represents a moving away from what has been called Freud's male bias. Klein has also been criticized for attributing a more developed ego to the infant than is accepted by mainstream psychoanalysts. She also claims that when the infant is frustrated, it develops the "schizoid position" and, as early as five months of age, it can take a "paranoid position." If the frustration persists in severity, this will cause "the depressive position" in the infant.[47] These constructs, which assume early ego development, are questionable. Can they be proven or disproven? What Klein contends, however, is that to the extent this early period is a satisfactory one, it will determine the adult's ability to attain healthy relationships. If the rage toward the mother was persistent, then this would cause depression, psychosis and paranoia, demonstrated later in life. Klein's contributions to the theory of neurosis, in the view of Anne E. Bernstein and Gloria M. Warner, both psychoanalysts, is that "the depressive position, with its concomitant fear of losing the primary object, gives impetus to the formation of the oedipal conflict as early as 1 year of age."[48] In effect, Klein's analytic work has served to focus more closely on pre-verbal and traumatic experiences in infancy.

Jay R. Greenberg and Stephen A. Mitchell in *Object Relations in Psychoanalytic Theory*, which is an exhaustive treatment of this subject, pithily summarize the essence of Klein's work and give her her due place in the history of Psychoanalytic ideas:

> Her discovery of early introjects and identifications, her expanded appreciation of phantasy, and her development of the concepts of internal objects and the internal object world provided powerful clinical tools for the psychoanalytic investigation of these earliest object relations. Her formulations concerning primitive persecutory anxieties, early defenses dominated by splitting and its elaborations, and depressive anxiety and reparation have contributed greatly to the study of dynamic processes within psychotic, neurotic, and normal mental functioning. Her development of play technique and her incisive descriptions of the insidious workings of greed and envy and their cen-

trality in establishing the most intransigent resistances in the psychoanalytic situation have greatly added to the range and efficacy of psychoanalytic technique.[49]

The catalogue of the British school would not be complete without acknowledging the work of Fairbairn, Guntrip, and Winnicott. All three, natives of Britain, were influenced by Klein. They built on her work, borrowed her concepts, and then developed their own theoretical perspective. Fairbairn, taking issue with Sigmund Freud's major contentions regarding human motivation and experiences, such as the libido theory and the theory of psychosexual development, argued that the main feature of libido is a function of the ego. In this view the ego, and therefore libido, is object-seeking rather than pleasure-seeking.[50] Basically, what Fairbairn is advancing is that from the time of infancy the individual is oriented toward others, that relation-seeking has a biological origin. In Fairbairn's theory of development, personality is conceived of in terms of object-relations, and consists of maturational sequences of relations to others. As Ernest Jones puts it, if it were possible to condense Fairbairn's views into one sentence it would be that:

> Instead of starting, as Freud did, from stimulation of the nervous system proceeding from excitation of various erotogenous zones and internal tension arising from gonadic activity, Dr. Fairbairn starts at the centre of the personality, the ego, and depicts its strivings and difficulties in its endeavour to reach an object where it may find support.[51]

Harry Guntrip, another leader of the object relations school, has been its foremost historian, synthesizer, and popularizer. But in carrying out these endeavors he has also modified Fairbairn's theory of ego–splitting and object relations. As Greenberg and Mitchell state, "Guntrip's history of psychoanalytic ideas is first and foremost a moral history."[52] Guntrip is concerned with the ultimate fate of mankind, because of the threat of nuclear war. He hopes that the insights provided by psychoanalysis can be utilized to prevent man's self-destruction. Guntrip's distinctive contribution to theory, in line with his concern for humane values, is his development of the concept of the "regressed ego." By this he means that when there is a fragmentation of the ego, as in the case of the schizoid, who has feelings of emptiness and weakness, this reflects "the withdrawal of energy from the real world into the world of internal object relations."[53] Guntrip believes that the traumas caused by poor mothering become essentially frozen in the unconscious, and this brings about a regressed ego and becomes the core of the pathological personality.

Donald W. Winnicott, the last in the British School to be discussed, was a pediatrician before he became a psychoanalyst. His works show a well-informed familiarity with the relationship between babies and mothers, if not an advocacy of this bond. Among the significant emendations that Winnicott makes is his observation that it is erroneous to assume, as traditional psychoanalytic theory and practice do, that a patient who enters treatment has a personality capable of interacting with others. Accordingly, most of Winnicott's work is concerned with the conditions that permit the child to develop an awareness of himself as distinct from other people.[54]

According to Winnicott, the kinds of experiences the mother provides for the infant, the degree of her devotion, the kind of world she presents to the child, will determine how the infant feels about itself. For the infant, the degree of satisfaction that the object provides—such as the breast and other satisfying experiences—will form the basis for feelings of omnipotence, feelings which are the foundation of healthy development. When the mother functions as a mirror, as Winnicott describes it, by being attuned to the baby's needs, then the child develops a positive sense of self.

Winnicott's particular approach is clear from his explanation of what a baby is. He has observed that "There is no such thing as a baby," meaning that "if you set out to describe a baby you will find you are describing a *baby and someone*. A baby cannot exist alone, but is essentially part of a relationship."[55] Winnicott finds that a period of "perfect environment" is necessary for a time, but there are times when the child needs solitude, a requirement for developing the capacity to be alone, to learn the realities of the outside world and those that are beyond its abilities to control.

Another facet of childhood which Winnicott observed and which has become celebrated for advancing the understanding of the early developments in children is the role of what he called the "transitional objects." The objects, which are "transitional," are items such as teddy bears, dolls, or blankets, to which the infant becomes attached, and which facilitate independence from the mother. Such objects have a symbolic nature in that they may stand for the mother, or for something else, but over which the child has control. Their value is that they aid the infant in making a shift from experiencing himself "as the center of a totally subjective world to the sense of himself as a person among persons."[56] Such creative acts become the basis for creativity in adulthood, and form the basis for the culture of society in general. These concepts led Winnicott to study the role of play and creativity, and their significance for later development. From such initial situations the infant is able to establish an "internal environment," which permits it to play "by itself."[57] Such experiences are essential to future creativity.[58] Although Winnicott focuses on the early relationship of infant and mother, he also takes into consideration the function of the father. The father is important for widening the child's intellectual horizon, encouraging creativity, and setting the guidelines for appropriate social behavior.[59]

To sum up, the members of the British School have both common denominators and differing emphases. The basic issue addressed by these theorists (aside from Anna Freud) is its conceptual focus on a person's relations with others, real or imagined. And their work has served to enrich psychohistory, as some historians have used the models they provided.

To date, relatively few psychohistorians have applied Klein's theories to their work. One who has is Judith M. Hughes, who has both written a book on the British School and applied their formulations in another volume. In *Reshaping the Psychoanalytic Domain: The Work of Melanie Klein, W.R.D. Fairbairn, and D.W. Winnicott*, Hughes presents an overview of the establishment of psychoanalysis in Britain, the growth of the field there, the influx of analysts from continental Europe, and the disputes which arose in the British Psycho-Analytical Society.[60] Although Hughes' emphasis is on one "school", she shows that the politics of psychoanalysis were hardly harmonious there. (This was the case in other countries as well.) However, with particular reference to British geography, Hughes notes that

"The three protagonists of this study stand as prime example of independence prospering under the protection of the English Channel."[61]

Essentially, "Reshaping the Psychoanalytic Domain", to the dismay of Anna Freud and the classical analysts, meant that the British School altered Freud's libido-drive model and the Oedipus Complex and gave primacy to the role of mothering. This led to stress on the analytic treatment of children and of psychotics (who previously had been considered unanalyzable). In line with Klein's greater emphasis on maternal care, she enhances the role of women in general. At the same time she rejects Freud's construct of penis envy, which by extension causes these innovations to have favorable implications for feminist thought.[62] Other implications of the paradigms of the British School, which are the links and the understanding of later adult behavior in light of early object relations, suggest new avenues of research for psychohistorians.

Hughes, in *Emotion and High Politics: Personal Relations at the Summit in Late Nineteenth-Century Britain and Germany*, examines the respective leaders of the two countries in light of object relations theory, and focuses on their mothering experiences.[63] The thesis of Hughes' innovative book in the field of diplomatic history is that the statesmen of Britain and Germany failed to understand each other because their experiences in their earliest periods of childhood were so at variance with each other that their interpersonal behavior was incompatible.

Germany was unified in 1870, and relations between it and Britain remained cordial until the 1880's. After that time, the enmity between them grew, culminating in war in 1914. The main and contending personalities studied by Hughes are, on the British side, Arthur J. Balfour, Joseph Chamberlain, William E. Gladstone, and Robert G. Salisbury. On the German side, they are, Otto von Bismarck, Bernhard von Bülow, Philipp Zu Eulenburg, Friedrich von Holstein and Kaiser Wilhelm II.[64]

In her appraisal of the national leaders, Hughes makes certain generalizations about their "tempers", or their characteristics. The British fare much better, for she regards them to have been tolerant of dissent and more collegial. The German "temper" was more suspicious, hostile, and authoritarian. After a description of what is considered to be "good enough" mothering which is D.W. Winnicott's construct, she raises a question fundamental to her thesis: "Is there reason, then, to believe that 'good enough' mothers dominated the British landscape?"[65] No British leader was as rageful as Bismarck, and his dislike of his mother has been well documented. Chamberlain, on the other hand, had a close and loving relationship with his mother and was called "sunny natured."[67]

Hughes' conclusion in this book is consonant with her thesis, and she holds that "tempers deeply rooted in childhood, more particularly in contrasting experiences of maternal care, set the parameters for interpersonal behavior among British and German statesmen."[68] This resulted in "incomprehension" between them, as they were just not on the same "mental track." Again, to cite Hughes: "Where the British hoped that patient negotiations might dispel suspicion, the Germans viewed a lack of ready compliance as a sure sign of enmity. In short, diplomatic discourse between the two summits echoed the clash of two dissonant tempers."[69]

In an apposite paper, Louise E. Hoffman, in "Object-Relations Theory and Psychohistory," provides a critical appraisal of the interface between the two approaches.[70] In this paper, Hoffman is critical, skeptical, and encouraging of those historians who have applied object relations theory, namely Loewenberg and Hughes.

Hoffman notes that psychohistorians have responded to changes in theory, but, in line with acceptance of the Oedipus complex, have tended to accentuate the leadership of males in history. In recent years, however, objects relations theory has found analytic supporters in the United States, and psychohistorians too have begun to use a wider variety of theories. But so far, very few psychohistorians have availed themselves of the new perspectives. After highlighting the theory, Hoffman first turns to an evaluation of the pertinent papers published by Loewenberg. Of Loewenberg's work, she says, "His work suggests advantages as well as limitations of integrating object-relations concepts with various psychoanalytic approaches."[71] Hoffman selects Loewenberg's "The Unsuccessful Adolescence of Heinrich Himmler," to discuss his study of the notorious SS leader. Hoffman notes that in this study,

Loewenberg resorted to a vast array of theories, including Freudian, Reichian, Eriksonian, ego psychology, as well as object relations. She says that Loewenberg relied on Himmler's diary, written when he was in his teens and early twenties, to explain his pathological behavior as the leader of the murderous SS. Loewenberg has applied the experiences of those who have had disturbances in early childhood, which then reveal themselves in those persons having poor affects, that is being emotionally cold and distant. Himmler is considered to have been such a type of person, which is in line with certain clinical studies of those who have had desolate object relations. To Hoffman, Loewenberg's interpretation is not tenable, and she says: "Unfortunately, the very nature of Himmler's personality impedes understanding. What Himmler did not feel, his diaries do not express. Vital information on his early relationship with his mother is almost utterly lacking."[72] Hoffman says that Himmler may have been schizoid, have had murderous rage, but the facts to support these assertions are not present. She concludes that "This suggestive theory augments Loewenberg's description of Himmler, but the evidence does not allow for a convincing explanation."[73]

In still another critique of an article by Loewenberg, "The Psychohistorical Origins of the Nazi Youth Cohort," Hoffman is more accepting of his use of object relations theory. Hoffman points out that for this subject Loewenberg has more sources available and that his interpretation is better demonstrated. The issue Loewenberg addresses in this paper is why Hitler and the Nazi party appealed to the young people in Germany after 1928. Some of his reasons include the fact that the generation born between 1900 and 1915 shared common traumatic experiences, such as material and psychological deprivation, "the fragmentation of families," and that these experiences led to feelings of anxiety and hostility in the young people.[74] Accordingly, the Nazi movement channeled its latent anti-social predisposition. In this instance, Hoffman not only approves of Loewenberg's use of theory, but recommends it for its direction, noting: "The result is a truly interdisciplinary point of view which draws on demographic data, political history, literature, clinical records of children under treatment, personal memoirs, and other sources, then uses methods and concepts from history, sociology, and psychoanalysis. This article exemplifies the integrated approach Weinstein and Platt (1975) advocated four years after Loewenberg's articles appeared, urging a shift from biography to collective experience and linking social reality with internal conflicts and drives".[75]

As for Hughes' *Emotions and High Politics*, Hoffman notes that in this work she provides a possible third approach, which is "neither pure biography nor social analysis but an interweaving of personal and family history with larger events."[76] Hoffman describes Hughes' thesis, indicating how she "explores the interactions among her subjects' earliest lives."[77] But Hughes recognizes that she would have liked more extensive documentation on her subjects' early childhoods, as well as on the family lives of each group of statesmen. Hoffman takes cognizance that in this work, the role of the father in raising the children is very secondary. In accepting the theories of Fairbairn and Winnicott, and diminishing the import of the Oedipus complex, Hoffman underlines this, and says: "Thus, the maternal relationship is first in priority, both temporally and emotionally, and sets the pattern for the child's interactions with others."[78] What this means—the focus on the mother by Hughes—is that "her interpretation entails a revision of the traditional image of the family and psychodynamics."[75]

As for the way Hughes uses theory, Hoffman says that she reads meaning into material that is just not there, that she "sometimes stretches"[80] its application. For example, Lord Salisbury's daughter who wrote a biography of him, in which her father said little of his mother, Hughes takes this to mean that they did not have a good relationship. Hoffman says of Hughes that her "style is retrospective," that she traces the history of these statesmen back to their infancy and childhood, to ascertain what shaped their character.[81]

With regard to Bismarck, whose alienation from his mother was well known, since he did not feel loved by her, Hoffman quotes Hughes, who writes that "he became a notoriously good hater," which also affected his political behaviour.[82]

In weighing the merits of object relations theory, Hoffman takes a position herself, but she does so along gender lines. She says: "If psychodynamic interpretations have a place in understanding history, then a theory in which the mother rather than the father is the crucial parent offers an opportunity to redress the male gender bias implicit in earlier explanations and to redirect attention toward experiences that previously were given little weight."[83]

Hoffman does not feel that just emphasizing the mother-infant bond is going to become the solution in psychohistorical work, because the matter of adequate documentation will persist. However, the range of issues and interpretations for the psychohistorian are now more varied. Hoffman concludes on an affirmative note, recommending object relations theory because: "This approach goes beyond the older psychoanalytic emphasis on innate drives and offers a way to recognize the uniqueness of particular individuals and events—a quality essential to historians, as Weinstein and Platt (1975) observed a decade ago."[84]

In sum, the above discussion of the theoretical developments in psychoanalysis, and its application to history have indicated the diversity of theoretical paradigms faced by psychohistorians, issues which, on the one hand, stem from a reading of Freud and on the other, that of subjective perspectives and responses to contemporary events. Psychoanalysis is marked by controversy, competing and divergent "schools", as is psychohistory. Psychoanalysis is also marked by individuals who have become charismatic leaders, and if they advance the field, they also fragment it.[85] Furthermore, for all the variegated responses, whether advancing psychoanalysis or bringing discredit to it, the fecundity of Freud's thought remains. Developments in psychoanalysis also affect psychohistory, and here too the responses and practices are related to the theoretical developments in that field. And some historians have undertaken psychoanalytic training and become practicing psychoanalysts.

3. The French Interpreters

The third epicenter of psychoanalysis is France. The rather widespread acceptance of psychoanalysis in France can be dated to the 1960s, especially to the turbulent days of May 1968 which acted as a catapult for the field. In comparison with the other countries just discussed, psychoanalysis was accepted slowly in

France. However, after the Second World War, the pace accelerated and a rich psychoanalytic literature flourished.

The initial cultural resistance to, and eventual acceptance of, psychoanalysis in France are reflective of its unique and particular traditions. Ironically, in terms of what took place, Freud was amazed at the seemingly rapid acceptance of psychoanalysis in the United States in the early 1900s. He even felt that a too ready acceptance signified that psychoanalysis was being diluted. In France, and in some other European countries, where it was resisted, Freud felt that it meant that psychoanalysis was taken seriously. At the present time, the former attitude of negation has reversed itself, and France is now one of the foremost centers of psychoanalysis and psychohistory.

That the process of cultural acceptance in France was slow is paradoxical. The very strength of its literary traditions, based on pride in the ability of the French *moralistes* who for centuries had been exemplars in introspectively examining human conscience, made for a climate in which a foreigner, such as Freud, had little to teach the French about human motivation. The Freudian doctrine, with its claim of being able to scientifically study the ways of the heart and the mind was considered to be not on a par with the French classics. And even Freud had first been inspired by Charcot. As H. Stuart Hughes observes, what had a people who had produced a Stendahl and a Montaigne to learn from a Viennese physician.[86]

Psychoanalysis in France between the two world wars was marginal to psychiatry and medicine, finding acceptance by just a few literary figures and artists, mainly the Surrealists. And when the bulk of psychoanalysts left their centers of origin in central Europe, which included the luminaries in the field, they bypassed France. In general, the vast emigration of intellectuals from central Europe to the English-speaking world served to reduce their provincialism. This great exchange of ideas had such beneficial consequences that it is considered to be the most important intellectual event of the era.[87]

Cultural pride and nationalism acted then to withstand psychoanalysis in France. Before World War II it was resented for its Germanic origins, and after the war it was disdained as a dubious American import, associated with permissive childrearing.[88] There were still other sources of opposition, religious and ideological, which were noted in the part on Freud's philosophy of history in chapter II, and which have general application to France as well. Unique to France was the role of the Communist party, which has been so prominent in French life for a number of decades. The Communist Party's position toward psychoanalysis was an antagonistic one, but in the 1960s its position softened. Some communist intellectuals even tried to reconcile Freud's thought with Marxism.[89]

Despite the cultural opposition, psychoanalysis was not completely disregarded, for in the period under consideration some of the most illustrious intellectuals were nevertheless influenced by Freud. There have been many psychoanalytic writers of stature in France, such as Didier Anzieu, Marie Bonaparte, Janine Chasseguet-Smirgel, Daniel Lagache,[90] Jean Laplanche, Jean-Baptiste Pontalis, Octave Mannoni, and Paul Ricoeur. Leading intellectuals who were influenced by Freud are Michel Foucault, Jacques Derrida, Louis Althusser, and Jean-Paul Sartre himself, to mention but a few.

Because of the time when psychoanalysis finally became a public issue, and since one person in particular was so responsible for dramatically bringing attention to the field, it is convenient now to highlight this man's ideas and influence. The most colorful, celebrated, and controversial figure on the psychoanalytic scene in France was Jacques Lacan. His role was closely tied to the vicissitudes of psychoanalysis in France. It was not until Lacan became popular in the 1960s that French psychoanalysis acquired international recognition.

A cogent biographical note on Lacan is that his background is notably eclectic. He was born in Paris (1901–1981), in a middle class Catholic family. He was the eldest of his siblings. His sister Madeleine, born in 1903, became a nun, and his brother, Marc-François, born in 1908, became a priest.[91] He himself was an atheist, abjuring all Christian beliefs and practices. In his youth, he excelled in German, and had a strong interest in philosophy. He received a medical degree, followed by neuropsychiatric training in the 1920s and in 1932 he wrote his medical thesis, which was a study of a paranoid personality. In this period, he both studied Spinoza and attended meetings of the monarchist and notoriously reactionary Action

Française, headed by Charles Maurras.[92] In 1932, he undertook an analysis with Rudolf Loewenstein, an eminent psychoanalyst from Berlin, who had settled in Paris. The analysis lasted six years, but is not considered to have been succesful, for it appears that Lacan was less than sincere in his commitment to being analyzed. In a confidential letter to Marie Bonaparte dated February 22, 1953, Loewenstein wrote to tell her what he thought of Lacan. He wrote: "He always constituted for me a source of conflict: on the one hand, his lack of character, on the other, his intellectual value, which I prize highly though not without violent disagreement."[93]

The analysis did not go well, as it appears that Lacan could not endure the length of the sessions, nor the length of time that therapy entailed. And it is alleged that Lacan undertook this training opportunistically in order to fulfill the requirements of the credentials.[94] According to Elisabeth Roudinesco, there was also a theoretical difference. Loewenstein accepted the concept of the death instinct, whereas Lacan did not.[95]

In the paramount matter of conducting psychoanalytic therapy, Lacan did not follow the fundamental principles established by Freud. Didier Anzieu, who had been Lacan's analysand, stopped in frustration, after only two years with him. Anzieu recounts that the initial sessions lasted for forty to forty-five minutes, set for appointed times. Then, the sessions became shorter, and shorter, until they lasted twenty minutes. Lacan would schedule many people so that "The waiting room became filled with persons anxious to know if they would be received—Lacan opened the door, designated the chosen one, who would retrace his steps ten or fifteen minutes later in order to leave."[96] Anzieu recalls that sometimes Lacan would cancel his appointment with him. Anzieu is aware that, because of his "negative transference" he could not complete his analysis. Anzieu also describes what occurred in his sessions, which is also not acceptable in a Freudian analysis. Anzieu recounts: "During the sessions Lacan was intermittently attentive. Sometimes, instead of sitting in his analyst's chair, he paced back and forth in the room in order to stretch his legs, to take a book; he sat at his work table and read, leafing pages covered with Chinese letters, which apparently, he was learning . . . Sometimes, his maid knocked on the door, to bring tea, sandwiches, the mail, or to alert him that he was wanted on the telephone. Lacan gave instructions for the answers or even went to answer himself."[97]

Although Lacan went on to generally have a poor press, he still has his partisans. An American, who lauds Lacan, and who went to Paris to be analyzed by him is Stuart Schneiderman. A former professor of English, Schneiderman had an analysis with Lacan and trained at the Ecole Freudienne, then returned to New York as a Lacanian analyst. He has written a book, *Jacques Lacan: The Death of an Intellectual Hero*, which is a paean to Lacan.[98] This book, however, is difficult to take seriously. It is humorous, nonsensical, irrational, and mystifying, on just about every page. These qualities of irrevence were cultivated and displayed by Lacan. The following quote gives a sampling of Schneiderman's view of Lacan, as it appears in the "prologue": "His writings are finely wrought, even overwrought, and they do not easily make sense. In this they resemble poetry, and like poetry they yield to critical thinking. Yet this resemblance is a ploy, a rhetorical ploy. This was my thought when I decided that it would be contradictory for me to continue explicating texts when I knew nothing of the experience from which the texts were drawn."[99]

Schneiderman approvingly says that Lacan "provoked a series of bitter struggles within the world of psychoanalysis," which then caused him to be expelled from the International Psychoanalytic Association.[100] He recognizes that Lacan was "outrageous." To use Schneiderman's own words, he says of Lacan: "He was prone to making scenes in public, to being abrupt and rude, to expressing his amorous intentions toward women in flagrant ways. (One, it is told, a taxi driver was so impressed by a love scene between Lacan and a woman in the back seat of his cab that he called for an appointment the next morning and went on to spend several years in analysis with Lacan)."[101]

The following quote, which describes Lacan as analyst is curious indeed. It is so substantive and perplexing that the entire paragraph is quoted:

> Lacan as an analyst was not trying to establish any sort of communication with his patients; nor did he think it a good idea that they understand each other. Like most analysts he encouraged free asso-

ciation but did not listen to it as if it were the ranting of someone involved in a gratuitous sort of self-indulgence. Lacan, like most analysts, listened to something other than what was said; he listened as if the remarks that were about him were really addressed to someone else and as if the remarks of the analysand that were supposed to be about himself were really about an other. This he did without saying very much. But acting much of the time as if he were a creature from another planet, even another galaxy, Lacan gave the impression that he was hearing something other than what you were saying. He never put himself on the same wavelength as his analysand, but remained always at cross purposes. He never tried to find areas of agreement and accord, but scrupulously maintained a fruitful, well-turned discord.[102]

In Sherry Turkle's *Psychoanalytic Politics: Freud's French Revolution*, the author develops her view that Lacan is a "French Freud," hence his stellar acclaim. Making comparisons between American and French emphases in psychoanalysis, Turkle observes how cultural specificity influences adaptation. Unlike an American, who for instance has been influenced by tales of the frontier, which in his psyche would mean the struggles of the ego in dealing with a difficult environmental reality, a French patient would have a different psychic susceptibility, one which since grade school was taught *explication de texte*, accentuated by literature.[103] With such a formation a French person "might be more receptive to a psychoanalysis which presents itself as a form of textual analysis on the unconscious."[104] It is this cultural background that Lacan was able to tap.

For Lacan, language is central to thought, but what further recommends him in France is his structuralism, in line with the Cartesian tradition. He is poetic, satisfying the French taste for a poetic psychology, and he is political, resonant with French intellectual life which is highly politicized and ideological.[105] And he is extremely controversial. Despite Lacan's centrality to French psychoanalytic culture, his interpretations and practice of psychoanalysis were so iconoclastic that in the early 1960s he and his followers were expelled from the International Psychoanalytic Association.

Characteristically, the reactions to Lacan are not neutral, varying from lauding him in superlatives to considering him to be prepostorous. As David J. Fisher, an American psychohistorian, psychoanalyst, and scholar of contemporary French intellectual thought succinctly puts it, "Jacques Lacan is the revolutionary figure of French psychoanalysis."[106] According to Fisher, Lacan oscillates between being a genius and a buffoon.

On the positive side, Lacan has made theoretical contributions by examining the issue of the relative importance between the individual and his society. To Lacan, the mental and the social are intertwined. He therefore tried to grapple with the way the internal psychic mechanisms developed, and tried to decipher the psycholinguistic modes of social and cultural expression. As Fisher notes, "Lacanian inquiry focuses on the perspective of how society and law enter the individual, with particular reference to the role of language and symbol for conferring social meaning."[107]

Lacan, in a key passage in a chapter entitled "La fonction créatrice de la parole," from his book *Les Ecrits Techniques de Freud*, indicates why language is so central to psychoanalysis:

> Every time that we have in the analysis of language to search for the meaning of a word, the only correct method is to make the sum of its uses. If you wish to know in the French language the meaning of the word 'main' (hand), you should draw up the list of its uses, and not only when it represents the bodily organ of the hand, but as well when it figures in 'main-d'oeuvre, mainmise, mainmorte, etc.' (manpower, manumission, mortmain, etc.). The meaning is given by the sum of its uses.
> We have to deal with this in analysis. We don't have to exhaust ourselves at all in finding the additional references. What need is there to speak of a reality that would support the so-called metaphorical uses? Any type of use, in a certain sense, is always metaphorical.[108]

Not only does Lacan acknowledge his great debt to Freud, but he is an advocate of fidelity to the Freudian text. The following passage has been selected to show just how Lacan regards Freud, and the importance which Freud himself placed on language. Lacan, referring to Freud's *The Interpretation of Dreams*, states:

> Freud shows us how the word, namely the transmission of a desire, can make itself recognized through anything, provided that this anything is organized in a symbolic system. That is the source that for a long time has been the undecipherable nature of the dream. And it is

for the same reason that we have not been able for a long time to understand hieroglyphics—they were not composed in their own symbolic system. It wasn't noticed that a small human silhouette, that could stand for a man, and, as such, could form part of a word as a syllable. Dreams are like hieroglyphics. Freud cites, as you know, the Rosetta Stone.[109]

On another issue, that of the self, Lacan posits that the self exits only in conjunction with society, but that now, in postindustrial society, the self is fragmented and conflicted. This position has a nuance which makes it differ from Freud's, whose intention it was to strengthen the capabilities of the ego. According to Lacan, the self does not exist in isolation, but in relation to "Others." By "Others" Lacan means that, for example, the child's desire for his parents, desires which cannot be satisfied, not even with psychoanalytic treatment. The frustration will persist, it is at the core of every person, and the parents will remain distant, symbolic objects. In this stand, Lacan is radical, for he argues that the aim of developing a coherent ego is not a valid goal. Indeed, he claims, the goals of adaptability and adjustment are really opportunistic attempts at social engineering, at accepting a conservative societal *status quo*. From the Lacanian perspective there is a contradiction in the way Freud is interpreted. On the one hand there is stress on uncovering the unconscious, with its liberating implications, and, on the other, insistence on adjusting to rational life. Taking such a position had political overtones for Lacan, who thereby criticized American theoretical developments. He did so because they appeared to him to have a need to create respectability for psychoanalysis, and in effect shackled the emancipatory features of Freudian creativity. In accordance with this view, Lacan provided therapy with no intention of strengthening the ego, the mental executive apparatus. For the advocates of ego psychology, Lacan had nothing but contempt.[110]

Clearly, Lacan is controversial, and his theoretical concepts are widely challenged. This is so even when he claims to be a faithful interpreter of Freudian thought. His clinical practice is generally not acceptable to mainstream psychoanalytic thought, and he is responsible for creating more splits and dissensions in France than exist in any other country. Where

Lacan is creative it is as a philosopher of psychoanalysis and as a critic of the field. He has attained this stature by borrowing widely from a gamut of disciplines, such as linguistics, surrealism, Hegelian and phenomenological philosophy, and of course psychoanalysis. But there are theoretical limitations. It is significant that in his major writings Lacan does not offer case studies. His theories are not supported by clinical evidence.[111] Although Lacan claims to foster a fidelity to Freudian ideas, his use of them is highly selective and arbitrary, and ultimately he departs from Freudian techniques.[112]

Yet, Lacan has had a stimulating effect on French psychoanalysis, his influence culminating in the heady days of May-June 1968. Lacan was one of the stars and charismatic figures of this period. His views converged with the outlook of this cultural revolution, which was like a surrealist happening. After 1968, the status of psychoanalysis changed profoundly in France, becoming far more widely accepted. And a distinctive feature of the nature of psychoanalysis in France was that, in comparison to the direction it had taken in the United States and Great Britain, it was more transdisciplinary.[113]

It is appropriate now to conclude with Fisher's assessment and summary of Lacan's role:

> If psychoanalysis is revolutionary in the contemporary French context, Lacan has played the ambiguous role of a Freudian Bonaparte. The next generation of French analysts and intellectuals will have to decide whether Lacan has perverted or extended the liberating techniques and spirit of psychoanalysis. This choice may turn on their ability to reconcile his libertarian methods and his verbal exhortations to freedom with his authoritarian personality and his dictatorial style.[114]

During World War II, when France was occupied, psychoanalysis received a serious set back as was the case throughout occupied Europe.[115] In Germany too, formerly one of the centers of the field, psychoanalysis was brought into line with Nazi ideology.[116] After the war, psychoanalysis slowly began to re-emerge.[117] With the publication of Lacan's works in the 1960s psychoanalysis became very popular, and in the three decades since then, psychoanalysis has acquired a centrality in intellectual thought formerly held by Marxism, existentialism and structuralism. In fact, Freud's thought may now hold in France, in the 1990s, "a centrality it probably never really possessed in the United States, even at the peak of its popularity."[118] In December 1994 a Freud Library of 12,000 volumes was opened. This Library, founded by the Societé Psychanalytique de Paris (The Psychoanalytic Society of Paris), included some fifty psychoanalytic and related journals, published in France and abroad.

4. Kohut and Self Psychology

Although there has been a proliferation of psychoanalytic theoreticians, there have been few who have oriented themselves to providing new theoretical directions for historians. An exception is Heinz Kohut (1913–1981), whose ideas have been accepted and applied by some historians. Kohut, though primarily concerned with theoretical applications to clinical problems, was a keen student of history, specifically devoting himself to writing about historical figures and issues. His connection with the field of history was hardly fortuitous, for it was intrinsic in his writings. In recognition of this interest, Kohut was specifically invited to address historians at a symposium sponsored by the Group for the Use of Psychology in History (GUPH) and the Center for Psychosocial Studies on the occasion of the annual meeting of the American Historical Association, held in Chicago in December 1974. The title of his paper was "The Self in History."[119] Again, such an invitation to a psychoanalyst to meet with a body of professional historians was exceptional. However, for all of Kohut's relevance to psychohistory, his meta-psychological formulations mark a departure from classical psychoanalysis and may be considered a challenge and opposition to psychoanalysis.

Kohut was born in Vienna, where he attended the Gymnasium, and at nineteen, entered the University of Vienna to study medicine. His early classical education, which included the study of numerous languages and a privileged social background, served to develop his interest in the arts. He graduated from the University of Vienna and received his medical degree in 1938. At the same time, he became interested in psychoanalysis and was analyzed by August Eichorn, who was close to Freud.[120] Although Kohut never met Freud, there is an interesting anecdote regarding how he once saw Freud. Kohut was advised to see Freud off at the train station in 1938. As Freud's train, bound for Paris, was pulling out of the station, he was looking out the window. Kohut tipped his hat to the elderly Freud, and Freud returned the gesture. This incident had much meaning for Kohut, as he was fond of telling this story. Several months later, Kohut too was forced to leave Vienna, and went to England. In 1940, he came to the United States and settled in Chicago. Charles B. Strozier, who knew Kohut personally and helped to publish his works, observed that Kohut was "consciously modeling himself on Freud."[121] Strozier also said that Kohut had "an early sense of purpose," and that he had "an inner fire and lofty ambition to be Freud's successor, long before those thoughts had any basis in actuality".[122] Strozier has a high opinion of Kohut, describing him as a great man, talented, charming and enthusiastic. However, with an obvious suggestion as to how his theories grew out of his own character, Strozier also says that Kohut's "self-centeredness could isolate people and cause wounds that lasted a lifetime."[123]

The issue of Kohut's theoretical reformulations were not just confined to professional circles, but were significant enough to attain wide public attention, as in the *New York Times Magazine* article "Oedipus vs. Narcissus" (11/9/80) by Susan Quinn.[124] The title of the article captures well the nature of the dispute, and the article highlights the theoretical differences. Quinn points out that Kohut's new analytic approach is called "self-psychology," because it stresses the narcissistic personality. Accordingly, Kohut feels that traditional psychoanalysis is no longer suitable to the kind of patient who was coming to therapy in the 1960s. With this rationale, Freud is regarded as having treated patients who typically suffered from hysterical symptoms, but now, in the second half of the twentieth century, such patients were rare. The reasons for the change is that the societal climate of sexual repression had diminished. According to Kohut, patients now were more apt to suffer "narcissistic character disorders."[125] In Kohut's view, the narcissistic person is one who has experienced rejection in early childhood and is marked by a generalized feeling of anxiety, cannot develop mature relationships, has insatiable needs to be admired, and whose alienation from others worsen as he grows older. The narcissistic disorder then is, as Kohut designates it, a "disorder of the self."[126]

Quinn argues that Kohut's early experiences sensitized him to "the theme of self-fragmentation"[127] which came to dominate his work. One experience is that as an only child he was forcibly uprooted from his native land, whose language and culture he was so passionately attached to. As Kohut formulated his constructs on narcissism, he moved ever further away from Freudian psychoanalysis.

Other theoreticians (such as Otto Kernberg) have also been concerned with the issue of narcissism, but they remained within mainstream psychoanalysis. Kohut rejected a central construct of psychoanalysis, the Oedipus complex, arguing instead that developmental conflicts arise because of "thwarted developmental needs,"[128] or extremely frustrating experiences in childhood. Since the narcissistic personality has been difficult to analyze, Kohut blames the theoretical inadequacy of the traditional approach for difficulty in analyzing the narcissistic personality. Instead of regarding conflicts as stemming from repressed sexual and aggressive drives, Kohut believes that they stem from inadequate responses to narcissistic aspirations. And the proper way to treat such patients is to understand them, in ways that they were not understood as children. And the way to reach them is by "empathy", a term that looms large in the Kohutian paradigm and which typifies his clinical approach. Simply put, it is the lack of empathy on the part of the parents which causes narcissistic personality disorders.[129]

With the publication of Kohut's *The Restoration of the Self* in 1977, the rift became more delineated. Many psychoanalysts rejected Kohut's work, even if they acknowledged that he brought new attention to the difficult patient. For example, Kernberg argued that what Kohut advocated ran counter to his clinical experiences with narcissistic patients, and that Kohut neglected feelings of aggression and hatred in the narcissistic person.[130] To charges which arose against Kohut that he was grandiose for not giving proper credit to those who had previously written on the subject and that he himself was narcissistic, Kohut invoked Freud, who he said had initially also faced enormous opposition to his ideas.[131]

Psychoanalytic Theory 151

Kohut's new theoretical directions have been indicated and his major works will now be cited, but emphasis in this section will be on Kohut's and his adherents' reaching out to the field of history. In 1971, with the publication of *The Analysis of the Self*, Kohut introduced his new formulations.[132] In this work, there was a lack of precision in his conceptual definitions, as he both seemed to accept established theory and proposed modifications. Among the many readers he thanks in his "acknowledgements," is Anna Freud.[133] As already indicated, in this book Kohut speaks about types of transferences, the grandiose self, narcissism, empathy, and art and creativity.[134] Again, in 1977, with the publication of *The Restoration of the Self*, the break was clear. In the "Preface", Kohut wrote that: "The present volume transcends my previous writings on narcissism in several directions. In the earlier contributions I presented my findings concerning the psychology of the self mainly in the language of classical drive theory."[135] And he makes the point, which is central to his theoretical approach that: "In comparison with my earlier contributions, the present work expresses more explicitly my reliance on the empathic-introspective stance, which has been defining my conceptual-theoretical outlook ever since 1959."[136]

As cited earlier, in 1974 Kohut spoke on "The Self in History" at a historical symposium. Before Kohut spoke, Ernest S. Wolf, a psychoanalyst affiliated with the Chicago Institute for Psychoanalysis, presented and summarized Kohut's main ideas. John Demos, a historian, moderated the symposium and was a warm exponent of Kohut's theoretical approach for the study of history.[137]

In his opening remarks, Kohut said that the intellectual development of his youth had been strongly influenced by a high school history teacher and that this teacher had inspired him. As Kohut began to expound on his theories, with regard to history and the study of groups, he posited a main point, which is that "the importance which the discovery of the remainders of the early object love and object hate had for adult psychopathology and for adult individual life would be matched by the importance which narcissistic motivations had for group behavior and for the behavior of man within groups."[138] With regard to narcissistic injuries, he said that great writers had anticipated some of his findings, as by Tolstoy, in *Anna Karenina*, in which a writer is panned by a reviewer because a few years earlier the writer had corrected one word that man had said, thereby publically humiliating him.[139] Such slights Kohut says, which are blows to one's prestige and sense of specialness applies to groups as well as to individuals. According to Kohut the study of group motivations from this perspective will add a new dimension to the data used by historians. Concerning historical aspects of narcissism, Kohut adds, "But I think that even those material forces if imbricated with the narcissistic dimension will go much farther in order to explain why people behave as they do, why they sometimes would rather die than live with an injury of this particular type."[140]

Kohut also argues for bridging the gap between historians and depth-psychologists so that each can reach out beyond his discipline. He says that they should work together and learn from each other, as they are on the same team in their quest for knowledge and that their working methods have much in common. In Kohut's opinion: "It seems to me that history and psychoanalysis are in many ways the most important sciences of the future."[141] The reason for this importance, says Kohut, is because of overpopulation, which is at crisis proportion in the world. In the future, people will have to have fewer children, as expansion into new continents has ceased. Accordingly, Kohut warns, "If humans are to survive in a way that has any relatedness to what we have prized up till now as being human I believe that the narcissistic motivation, the motivation of the individual, must come into the ascendency."[142] In conclusion he said that he hoped to see formed a "new science of the future which is neither history nor depth-psychology but which is a new fusion between these two disciplines."[143]

At the conclusion of Kohut's talk, an interesting question and answer period followed. Demos spoke too, expressing his support for Kohut's ideas and criticizing Freud for his theoretical limitations in many areas, but especially for his concepts on female psychology. Demos considered that Kohut's ideas brought about "new possibilities and potentialities that are opened up for historical research by the investigation of the developmental line of narcissism."[144] Then, Demos took aim at a fundamental construct of psychoanalytic theory, which serves to exemplify the theoretical differences between the two camps. Demos said: "And I am making here an implicit or perhaps an explicit contrast or comparison with the whole theory of object love and hate which is the basis for orthodox psychoanalytic and psychohistorical work."[145] Demos continued in this vein, saying that the traditional psychohistorical approach to leaders was "incomplete," "discontinuous or dissatisfying."[146] On the other hand, he said, "The narcissistic emphasis may therefore prove to be very fruitful in that context."[147] Furthermore, in recommending Kohut's approach he said, "the theory of narcissism as it is currently being developed and applied in psychoanalysis makes no preference between male and female."[148] Demos claimed that Freud's theories were inadequate for the study of women, and that narcissism avoids this particular trap because it is not dependent on the same anatomic and biological distinctions that classical Freudian theory makes."[149]

Ernest S. Wolf, affiliated with Kohut as an exponent of Self-Psychology, in his "Psychoanalytic Selfobject Psychology and Psychohistory," also addresses historians.[150] He highlights Kohut's conceptualizations and advances its applications to the study of history. Advocating Kohut's views, Wolf criticizes Freud for not having gone further in elaborating on the importance of empathy. And, says Wolf, classical psychoanalysis does not go far enough in recognizing how essential this aspect is, but Kohut emphasizes the significance of empathy in the clinical situation. With specific criticism of the psychic constructs of id, ego, and superego, Wolf replaces it by saying that "we talk about the self and about selfobjects."[151]

After reviewing the new concepts, Wolf explains why they are recommended to historians. He says that "empathy-based interpretations" are preferable to the traditional "theory-based interpretations" for psychohistorical research.[152] Wolf underlines this by stating that "the application of certain psychoanalytic theories to historical data yields interpretations about the meaning of historical events that are theory near but experience-distant."[153] Wolf elaborates on this approach and adds that the psychohistorian should favor "the kind of deep immersion into his historical material that would evoke in him an emotional involvement and reactions to which he would gain access by introspection."[154]

After summarizing the value of Kohut's clinical innovations, Wolf noted that an understanding of narcissistic injuries can help to understand group behavior and the role of leaders. For example, when a group finds itself threatened, it needs special "self objects to shore up the crumbling group-self", leading to a need for a messianic leader. Winston Churchill, says Wolf, was such a leader for Britain during World War II.[155] In line with Kohut's thinking, Wolf has high praise for the importance of empathy, which means "to really listen to and attempt to understand another person" and that will lead "to bridge the boundaries of race, religion, and nation, of generation, epoch, and time bound past ages, that is, to transcend individual and group self."[156] Indeed, Wolf has high expectations for this ideal, for he concludes by claiming that "the developing psychoanalytic selfobject psychology can become a powerful tool for illuminating difficult questions in history and the social sciences."[157]

In still another essay, "Self Psychology and the Sciences of Man," Kohut examines historical issues in light of his theories. He begins his essay by stating his fundamental theoretical proposition: "The basic premise of the psychoanalytic psychology of the self is the defining position it assigns to empathy and introspection."[158] Here again, although he recognizes Freud's contributions, Kohut considers his own work a major advance in psychoanalysis. He writes, "Self psychology is instrumental in ushering in a new phase in the history of psychoanalysis: the move from a preoccupation with the elaboration and refinement of the established theories to one of renewed emphasis on the gathering of primary data, a return to the emphatic observation of inner experience."[159]

After reviewing his theoretical innovations, Kohut applies his findings to literature, art, and history. In literature, he examines the widely accepted psychoanalytic interpretation of Shakespeare's character Hamlet, which considers his conflict to be oedipal in nature. Kohut rejects this explanation in favor of what he considers to be Hamlet's needs, arguing that his parents had been inadequate to him.[160] Kohut makes a transition from literature to history, and offers some parallels between Hamlet and Denmark and Hitler and Germany. As Kohut observes, although there are similarities in both situations, differences exist. He is mainly concerned with a moment in German history when there was a "serious disturbance" in the strength and cohesion of the German group self, which "was experienced without the empathic sustaining voice of the truly creative individuals among the artists or political leaders or from the world that surrounded Germany during the 15 years between the peace of Versailles and the assumption of power by the Nazi party."[161] Kohut admits that to understand the Nazi phenomenon is so enormous that it is something he cannot do, but it is also "beyond the powers of the depth psychologist."[162] Kohut's position on this is that he can only try to convince historians and political scientists what they should do, but he is certain that "the psychological explanations which self psychology can offer are in essence correct."[163]

Kohut expounds his line of approach about the German people at a critical time in their history. He makes many recommendations and raises many questions, and returning to the case of Hamlet, asks a question which indicates his path: "Was Hamlet's self stronger than that of Germany's group self?"[164] Like Hamlet, Kohut says, Germany had experienced a great defeat after World War I. All the details of Kohut's presentation cannot be discussed here, but among his key points on this subject are the "chronic weakness of the German group self," and lack of "sustained self objects," which caused the group "serious fragmentation."[165]

Kohut discusses the role of art during the Weimar period, which he says the psychohistorian should pursue. His point is that the artists were out of touch with the people, and the Nazis knew this, hence they publicized it as degenerate. Additionally, Kohut says, the educated classes, political thinkers, and the artists, writers, and musicians "failed to provide the German group self with the needed resonance that would have encouraged development toward a new self image."[166] Kohut suggests that what Germany needed in the 1930's was a Churchill, who knew how to rally his people in a constructive way.[167]

Kohut compared the leadership of the Weimar regime, which followed the defeated monarchy of Germany in 1918, to an incompetent analyst. And since that portion of the people whose "self had been most severely damaged by the war" had formed no workable transference to the new regime, that leadership had responded negatively labeling these people as "unanalyzable."[168] Only when the threat became ominous did they respond and "offer some remedial understanding," but it came too late. Kohut says that all leaders failed. Hitler, however, succeeded, because he was a charismatic leader. Finally, Kohut contends, "it was the abysmal failure of constructive empathy in Germany and in its European surroundings that made Hitler possible."[169] And in his closing paragraph, Kohut faults Freud for not better recognizing the coming world catastrophe, in effect, because he did not recognize the significance of narcissistic injury and of the self.[170]

The last of Kohut's papers to be cited, "*Creativeness, Charisma, Group Psychology: Reflections on the Self-Analysis of Freud*, not only concerns his views of Freud and the creativity that resulted from Freud's beneficial relationship with Wilhelm Fliess, but its example for future advances in knowledge.[171] Kohut indicates an interest not only in the individual, but in groups and their behavior. The promise of such an undertaking of any group ever being able to overcome its inner resistances and thus make a decisive step toward the understanding of the dynamics of its behavior, such as the sources of its conflicts and ambivalences, then that group "will have laid the foundations for a valid psychological understanding of history."[172]

Thomas A. Kohut, the son of Heinz Kohut, is a historian and has continued in his father's footsteps, applying self-psychological theories to the study of history. Kohut's article on the subject "Psychohistory as History" was published in the *American Historical Review*, in 1986.[173] What makes the younger Kohut's work especially noteworthy is that he is both a professor of history as well as a practicing psychoanalyst, and he applies his clinical work to his study of historical figures.

Kohut, in line with his father's methodology is critical of "traditional" psychohistory. His essential opposition is that psychohistory relies too much on psychoanalytic theory. As he says, "figures and events from the past are not comprehended or made comprehensible on their own terms but are understood and explained primarily by psychological theory."[174] Psychohistorians, he adds, study the past with preconceived ideas, and the explanations they offer are the result of a theoretical model, not from the specific evidence available. His second objection is that unlike traditional historians who use only the evidence that is available to them, psychohistorians by relying on theory "accept evidence from the present to validate their interpretations."[175] To prove his contentions, Kohut singles out Erikson's *Young Man Luther*. He says that "Erikson made no systematic attempt to prove solely with evidence from the past that Luther experienced a crisis of identity or that such a phenomenon existed in Luther's time."[176] Another fundamental objection Kohut makes of Erikson's *Young Man Luther* is that it "is a vehicle that Erikson used to popularize his views on identity and on the crisis of identity that often accompanies the transition from adolescence to adulthood."[177]

However, what is essential in Kohut's methodology is the role of empathy, for the clinician and the historian. Elaborating on this key point, he argues that empathy is the ability to be aware of subjective responses and to be able "to experience, although to a necessarily attenuated degree, the experience of another."[178] And, he adds, for therapist and historian, "understanding is achieved when the investigator puts himself in the place of the other and imagines why—given the time, place, circumstance, and experience of the other—it makes sense that he felt, thought, and acted as he did."[179] Kohut claims that by not relying on theory, but on "empathy," "the historian can remain a historian."[180] To underscore this point, Kohut adds that the historian "can continue to use traditional historical methods and, in doing so, function in a way that is fundamentally compatible with the way in which the psychoanalyst functions as a clinician."[181]

As indicated above, Kohut has had clinical experience, and training as a research candidate at the Cincinnati Psychoanalytic Institute. He refers to a patient and to himself as historical figures. Kohut recounts how a patient, who had felt abandoned in his childhood, reacted when he told him that he was going on vacation. This triggered a reaction in the patient, who, fearing desertion by the analyst, left the room. The point that Kohut makes is that "empathy" rather reliance on theory, helped him to understand the patient's dynamics.[182] This experience became a lesson to apply when he was studying Kaiser Wilhelm II. The Kaiser, as he often did, reacted inappropriately to a failed German expedition to the South Pole in 1903. The Kaiser's outburst was intense, and feeling personally humiliated, he wanted to punish the leader of the expedition. Fortunately, his friend Philipp Eulenburg, who was with the Kaiser, understood the meaning of the Kaiser's reaction, and explained it to him. Kohut says that he understood the behavior in both situations as "a wish to do to others what has been experienced as having been done to the self."[183] In sum, in Kohut's exposition of his methodology, empathy takes precedence over theory, and the psychoanalytic approach to history is dismissed. Kohut states at the end of the article that "historians neither need to nor should depend on the psychohistorical method in studying the past's psychological dimension."[184]

Where does Heinz Kohut's self psychology stand in relation to psychoanalysis? Kohut's work has attracted much attention and a number of adherants, but it has not supplanted psychoanalysis. And in comparison with psychoanalysis, self psychology seems quite limited. In an evaluation of that work, Marshall A. Greene in "The Self Psychology of Heinz Kohut: A Synopsis and Critique," demonstrates its inadequacies.[185] Greene notes that initially there was great interest in Kohut's work, but that ultimately it was not a significant breakthrough. Greene even criticizes Kohut's writing style, describing it as "turgid", and he says that he uses "confusing terminology."[186] Greene points out that Kohut "defined terms in one way and then used them in another."[187] For example, the term "self", which he defined the way Hartmann did, but eventually "used it to mean almost the totality of the psychic apparatus."[188] Greene, to cite only the essential points of his extensive critique, says that Kohut's discussion of narcissism ignores the important role of aggression. Greene argues that "paradoxically, it is the complexity of psychoanalysis rather than the difficulties in understanding the much simpler self psychology that makes comparison difficult."[189]

To serve as a frame of reference for the respective concepts which follow, an outline of psychoanalysis was presented in Chapter II. In its main difference, self psychology is a theory of deficit, stemming from insufficient care in early childhood. Psychoanalytic theory is concerned with early childhood issues too, but is conceptualized in terms of conflicts, such as the defenses (subjective in nature), the feelings of aggression, the id and the ego, and the developmental focus is on the various psychosexual stages. The psychic apparatus is regarded differently too. In self psychology, there is the "bipolar self," which aims at achieving particular goals in reality.[190] In psychoanalysis, the psychic apparatus is seen as being tripartite, and the drives are the motivating factors. In the treatment of the patient in self psychology, a withdrawal by the patient is regarded as a failure of empathy on the part of the therapists. In psychoanalysis, the clinical focus is on intrapsychic conflicts and defenses. Kohut emphasizes the technique of empathy, but psychoanalysis accentuates analyzing the patients transferences and resistances. The fundamental goal in psychoanalysis is to make the "unconscious conscious," but in self psychology, an analysis is completed when, in Kohut's words "by achieving success in the area of compensatory structures it has established a functioning self—a psychological sector in which ambitious, skills, and ideals form an unbroken continuum that permits joyful creative activity."[191] In his conclusion, Greene expresses doubt about the plausibility of Kohut's theoretical constructs as borne out by his clinical data. And, Green says, self psychology is distinct from psychoanalysis and "it should be evaluated on the same basis any any other nonanalytic psychology: on its use of clinical data and not on its fit with psychoanalytic metapsychology."[192]

What is the merit of self psychology? What may be said of it is that it has brought attention to the mental health field of a wider segment of patient population, those very difficult to treat and having severe narcissistic disorders.[193] But Kohut has not succeeded in supplanting traditional psychoanalytic theory, ultimately because psychoanalytic theory is so much broader in range and depth. As for its use in history, although some historians have applied it, it has not become mainstream, and is not likely to become so.

Notes

1. Sigmund Freud, *Group Psychology and the Analysis of the Ego, Standard Edition*, Vol. 18, The Hogarth Press, 1957, pp. 93-99.
2. Reuben Fine, *The Development of Freud's Thought*, Aronson, 1973, p. 243.
3. Heinz Hartmann, *Ego Psychology and the Problem of Adaptation*, International Universities Press, 1958, p. 24.
4. *Ibid.*
5. *Ibid.*, p. 8.
6. Gertrude and Rubin Blanck, *Ego Psychology: Theory and Practice*, Columbia University Press, 1974, pp. 28-29.
7. Hartmann, *Ego Psychology*, p. 35.
8. Reuben Fine, *A History of Psychoanalysis*, Columbia University Press, 1979, pp. 358-359.
9. *Ibid.*, p. 337.
10. Fred Weinstein and Gerald M. Platt, *Psychoanalytic Sociology: An Essay on the Interpretation of Historical Data and the Phenomenon of Collective Behavior*, The Johns Hopkins Press, 1973, pp. 16-17.
11. Richard L. Schoenwald, "Using Psychology in History: A Review Essay," *Historical Methods Newsletter*, Vol. 7, 1973, p. 12.
12. Fred Weinstein and Gerald M. Platt, "The Coming Crisis in Psychohistory," *The Journal of Modern History*, Vol. 47, June 1975, p. 209.
13. *Ibid.*, p. 212.
14. *Ibid.*, p. 215.
15. *Ibid.*, p. 226.
16. *Ibid.*, p. 227.
17. Fred Weinstein, "The Transference Model in Psychohistory: A Critique," *The Psychohistory Review*, Vol. V, March 1977, p. 15.
18. *Ibid.*, p. 17.
19. Peter Loewenberg, "Psychoanalytic Models of History: Freud and After," in *Psychology and Historical Interpretation*, ed. William M. Runyan, Oxford University Press, 1988.
20. *Ibid.*, pp. 126-128.

21. Weinstein argues that there should be no precondition of psychoanalytic training for doing psychohistory, strongly disagreeing with psychoanalysts who contend that such training is necessary for being able to utilize analytic concepts competently. See Weinstein and Platt, *Psychoanalytic Sociology*, p. 1.

22. Loewenberg, "Psychoanalytic Models of Psychohistory," p. 128.

23. *Ibid.*, p. 128.

24. *Ibid.*, p. 130.

25. *Ibid.*, pp. 130-141.

26. *Ibid.*, p. 146.

27. *Ibid.*, p. 147. On the issue of such responses, see also by Harold F. Searles his chapter 18, "Countertransference and Theoretical Model," in *Countertransference and Related Subjects*, International Universities Press, 1979, pp. 373-379.

28. Loewenberg, "Psychoanalytic Models of Psychohistory," pp. 147-148.

29. *Ibid.*, p. 148.

30. *Ibid.*

31. *Ibid.* A relatively early paper by an historian who makes a case for employing ego psychological methodology in historical inquiry, is Cushing Strout, "Ego Psychology and the Historian," *History and Theory: Studies in the Philosophy of History*, Vol. 7, No. 3, 1968, pp. 281-197.

32. *Ibid.*, p. 150.

33. *Ibid.*

34. *Ibid.*, p. 151.

35. Although Jones was a member of Freud's inner circle, in the 1930s Freud privately became critical of Jones and made many disparaging remarks about him in his letters to Max Eitingon, The Freud-Eitingon Correspondence, The Freud Museum, London.

36. Anna Freud, *Introduction to Psychoanalysis: Lectures for Child Analysis and Teachers, 1922-1935*, International Universities Press, 1974, pp. 73-90. The work cited here, which contains some revisions, is based on the author's previous studies on the above mentioned subjects.

37. Anna Freud and Dorothy Burlingham, *War and Children* ("Freud-Burlingham Reports"), Medical War Books, 1943, pp. 15-46.

38. Anna Freud, *The Ego and the Mechanisms of Defence*, trans. by Cecil Baines, International Universities Press, 1946, p. 3.

39. *Ibid.*, p. 4.

40. *Ibid.*, pp. 117-146. See also the biography by Elisabeth Young-Bruehl, *Anna Freud*, Summit Books, 1988.

41. Melanie Klein, *Envy and Gratitude: A Study of Unconscious Sources*, Travistock Publications, 1954, pp. 3-24.

42. Phyllis Crosskurth, *Melanie Klein: Her World and Her Work*, Alfred A. Knopf, 1986.

43. *Ibid.*, p. 154.

44. *Ibid.*, pp. 3-4

45. *Ibid.*, pp. 41-49.

46. *Ibid.*, p. 218.

47. R.D. Hinshelwood, *A Dictionary of Kleinian Thought*, Free Association Books, 1989, pp. 372-373. This work, a compilation of Kleinian concepts and terms, is also helpful in that it provides glossaries of leading contributors to the Kleinian school. These include Wilfred Bion, who conducted group therapy, and studied group behavior, and Hanna Segal, who treated schizophrenics. See also, Leon Grinberg, Dario Sor, Elizabeth Tabak de Bianchedi, *New Introduction to the Work of Bion*, Jason Aronson, 1993.

48. Anne E. Bernstein and Gloria M. Warner, *An Introduction to Contemporary Psychoanalysis*, Jason Aronson, 1981, p. 100.

49. Jay R. Greenberg and Stephen A. Mitchell, *Object Relations in Psychoanalytic Theory*, Harvard University Press, 1983, p. 145.

50. *Ibid.*, p. 155.

51. Preface by Ernest Jones in W. Ronald D. Fairbairn, *An Object-Relations Theory of the Personality*, Basic Books, 1954, p. v.

52. Greenberg and Mitchell, *Object Relations*, p. 210.

53. *Ibid.*, p. 211.

54. *Ibid.*, p. 191.

55. Donald W. Winnicott, *The Child and the Outside World: Studies in Developing Relationships*, Basic Books, 1957, p. 137.

56. Greenberg and Mitchell, *Object Relations*, p. 195.

57. Brooke Hopkins, "Keats' 'Negative Capability' and Winnicott's Creative Play," *American Imago*, Vol. 41, Spring 1984, p. 87.

58. *Ibid.*, p. 88.

59. Winnicott, *The Child*, p. 15, 184. See also the chapter "What About Father," in Winnicott's *The Child, the Family, and the Outside World;*, Penguin Books, 1975.

60. Judith M. Hughes, *Reshaping the Psychoanalytic Domain: The Work of Malanie Klein, W.R.D. Fairbairn, and D.W. Winnicott,* University of California Press, 1989.

61. *Ibid.*, p. 8.

62. *Ibid.*, p. 44-56.

63. Judith M. Hughes, *Emotion and High Politics: Personal Relations at the Summit in Late Nineteenth Century-Century Britain and Germany,* University of California Press, 1983, pp. 4-10.

64. *Ibid.*, p. 2.

65. *Ibid.*, p. 164.

66. *Ibid.*

67. *Ibid.*, p. 192.

68. *Ibid.*, p. 210.

69. *Ibid.*

70. Louise E. Hoffman, "Object-relations Theory and Psychohistory," *Bulletin of the Menninger Clinic,* Vol. 49, No. 2, 1985.

71. *Ibid.*, p. 116.

72. *Ibid.*, p. 117.

73. *Ibid.*

74. *Ibid.*, pp. 117-118. It should be noted that Loewenberg, in his article on the Nazi youth cohort, does emphasize the role of the father, but Hoffman ignores his focus.

75. *Ibid.*, p. 118.

76. *Ibid.*

77. *Ibid.*

78. *Ibid.*, p. 119.

79. *Ibid.*

80. *Ibid.*

81. *Ibid.*, p. 120.

82. *Ibid.*

83. *Ibid.*

84. *Ibid.*, p. 121. For a noteworthy application of the Kleinian concept of splitting in the interpretation of mysogyny in art, literature and myth in the Middle Ages, see two articles by Ildiko Mohacsy, "The Legend

of the Unicorn: An Illumination of the Maternal Split," *Journal of the American Academy of Psychoanalysis*, Vol. 12, No. 3, pp. 387-412, 1984, and "The Medieval Unicorn: Historical and Iconographic Applications of Psychoanalysis," *The Journal of the American Academy of Psychoanalysis*, Vol. 16, No. 1 pp. 83-106, 1988.

85. Reuben Fine, *The Psychoanalytic Vision*, The Free Press, 1981, pp. 330-333.

86. H. Stuart Hughes, *The Obstructed Path: French Social Thought in the Years of Desperation, 1930-1960*, Harper and Row, 1968, pp. 9-10.

87. *Ibid.*, p. 8. Larry Shiner, the editor of *The Psychohistory Review*, published a special issue with a focus on psychohistory in France, but also touching on England. In addition to his "Introduction: Psychohistory in France and England," pp. 1-2, he also has written a review essay, pertinent to the works discussed in this chapter, "The History of Psychoanalysis in France," pp. 107-117. Other relevant articles are Elizabeth W. Marvick, "New Lives: Differential Receptions of Psychobiograpical Writings by Twentieth-Century Historians," pp. 3-66; Micheline Guiton, "François Mitterand: Personality and Politics," pp. 27-72; Jacques Le Rider, "Viennese Modernity and Crises of Identity," Vol. 21, No. 1, Fall 1992, pp. 73-106.

88. Sherry Turkle, *Psychoanalytic Politics: Freud's French Revolution*, Basic Books, 1976, p. 6.

89. *Ibid.*, p. 70.

90. In the Que Sais-Je? series there is Daniel Lagache, *La psychoanalyse*, Presses Universitaires de France, 1979.

91. Elisabeth Roudinesco, *Jacques Lacan & Co.: A History of Psychoanalysis in France, 1925-1985*, Trans., with a Foreword, by Jeffrey Mehlman, University of Chicago Press, 1990, pp. 102-104.

92. *Ibid.*, p. 104.

93. Cited in David J. Fisher, a Book Review of *Jacques Lacan & Co.: A History of Psychoanalysis in France, 1925-1985*, by Elisabeth Roudinesco, in *Psychoanalytic Books*, Vol. 5, 1994, p. 373.

94. *Ibid.*, p. 372.

95. *Ibid.*

96. Marion M. Oliner, *Cultivating Freud's Garden in France*, Jason Aronson, 1988, p. 123.

97. *Ibid.*, p. 124.

98. Stuart Schneiderman, *Jacques Lacan: The Death of an Intellectual Hero*, Harvard University Press, 1983.

99. *Ibid.*, pp. v–vi.

100. *Ibid.*, p. vi.

101. *Ibid.*, p. 12.

102. *Ibid.*, p. 119.

103. *Ibid.*, p. 49.

104. *Ibid.*

105. *Ibid.*, p. 50.

106. David J. Fisher, "Lacan's Ambiguous Impact on Contemporary French Psychoanalysis," *Cultural Theory and Psychoanalytic Tradition*, Transaction Publishers, 1991, p. 4.

107. *Ibid.*, p. 5.

108. Jacques Lacan, *Le Séminaire de Jacques Lacan*, Livre I, edited by Jacques-Alain Miller, *Les Ecrits Techniques de Freud*, Editions du Seuil, 1975, p. 262.

109. *Ibid.*, p. 269. See also John P. Muller and William J. Richardson, *Lacan and Language: A Reader's Guide to Ecrits*, International Universities Press, 1982; Jacques Lacan *Television: A Challenge to the Psychoanalytic Establishment*, trans. by Jeffrey Mehlman, ed. by Joan Copjec, W.W. Norton, 1990. Three papers were presented at a symposium, "Freud and Language: Contributions of Jacques Lacan—Theory and Therapy," who considered Lacan's contributions, including those of language and speech, the role of words in the analytic relationship, and that of clinical application. These papers were delivered at the 86th Annual Convention of the American Psychological Association, held in Toronto, Canada, in 1978. The papers are as follows: William J. Richardson, "Lacan's View of Language and Being;" John P. Muller, "Ego and Subject in Lacan;" James E. Gorney, "The Clinical Application of Lacan in the Psychoanalytic situation," *The Psychoanalytic Review*, Vol. 69, No. 2, Summer 1982, pp. 229-248.

110. Fisher, "Lacan," pp. 8-11.

111. *Ibid.*, p. 11.

112. Lacan's ideas, and those of structuralism are critically discussed by Stanley L. Olinick, "Psychoanalysis and Language," *Journal of the American Psychoanalytic Association*, Vol. 21, 1984, pp. 617-653.

113. Aland Roland, Editor, *Psychoanalysis, Creativity, and Literature: A French-American Inquiry*, Columbia University Press, 1978, p. 3.

114 Fisher, "Lacan," pp. 16-17. Another critical exposition of Lacan, by an author who wonders why Lacan was able to keep a following for so

166 *Psychoanalytic Theory*

long, is François Roustang, *The Lacanian Delusion*, trans. by Greg Sims, Oxford University Press, 1990.

115 For an examination of the growth of psychoanalysis in France, with attention to the crisis caused by World War II, see Alain de Mijolla, "La psychanalyse en France (1893-1965)," in *Histoire de la psychanalyse*, Vol. II, ed by Roland Jacard, Hachette, 1982, pp. 5-118. This volume contains helpful essays on the growth of psychoanalysis in numerous countries, including Japan, Argentina, Italy, and Hungary.

116. Works which examine and document this phenomenon are, *Die Rezeption der Psychoanalyse in der Soziologie, Psychologie und Theologie im deutschsprächigen Raum bis 1940*, ed. by Johannes Cremerius, Suhrkamp Verlag, 1981; Geoffrey C. Cocks. *Psychoanalysis in the Third Reich: The Göring Institut*, Oxford University Press, 1985.

117. For the slow recovery of psychoanalysis in Germany after World War II, and for a survey of its growth in postwar France, see Edith Kurzweil, *The Freudians: A Comparative Perspective*, Yale University Press, 1989, pp. 294-303.

118. Eugene Webb, *The Self Between: From Freud to the New Social Psychology of France*, University of Washington Press, 1993, p. 3.

119. Heinz Kohut, "The Self in History," A Symposium Discussion, *Newsletter of the Group for the Use of Psychology in History*, Vol. 3, No. 4, pp. 3-10.

120. Charles B. Strozier, "Glimpses of a Life: Heinz Kohut (1913-1981)," in *Progress in Self Psychology*, Vol. 1, Ed. Arnold Goldberg, The Guilford Press, 1985, p. 6. Strozier, as an historian and former editor of *The Psychohistory Review*, has been a foremost exponent of Kohut's work. See his "Heinz Kohut and the Historical Imagination," *The Psychohistory Review*, Vol. 7, No. 2, Fall 1978, pp. 36-39; and the "Special Issue: Self Psychology and Psychohistory," in which Strozier contributed "The Soul of Wit: Kohut and the Psychology of Humor," *The Psychohistory Review*, Vol. 15, No. 3, Spring 1987, pp. 47-68. Strozier also has edited, with Daniel Offer, with a Foreword by Peter Gay, *The Leader: Psychohistorical Essays*, Plenum Press, 1985, which contains essays from a Kohutian perspective on leaders such as Lincoln, Gandhi, and Wilson. Strozier has also written a biography in this vein, *Lincoln's Quest for Union: Public and Private Meanings*, University of Illinois Press, 1987.

121. Strozier "Glimpses," p. 7.

122. *Ibid.*

123. *Ibid.*, p. 8.

124. Susan Quinn, "Oedipus vs. Narcissus," *The New York Times Magazine*, No. 9, 1980.

125. *Ibid.*, p. 123.

126. *Ibid.*

127. *Ibid.*

128. *Ibid.*, p. 126.

129. *Ibid.*, p. 128.

130. *Ibid.*, p. 130.

131. *Ibid.*, p. 131. See also, Otto F. Kernberg, *Borderline Conditions and Pathological Narcissism*, James Aronson, 1975.

132. Heinz Kohut, *The Analysis of the Self: A Systematic Approach to the Psychoanalytic Treatment of Narcissistic Personality Disorders*, International Universities Press, 1971.

133. *Ibid.*, p. xi.

134. *Ibid. passim.*

135. Heinz Kohut, *The Restoration of the Self*, International Universities Press, 1977, p. xiii.

136. *Ibid.* See also, Heinz Kohut, *How Does Analysis Cure?* Ed. by Arnold Goldberg, with the collaboration of Paul Stepansky, University of Chicago Press, 1984.

137. Kohut, Symposium Discussion, *Newsletter*, Vol. 3, No. 4, p. 3.

138. *Ibid.*, p. 4.

139. *Ibid.*

140. *Ibid.*, p. 5.

141. *Ibid.*

142. *Ibid.*, p. 6.

143. *Ibid.*

144. *Ibid.*

145. *Ibid.*

146. *Ibid.*

147. *Ibid.*

148. *Ibid.*

149. *Ibid.*

150. Ernest S. Wolf, "Psychoanalytic Selfobject Psychology and Psychohistory," in *New Directions in Psychohistory*: The Adelphi Papers in Honor or Erik H. Erikson, ed. Mel Albin, D.C. Heath, 1980, p. 37.

151. *Ibid.*, p. 38.

152. *Ibid.*, p. 39.
153. *Ibid.*
154. *Ibid.*
155. *Ibid.*, p. 45.
156. *Ibid.*, p. 37.
157. *Ibid.*, p. 46.
158. Heinz Kohut, "Self Psychology and the Sciences of Man," *Self Psychology and the Humanities: Reflections on a New Psychoanalytic Approach*, ed. and intro. by Charles B. Strozier, W.W. Norton & Company, 1985, p. 73.
159. *Ibid.*
160. *Ibid.*, pp. 76-79.
161. *Ibid.*, p. 81.
162. *Ibid.*
163. *Ibid.*
164. *Ibid.*, p. 84.
165. *Ibid.*, p. 87.
166. *Ibid.*, p. 90.
167. *Ibid.*, p. 91.
168. *Ibid.*, p. 92.
169. *Ibid.*, p. 93.
170. *Ibid.*, p. 94.
171. Heinz Kohut, "Creativeness, Charisma, Group Psychology: Reflections on the Self-Analysis of Freud," in *Freud: The Fusion of Science and Humanism*, eds. John E. Gedo and George H. Pollock, in *Psychological Issues*, Monograph 34/35, International Universities Press, 1976, pp. 392-393.
172. *Ibid.*, p. 425.
173. Thomas A. Kohut, "Psychohistory as History," *The American Historical Review*, Vol. 91, No. 2, April 1986.
174. *Ibid.*, p. 338.
175. *Ibid.*
176. *Ibid.*

177. *Ibid.*, p. 339.

178. *Ibid.*, p. 344.

179. *Ibid.*

180. *Ibid.*

181. *Ibid.*, pp. 349-350.

182. *Ibid.*, pp. 350-351.

183. *Ibid.*, p. 351.

184. *Ibid.*, p. 352.

185. Marshall A. Greene, "The Self Psychology of Heinz Kohut," *Bulletin of the Menninger Clinic*," Vol. 48, No. 1, 1984, *passim*.

186. *Ibid.*, p. 37.

187. *Ibid.*, p. 38.

188. *Ibid.*

189. *Ibid.*, p. 45.

190. *Ibid.*, p. 46.

191. *Ibid.*, p. 47.

192. *Ibid.*, p. 52.

193. By now, there is a literature that elaborates on and provides clinical guidelines to psychotherapists utilizing Kohutian concepts for a wide range of patients. See Hyman L. Muslin, a psychoanalyst and also a leading proponent of self psychology, who has written a work integrating the theory with clinical practice, in collaboration with Eduardo R. Val, *The Psychotherapy of the Self*, Brunner/Mazel, 1987. Muslin also has applied Kohutian concepts to historical figures and to literary criticism, see "Shakespeare and Psychology of the Self: The Case of Othello," in *Kohut's Legacy: Contributions to Self Psychology*, eds. P.E. Stepansky and A. Goldberg, The Analytic Press, 1984, pp. 215-231; with Thomas Jobe, *Lyndon Johnson: The Tragic Self*, Plenum Press, 1991. For a collection of essays which give an overview of all the theoretical approaches discussed in this chapter, as well as Freudian and Sullivanian paradigms, see Arnold Rothstein, ed., *Models of the Mind: Their Relationships to Clinical Work*. International Universities Press, 1985. On the uses of various methodologies employed for studying leaders, Bruce Mazlish accepts the Kohutian model, as well as others, for studying presidents (George Bush and Bill Clinton) and those with presidential aspirations (Ross Perot) when sources on their early childhood is lacking, in "Some Observations on the Psychology of Political Leadership," *Political Psychology: Journal of the International Society of*

Political Psychology, Vol. 15, No. 4, December 1994, pp. 745-753. Reflecting the growing diversification in the field, the American Psychoanalytic Association has included many new terms in its revised glossary, and which now includes terms from the works of Carl Jung, Heinz Kohut, Wilfred R. Bion, and others of the object relations school. See, ed. by Burness E. Moore and Bernard D. Fine, *Psychoanalytic Terms and Concepts*, Yale University Press, 1990.

Chapter 6

Psychohistory: Genre and Interpretations

1. Biographical Studies

The forte of psychohistory is biography. For this category in the field of psychohistory, the others being childhood, the family, and the group, the theory is the most developed, and it is in this category that the most psychohistorical work has been done. Moreover, it is in the study of the individual that the superiority of the psychohistorical approach is clearly demonstrated over that of the traditional approach. The insights, the depths, and the dimensions that this approach affords just cannot be duplicated by the conventional methods of history. There is much overlapping in the various categories, a feature that is both valuable and enhancing, as will be shown. The psychobiographical study of the individual is also referred to as life history.

By now, psychobiographical studies have been written on individuals of all periods. However, it is individuals in the modern period who have received the most attention by psychohistorians. As with the study of history in general, there has been greater interest in the contemporary period, the great divide in this periodization being the French Revolution, with a convergence on the Twentieth Century. And within this century, the era of the Second World War has been a period of special concern to psychohistorians. Concurrent with this interest in the contemporary period is that more source material is available than for past historical periods.

In line with this focus, comparatively few national leaders have been the objects of special study. By country, they are the leaders of France, Germany, Russia, and the United States.

These include Robespierre and Pétain, Bismarck and Himmler, Peter the Great and Stalin, Lincoln and Wilson. However, one individual in particular—and his movement—has come under intense investigation, and that is Adolf Hitler.

The study of Hitler has attracted a galaxy of scholars. Because of the ramifications of Hitlerism, and its global magnitude, this phenomenon has been the object of much discussion. But the special value of discussing the work on Hitler in the context of this chapter is illustrative, for by comparatively examining the studies on him, the psychohistorical study of the individual is put into better relief.

One of the earliest books written in the post-war period, which was well received and popular, was the biography by the British historian Alan Bullock, *Hitler, A Study in Tyranny*. It is an epic work of over eight-hundred pages, exhaustively researched, informative and balanced. However, because it is written in the traditional mold, the work does not come to grips with the pathological manifestations of Hitler's personality, nor with the reasons for his appeal. To be sure, Bullock does mention Hitler's childhood and his parents, discusses his career and his rise to power, and the course of Hitler's direction of the war from 1939 to 1945, but Bullock's study is essentially descriptive in nature.

In regard to Hitler's developing support among the German people, and in contrast to a psychohistorical approach, Bullock even states that "If at times, especially between 1938 and 1945, the figure of the man is submerged beneath the complicated narrative of politics and war, *this corresponds to Hitler's own sacrifice of his private life (which was meager and uninteresting at the best of times)* [italics mine] to the demands of the position he had created for himself."[1] And although Bullock adds that in "the last year of his life," as the Reich was collapsing, "the true nature of the man is revealed again in all its harshness,"[2] he does not deal with Hitler's mental illness. In discussing Hitler's formative years, the ones in his youth in Vienna and his stint as a soldier in World War 1, Bullock takes the so-called "common sense" approach. He deduces that:

> Those years between the end of 1908 and the end of 1918 had hardened him, taught him to be self-reliant, confirmed his belief in himself, toughened the power of his will. From them he emerged with a

stock of fixed ideas and prejudices which were to alter little in the rest of his life: hatred of the Jews; contempt for the ideals of democracy, internationalism, equality, and peace; a preference for authoritarian forms of government; an intolerant nationalism; a rooted belief in the inequality of races and individuals; and faith in the heroic virtues of war.[3]

The issues taken up by Bullock are the essential characteristics of Hitlerism, but his narrative is descriptive and the dynamics of Hitler's personality are missing.

In comparison, psychohistorians pay attention to the very manifestations that the traditional historians avoid. A study that was commissioned in 1943 by an American military intelligence agency and written by a psychoanalyst throws an entirely different light on Hitler. This study, written by Walter C. Langer, *The Mind of Adolf Hitler: The Secret Wartime Report*, was declassified and finally published in the 1970s. Langer, in attempting to get at the measure of the man, delves into Hitler's personal and family conflicts, his sexual pathology, and the psychic roots of his anti-Semitism. Langer even goes to the extent of indicating Hitler's probable behavior. With the defeat of Germany becoming imminent, Langer predicted that Hitler would probably commit suicide. Langer surmised that Hitler had an inordinate fear of death, "but being a psychopath he could undoubtedly screw himself up into the superman character and perform the deed."[4]

On Hitler's anti-Semitism, Langer attributes this to being, along with many other phobias, "an identification with the aggressor," an unconscious acting out of the fears that he had about the stronger Allies. Hitler practiced "on the Jews in reality the things he feared the victors might do to him in fantasy," affording "him an opportunity of appearing before the world as the pitiless brute he imagines himself to be."[5] As was mentioned earlier, there is an overlapping in the categories of psychohistory, the study of the individual dovetailing with that of the group. Accordingly, in a significant passage, Langer summarizes the reasons for Hitler's appeal to the German people. Langer notes that:

> It is Hitler's ability to play upon the unconscious tendencies of the German people and to act as their spokesman that had enabled him to mobilize their energies and direct them into the same channels

through which he believed he had found a solution to his own personal conflicts. The result has been an extraordinary similarity in thinking, feeling, and acting in the German people.[6]

The psychohistorian Robert G. L. Waite, who wrote an Afterword in Langer's book, elaborated on the thesis he presented in this essay in his book *The Psychopathic God: Adolf Hitler*. Waite's thesis is that Hitler had a borderline personality, and that he tried to cope with his psychopathy by engaging in political activity. Waite, who makes an extensive and detailed reconstruction of Hitler's personality, pays much attention to this psychosexual development, and the perversions and phobias he exhibited in adult life. He shows that Hitler was beset by feelings of guilt and intense self-hatred, and that these feelings were projected onto Germany. In his unconscious, his mother was identified with Germany, and his father with Austria. Hitler loved his mother with an intense "primitive idealization," and he hated his father, although he did not say this publicly.[7] On a deeper level, Waite points out, "he despised them both."[8] As for his relentless anti-Semitism, it was a projection of his intense self-hatred, stemming from his conflict with his father. And just as he had suffered a narcissistic wound, intensified by being gassed during World War I, Hitler intuited that Germany suffered from a similar blow to its self-esteem because of its defeat in that war. Waite's detailed study of Hitler's personality, and the reasons for his appeal, has a transcending value, for it relates in general to the issue of the charismatic leader and his inspiration of mass movements.

Rudolph Binion, in *Hitler Among the Germans*, undertakes a psychohistorical approach based on the repetition of childhood trauma repeated in adult life. Binion points out that Hitler strongly identified with his mother. Of particular significance were her treatments for breast cancer administered by the Jewish physician, Dr. Eduard Bloch.[9]

In a meticulous piece of detective work, Binion concludes that Bloch unintentionally poisoned her with iodoform. Later, as a soldier, Hitler himself was poisoned by gas, which revived the trauma of his mother's death. These events led Hitler to become anti-Semitic, even though he had once been grateful to Bloch. He came to associate gassing with Jews, which motivated him to avenge the trauma. Ultimately, it led to the creation of the gas chambers of World War II. Binion also pays attention to Hitler's appeal "among the Germans," as his title indicates. Consequently, Hitler prevailed in that his "uncanny personal power over Germans came from his having coordinated his private traumatic fury with the national traumatic need."[10]

Another approach to Hitler is that of Helm Stierlin, a German physician, who wrote *Adolf Hitler: A Family Perspective*. Stierlin, both medically and psychoanalytically trained, came to the study of Hitler from his experience as a psychoanalyst and family therapist. He was influenced by the tragic experience of having lived in his youth under Hitler.[11] In treating and studying families, Stierlin observed that there are certain basic foci, such as the separation of parents and adolescents, the "dynamics of shame, guilt, and loyalty in family relations."[12] It is this conceptual framework that he applied to the study of Hitler.

Stierlin, who builds on and credits Binion's work, cites him for noting Hitler's unusual attachment to his mother. Quoting Binion's study, Stierlin establishes a premise for Hitler's adult motivations and behavior in connection to his mother: "Adolf was her compensation for her triple loss; she guarded him as anxiously as she did even while she unconsciously relived her triple loss; *thus he sucked in that maternal trauma with his mother's milk*"[13] [Stierlin's italics]. This notion led Stierlin to one of his key points regarding Hitler. In Chapter 2, "Hitler Bound and Delegated by His Mother," Stierlin argues that Hitler was used by his mother to satisfy her psychological needs, that he came to serve "as delegate."[14] In itself, this is a common feature of family life, but in Hitler's case this took on a pathological quality.[15]

Hitler's father Alois, although a successful official in the Austrian empire, was abusive and neglectful. He was not a good model of male-female relationships for the young Hitler. While Hitler regarded his father as domineering, autocratic, and manipulative, it was his mother, "the weak, submissive self effacing Klara, who therefore became Adolf's main delegator."[16] His mother, who lost her first three children, came to lavish much affection on Adolf, and Stierlin says "she recruited Adolf as fighter for *her Lebensraum*, [Stierlin's italics] i.e., as a delegate who competed on her behalf for a share of the scarce—material as well as non-material—goods of the world."[17] Furthermore, Stierlin says, "she possibly recruited him to defeat, if not destroy, her exploiting and disloyal husband—even though, and probably because, she overtly remained to the end Alois' submissive maid."[18]

Stierlin recognizes that the evidence for Klara's feelings and fantasies are sparse, but he turns to John Wilkes Booth's mother, as an example of a "delegating mother who also fatefully influenced history,"[19] her son having assassinated Abraham Lincoln. In this instance, there is more evidence to support the schema.

Hitler was a failure as an artist, as a painter, and as an architect. He continued to view himself as such until the end of the Third Reich. Stierlin says, however, that Hitler retained the artist's temperament and excelled in the art of "political stagecrafting," "myth-making," or "myth-selling," and as an orator and actor. Ultimately, however, Hitler suffered a "suicidal drive," celebrating a cult of death, "as when he orchestrated massive funeral processions or memorial services for war heroes and martyrs of the Nazi movement, complete with dipped banners, gigantic choruses, sombre marching music, and muted drums."[20] Typically, Hitler preferred evening or night hours to stage his rallies and processions, "since a quality of moody darkness added to the effect."[21] In this respect, as well as in his stagecrafting, he imitated Richard Wagner, his admired model, bringing about his own "Götterdammerung" and "Niebelungentod."[22]

Stierlin also argues that Hitler, as his mother's delegate, was burdened as well as privileged in this relationship. The hatred Hitler came to feel for others was a displacement of his hatred for his parents, especially his mother. Unconsciously, Hitler came to feel that he was exploited and unjustly treated by his parents. This relationship led him "to displace his retaliatory fury onto others and eventually onto the whole non-German world, thereby compounding a millionfold the injustice he had suffered, but keeping the original loyalty bond intact and unquestioned."[23] Hitler was extremely narcissistic, and he lacked compassion and empathy. When his mother died, according to Stierlin, despite his public profession of grief, Hitler really did not mourn her. His personal experiences also resonated with his followers, for Hitler was not only his mother's delegate, "but also that of the German people."[24] In connection with mourning and group dynamics, Stierlin says that Hitler "failed to confront and reexperience what tied him to his lost object: love, devotion, ambivalence, rage and other emotions. Here, too, the Germans acted like Hitler. Rather than mourning *their* losses and confronting *their* pains [italics Stierlin's], they tried to deny them with Hitler's help."[25]

It is difficult in a brief synopsis to do justice to the works of the psychohistorians just presented. Their findings are especially insightful and textured, and they present interpretations of Hitler that are consistent with general knowledge about human functioning. They take into consideration Hitler's psychosexual development, his sexual pathology, his unconscious motivations, and they deal with the oedipal character of his rages. Hitler was overly attached to his mother and extremely hostile to his father. He associated the Jews with hated father figures. Not only do psychohistorians deal with Hitler's conflicts and anti-Semitism, but they also link them with Hitler's ability to exploit the unconscious conflicts of the German people. Furthermore, this explanation of Hitler's behavior is related to his social context.

A few other leaders, contemporary with Hitler, who have been the subject of much study because of their pivotal historical roles will now be discussed briefly, but again, the focus will be on the interpretations of psychohistorians. Although these historical figures loom large, and are controversial, they have not been studied to the same extent as Hitler. Stalin, who ranks as one of the greatest tyrants of Western history has been studied psychoanalytically by Robert C. Tucker, in *Stalin as Revolutionary, 1879-1929: A Study in History and Personality.* In his "Acknowledgements," Tucker says that he owes a "large debt to Erik H. Erikson's thought," and that he has had much help from prominent psychoanalysts, such as Otto F. Kernberg, in its preparation.[26]

Tucker says that he "does not view Stalin as a psychiatric case,"[27] placing him in the historical context of a Georgian, subjugated by Russia. He covers the growth of Bolshevism, and Stalin's relationship with Lenin and other revolutionaries. However, Tucker also deals with Stalin's childhood, and his relationship with his parents. Stalin's feelings for his father were not positive, for he was a heavy drinker and he beat him and his mother. Stalin's relationship with his mother was better, but she also beat him, and wanted him to become a priest.[28]

Tucker advances that Stalin had a paranoid personality, and that after he attained power anyone he deemed to slight him, or have contempt for him, and there were many who did not respect him, was labeled a "class enemy," which held ominous consequences. Eventually, a cult of the personality developed. This was encouraged by Stalin, who wanted to be esteemed like Lenin, but in contrast to Lenin, he had an enormous need for personal adulation.[29] Tucker comments on one of Stalin's responses to the less than spontaneous outpourings of congratulatory eulogies on his fiftieth birthday in 1929, to which he replied with a public message of thanks. He said that the credit for his leadership belonged to "the great party of the working class which bore me and reared me in its own image and likeness."[30] He referred to the Communist Party as "our glorious Leninist party" and added, "I make bold to tender you my Bolshevik thanks."[31]

In the second paragraph of this statement he declared dramatically: "you need have no doubt, comrades, that I am prepared in the future, too, to devote to the cause of the working class, to the cause of the proletarian revolution and world communism, all my strength, all my ability, and if need be, all my blood, drop by drop."[32]

Tucker notes that Stalin's response revealed a false modesty, and he makes an additional interpretation: "Secondly, the remarkable imagery of birth and rearing by implication placed the party and Stalin in a mother-son relationship and thereby suggested that he saw in the party—or wanted to see—another source of the trust, loving devotion, and complete admiration that he had originally received from his mother. In place of the doting mother of his childhood, he needed a doting party."[33]

What was so serious, given Stalin's pathological character, was that he easily felt "betrayed." As he said, in a speech in 1928, what was a frequent theme for him "We have internal enemies. We have external enemies."[34] Yet, Stalin's animosity did not extend to foreign national leaders who opposed communism. For instance, the American ambassador Averell

Harriman, who really was a 'class enemy,' commented on how considerately and courteously Stalin treated him.[35] Instead, because of his insecurities, Stalin vented his rage against persons in his own entourage. Tucker explains how Stalin rationalized his behavior:

> For if they were class enemies, they fully deserved to be mercilessly exposed and harshly punished. But equally important, the categorizing of his critics as class enemies was for Stalin a necessary way of rationalizing their derogatory attitudes toward him. He thereby warded off any need to confront himself in a self-questioning way and accept the painful possibilities that these attitudes had some foundation.[36]

The notorious purges by Stalin in the 1930s were noted for the wholesale killing of the most dedicated Bolsheviks. Eventually, Stalin, as the ruler of the Soviet Union, the head of international communism, and a leader of the victorious coalition against Hitler's Germany, was considered a charismatic leader.

Another controversial leader and head of state, about whom much has been written, although not from a psychohistorical viewpoint is Marshal Philippe Pétain. Pétain, victor of the great battle at Verdun in World War I, Minister of War in 1934, Ambassador to Spain in 1939, became head of the fascist Vichy government in 1940, following the fall of France. For the regime he headed, and for his collaboration with the German occupational forces during World War II, he was tried for treason by a French tribunal after the war, convicted in 1945, and sentenced to death. However, because of his advanced age—he was eighty-nine—his sentence was commuted to life imprisonment. He remained in prison for the rest of his life, and died in 1951.

There is a large literature on Pétain, but most of it is polemical, considering him to be either a traitor or a savior. To some extent, all try to explain his unusual denouement. The question is why he acted as he did in 1940, which led to his fall from grace. The underlying question of Pétain's anomalous, if not aberrant, behavior is a psychohistorical one, and involves his psychic motivation.[37]

Pétain demonstrated a consistent passive aggressive pattern of behavior. He was ambitious, but also self-effacing, reserved, and fatalistic. In the way he rose through the ranks, accepted political assignments, took power in 1940, and accepted his verdict in 1945, he demonstrated a self-sacrificing manner.[38] He frequently said, and with satisfaction, "They only call me in disasters."[39]

This pattern of behavior also pertains particularly to his relationships. Although traditional historians record the salient events in Pétain's life, they do not relate them psychodynamically to his character. Of paramount importance is the fact that Pétain's mother died when he was seventeen-months old. His father remarried shortly thereafter, and Pétain was forced to leave his parental home. By the age of four, in the critical pre-oedipal period, he had been 'rejected' by his mother, his step-mother, and his father. For a few years he lived with his grandparents, but at the age of eleven he was sent to a boarding school. At twenty, he entered Saint Cyr, the French military academy. Upon graduation, he entered the army.

The trauma and neglect he experienced in his youth indelibly marked all his relationships. Significantly, he married, for the first time, when he was sixty-four years of age. There was a connection (overlooked by historians and publicists) between the trauma that Pétain experienced in infancy and the fact that he married so late in life. The woman he married, Alphonsine-Berthe-Eugènie Hardon was a divorced mother.[40] Pétain, who was raised as a Catholic, and had an extensive Catholic education, could only marry her in a civil ceremony in 1920. In doing so, Pétain acted in defiance of his Catholic background. With the marriage, Pétain gained a son, with whom he identified and with whom he could be paternal, as well as a mother and a wife.[41]

As Pétain became a public figure in the 1930s, he made many speeches of a political nature. In these speeches to the French people, he glorified regenerative suffering. For example, speaking to war veterans no less, well before the defeat of 1940, he asserted: "It is a recognized fact that defeat always awakens the French people."[42] In effect, he was propagating a form of moral masochism. Pétain was described by those who knew him as authoritarian, reserved, cold, and secretive. In his political ideology, he was a monarchist and an anti-democrat, who favored the traditions antedating the French Revolution of 1789.[43]

A unique source of information which has served to further shed light on Pétain's psychology and his motives for his most fateful and controversial decisions, is the nearly forty-year correspondence with his wife, which became available to scholars in 1981.[44] The feelings and thoughts expressed by Pétain in this correspondence are consistent with his public stance, as demonstrated during his military and political career. Pétain often spoke of personal suffering and sacrifice in the letters, which reveal a sado-masochistic component.[45]

Pétain, readily accepted the defeat of France, and this led to the fall of the republican government. The Vichy State, which he headed, eventually contributed to a civil war. The Vichy regime, under the guise of installing a "New Order," became repressive, and was morally compromised by its collaboration with Nazi Germany and by its opposition to the Allies, namely Great Britain, the United States and the Soviet Union. This collaboration led to Pétain's fateful political decisions of 1940, and throughout the years of his Vichy State, which culminated in his trial in 1945.[46] Because of his childhood feelings of rejection and suffering, he sought martyrdom and self-sacrifice. On taking power at a time of national catastrophe, he came to be regarded as a savior, a judgment which he accepted. At this time, he identified with Jesus Christ, for he said to an aide, "I believe I shall carry my cross until my death."[47] His defense attorney, Jacques Isorni, said that when Pétain made the decision not to leave France in 1942, he did this ". . . out of his love for the French people. He sacrificed himself totally for them. He gave them the gift of his person."[48] As for Pétain's accepting the verdict of guilty in 1945, Isorni recognized this as "almost a seeking of the crown of thorns."[49] As an indication that he wished to be punished, he accepted his sentence with resignation. Psychically, because of Pétain's rage and hostility, and his consequent feelings of guilt, he needed to be punished and to atone. Among the many statements Pétain made while in prison, two bear out his feelings of acceptance and guilt. On July 10, 1947, members of a parliamentary commission investigating the causes of the defeat of France in 1940, held a hearing with Pétain on Ile d'Yeu, where he was imprisoned. Pétain, then ninety-one years old, had received a warning from Isorni not to answer questions, but he held a session which lasted for two hours. This last public statement dealt with his past behavior. Pétain's statements revealed his timidity, cautiousness, secrecy, passivity, sense of martyrdom, shrewdness and dignity. They also reveal a defiant attitude toward his questioners. When Pétain was asked how he found conditions in prison, he pointedly replied: "I never complain."[50] He appeared to accept his condemnation, and his final words to the parliamentarians were: "I have taken the position to ask for nothing, to make no comments. I have accepted the sentence. I will go to the end, until my death. If I must finish my life in this situation, I accept it in advance. I can say no more."[51] Pétain, in effect, admitted his guilt.

The other statement is in a letter to his wife, dated February 16, 1947, in which Pétain raises a key question about himself and which goes to the core of his motivation. He writes: "ce qui me trouble c'est de terminer ma vie avec l'idée que je suis en prison. Ai-je donc vraiment mérité un tel sort?" (that which troubles me is to end my life with the idea that I am in prison. Have I really deserved such a fate?)[52] Pétain thus posed a rhetorical question about his role followed by neither an answer nor a defense. He unconsciously admits his guilt and responsibility.

American leaders, especially presidents of the United States, have also been subjects of psychohistorical study. American presidents were not as charismatic to the same degree as European revolutionary leaders, but is it important to juxtapose the different historical and national situations. Generally, political conditions in the United States have been more stable, at least in the twentieth century, than in Europe. Most psychobiographical studies of American presidents have focused on the twentieth century. A good example is Woodrow Wilson, who has been the subject of much attention and debate by psychohistorians.

The psychohistorical studies of Wilson consider his self-destructive behavior, which ran alongside a history of distinguished achievements. But what makes the historiography of Wilson unique is that Freud also wrote about him. In collaboration with William C. Bullitt, Freud wrote *Thomas Woodrow Wilson*, which was not published until 1957.[53] Bullitt, the American Ambassador to France from 1936 to 1940, helped Freud escape from Austria in 1938, and he enlisted Freud's help in his biographical endeavor. Both, for different reasons, were critical of Wilson. The thesis of their book is that Wilson was a passive person, who learned how to use words, as in preaching or giving speeches, but he did not know how to fight. He therefore could not enforce his Fourteen Points, nor obtain a "just and lasting peace."[54] Despite the power and resources of the United States, Wilson was unable to deal effectively with either Georges Clemenceau or Lloyd George, the allied leaders. Wilson's passivity, according to Freud and Bullitt, stemmed from his close identification with his father, whom he exalted. This led to his "exalted super-ego."[55] Not only was Wilson neurotic at times, but at "the end of his career he nearly plunged into psychosis."[56]

Another study, that is a classic, is by Alexander and Juliette George, *Woodrow Wilson and Colonel House: A Psychological Study*, published in 1964. The authors contend that Wilson's unconscious conflict with his father was displaced onto his opponents at critical junctures in his career. Starting with his tenure as President of Princeton University in 1906, Wilson demonstrated an obstinate pattern of behavior. In his zeal as a reformer, he could not compromise, and inevitably failed. Such actions were repeated elsewhere, and in 1919 they led to his sabotaging of America's entry into his cherished League of Nations.[57]

A different emphasis, as the title indicates, is the work of Edwin A. Weinstein, a physician, *Thomas Woodrow Wilson: A Medical and Psychological Biography*. Weinstein argues that Wilson's problems were caused by brain dysfunction, because of dyslexia as a child and that his depression was expressed psychosomatically. Wilson, Weinstein says, had several strokes, the first when he was a professor at Princeton University. A massive stroke in 1919 "caused enduring mental changes."[58] Weinstein in 1988 published a paper in which he discussed the motives of Bullitt and Freud in writing on Wilson, authors with whom he disagreed. Weinstein believed that there were personal reasons for writing this book by Bullitt, and that Bullitt felt that Wilson did not sufficiently appreciate his diplomatic skills. In Freud's case, it was that he held Wilson accountable for the hardships caused by the Treaty of Versailles in Austria and Germany.[59]

Weinstein, in providing a medical history of Wilson, says that, in addition to strokes, "he had a long history of hypertension, and had had a retinal hemorrhage in his left eye in 1906 with persisting and severe loss of vision. During his presidency ophthalmological examinations by Dr. George de Schweinitz showed advanced retinal arteriosclerosis, angiospasticity and exudates. From 1918, Wilson had complained of memory loss, showed diminished emotional control, and had become more egocentric, secretive, and suspicious. I originally thought that Wilson had carotid artery disease with embolization, but now accept the view of Dr. James Toole that he had small vessel disease with lacunar infarcts."[60]

Weinstein attacks Bullitt and Freud by saying that their book "should be appreciated in the context of psychiatric and psychoanalytic thought in the 1920s and early 1930s which antedated ego psychology."[61] And while Weinstein acknowledges that Wilson's state of health and mental condition affected him at the Paris Peace Conference, the Freud/Bullitt book is relegated to "the history of psychobiography."[62]

A further addition on the Freud-Bullitt collaboration is the probe by Silas L. Warner, whose title ridicules their work, "Fourteen Wilsonian Points for Freud and Bullitt."[63] A key point in Warner's investigation of the circumstances which led to their collaboration is that Bullitt had been analyzed by Freud from 1926 to 1930.[64] Although both denied this, Warner claims to have verified the treatment from statements by Anna Freud and many others.[65] In Warner's opinion, Bullitt and Freud undertook this project because they both disliked Wilson. However, there is more, as Warner offers his own psychological explanation. "I believe that Wilson's personality represented the repudiated, detested self of both Freud and Bullitt. They were both unconsciously compelled to attack and disavow this negative self by attacking Wilson."[66] Warner considers their view as "projective identification" asserting that there was a problem of "transference and countertransference."[67] Hence Freud's analysis of Bullitt was a failure. For these controversial interpretations, Warner offers no documentation.

A Kohutian approach by Joseph A. Bongiorno, "Woodrow Wilson Revisited: The Prepolitical Years," proposes that Wilson had problems of self-esteem. In this sense, when Wilson experienced stress, he responded "not from strengths but from his vulnerability, which temporarily became the leading edge of his personality."[68] However, Bongiorno says, even if Wilson had conflicts with his father, the nature of his relationship with him "enabled him repeatedly to rebound from defeat and which constituted the nucleus of his greatness."[69]

Although there is a diverse body of work on Wilson, and a variety of theoretical approaches, there is also a consensus on the nature of Wilson's behavior and the roots of his problems. Dorothy Ross, in "Review Essay/Woodrow Wilson and the Case for Psychohistory," examines the historiography on Wilson, much of it mentioned above. She notes that all these biographers, namely Freud and Bullitt, the Georges, and Weinstein, recognized that Wilson acted in a self-defeating manner while he was at Princeton. This reoccurred in the way he negotiated the Treaty of Versailles and the way he sought its ratification in the United States.[70] These biographers also agree that what contributed to Wilson's failings was his "overconfidence, egotism, unrealistic faith in his own judgements and powers, and stubborn adherence to his principles, combined with ambition and desire for power."[71]

As more documentation has become available, interpretations of Wilson's personality have changed. Since Weinstein had sources that were not yet available to the earlier biographers, he was able to go further than the others. Ross, however, has reservations about Weinstein's analysis. The new evidence points to a less conflicted relation with the father and a more important role for the mother. It also suggests that the power struggles that took place at Princeton had a basis in reality. Ross's objection to Weinstein's description of Wilson is that "Weinstein inadvertently leaves the reader wondering how such an unstable person as Wilson accomplished what he did."[72] In line with more recent theoretical directions, Ross contends that as the mother-son relationship and the issues of narcissism are considered to be more consequential, ego psychology will be instrumental in reaching "a more subtle and integrated view of Wilson's personality."[73] Regarding future portrayals, Ross says that "the degree and location of Wilson's psychological difficulties cannot begin to be assessed until they are seen in the context of his strengths."[74]

The last president to be discussed here, about whom there is a large body of psychohistorical work, is Richard M. Nixon. As the title of one article indicates, "Nixon and the Psychohistorians" by James P. Johnson, Nixon has been a subject of particularly intense inquiry because his denouement was so anomalous.[75] Nixon is the only president in American history to resign from office because he faced impeachment. The debacle which marked his administration, the Watergate Scandal, in addition to being a felonious break in and burglary of the opposition Democratic Party headquarters, turned into a constitutional conflict. When Nixon tried to cover up the scandal, claiming presidential prerogative, the Congress of the United States, in line with its constitutional authority, prepared to impeach him.

Paradoxically, one differentiating aspect of the Nixon presidency is that it acted as a fillip for the field of psychohistory. Because of Nixon's continuous aberrant behavior, which earned him the epithet "Tricky Dick," he invited the attention and psychological scrutiny of the mental health field. Nixon became extremely sensitive to mental assessments of him, and disdained psychiatrists.[76] Defensively, and perhaps for the first time, a national leader, made disparaging remarks about the field of psychohistory.[77] Nixon's long public career was marked by so many "crises" and curious tactics, that it aroused the curiosity of the public, the press corps, of academics, and of psychologists.

Mindful of his growing notoriety, Nixon wrote a book in 1962, which he ironically entitled *Six Crises,* and which was a defense of his actions at critical times.[78] Nixon was president from 1969 to 1975. He published his autobiography, *RN: The Memoirs of Richard Nixon*, in which he portrayed himself as a fighter, who was constantly pitted against great odds, yet who prevailed against his enemies.[79] Aware that he aroused perplexing feelings and equivocation, he became sensitive to studies of his personality. Johnson quotes a Nixon associate, who informed a former Nixon law partner that Nixon was participating in a panel that would include a psychiatrist. He was told that Nixon would not accept such an arrangement. One associate said to the other, "Jesus Christ, you're not going to believe this but Nixon hates psychiatrists. . . . He's got this thing, apparently. They make him very nervous."[80] Psychohistorians

Psychohistory: Genre and Interpretations 187

have noted in fact that Nixon, who has denied being paranoid, "has an extraordinary need to fight against real or imagined enemies."[81] It was widely observed that Nixon was an unusually aggressive person, but he justified his behavior "by asserting that the struggle is for a worthy cause—even the life of the nation—and that his enemies will stop at nothing to defeat him."[82] In fact, Nixon's political career, beginning with his campaign for Congress in 1946 was marked by smearing and discrediting his opponents, all under the guise of fighting national and international communism. Nevertheless, after he became president, he improved relations not only with the Soviet Union, but, astoundingly, and with much fanfare, with the Communist China of Mao Tse Tung.

Bruce Mazlish considers Nixon's Quaker background, his religiosity, his attitude toward authority, his courtship of his wife, his amateur acting in college, and his struggle to establish himself as a young lawyer. Mazlish, considering the various aspects of Nixon's personal history, seeks to illuminate the question of who was the "real Nixon."[83] Although every facet of Nixon's life is grist for the mill, one telling aspect of his career is his penchant for concentrating on the need to speak effectively and convincingly. Not only did Nixon engage in amateur acting while in college, he was also on the debating team. In 1952, relatively early in his career, while he was vice president during Eisenhower's presidency, he made his celebrated "Checkers speech" in which he defended himself against charges of corruption. His "performance" was so convincing that Darryl Zanuck, one of the most famous Hollywood film producers telephoned him to praise his speech. Zanuck called it "The most tremendous performance I've ever seen."[84] Mazlish notes that Nixon was constantly concerned with acting and that he "believed intensely in his own verbal and acting skills."[85] Nixon, however, honed his verbal abilities for hostile and aggressive purposes, preparing himself for the political arena. In most of his encounters, he defeated his opponents, until his debate with John F. Kennedy in 1960. Although he was confident that he would win, in this instance he failed and Kennedy won the election.

Mazlish says of Nixon's many encounters that "making his full use of his verbal and acting skills in debate provided a wonderful release."[86] In general, Mazlish considers Nixon an aggressive person, but who regarded himself as "high principled" and "fair minded."[87] Due to the way Nixon viewed his circumstances, he felt that he had to defend himself against opponents who themselves were unfair and sought to smear him. Although Mazlish emphasizes Nixon's personal psychodynamics, he recommends that a fuller explanation should include the role of the public he led. For example, Nixon's self-righteous posturing and his view of himself as a man of principle, according to Mazlish, "corresponds to the image of self-righteousness projected by America as a whole"[88] at this time. And, this "correspondence" with the public brought Nixon his political success.[89]

In conclusion, Johnson's interpretation of Nixon's memoirs, is his finding that the "result confirms the psychohistorical corpus about the president's need, even compulsion, to sweat and strain against enemies, real and imagined, and somehow to overcome or get revenge for some past hurt."[90]

2. Group Dynamics

The study of groups is another important domain of psychohistory. It encompasses the interactions of leader and led, collective acts, institutions, events, and nations. Such processes are of intrinsic and fundamental concern for the historian. Moreover, the perennial question for all historians is the issue of who makes history—the individual or the group? And it is in the interaction of the individual with the group that results in the processes of history.

Psychohistorians are concerned with how groups are affected by traumatic experiences such as revolutions, wars, and epidemics, all of which cause mass hysteria. The goal of studies of groups is to try to understand the collective motivations for common actions and feelings, and how they are shaped by historical circumstances. Erikson pointed the way with his life histories of Luther and Gandhi. He contended that in solving their own problems great men were also solving the problems of the group. Individual history thus illuminates group history.

In the field of psychohistory, psychobiography is prominent. And national leaders, such as Hitler, have drawn much attention from psychohistorians. In tandem with this interest, there has been the central issue of the relationship between the leader and the led. Collective behavior is therefore a major interest for psychohistorians. The development of fascism, or totalitarianism in general, has stimulated a need to understand these phenomena. Why were people deceived by detrimental leaders? Still another reason for the perennial interest in the European dictators, spawned following World War I, is that they have cast a long shadow, which continues to affect societies in the present. With the conflagration sparked by Hitler's expansionism, World War II affected every continent in the world.

The first psychohistorians were Central European psychoanalysts, who grappled with the meaning of fascism. Freud followed the course of World War I, and recorded some of his observations in a diary; these issues then found expression in several of his works.[91] Erikson also wrote on Hitler and the German national character. However, many of the psychoanalysts who established the foundations for studying and understanding the manifestations of National Socialism lacked historical training. As Louise E. Hoffman says in "Psychoanalytic Interpretations of Adolf Hitler and Nazism, 1933–1945: A Prelude to Psychohistory," psychohistory "may be said to have emerged out of the psychoanalytic investigations of Adolf Hitler by his contemporaries."[92] Not only was Hitler's personality studied, but his political techniques were also examined. Hoffman observes that "these writers provided a perspective that most historians of the time had overlooked, but that was still partial and liable to distortion."[93] Nevertheless, the work of the most prominent psychoanalysts of the time, including Ernest Jones, Raymond de Saussure, and Wilhelm Reich, contributed to a theory of totalitarianism. Eventually, their work became more sophisticated and, as Hoffman says, "The confrontation with Nazism advanced psychohistorical investigation by stimulating cooperation among psychoanalysts, political scientists, sociologists, and historians; interdisciplinary enterprises became even more common after the war."[94]

Leaders are reflective of their time, circumstances, and groups. Bruce Mazlish, who has written widely on the methodology of group psychohistory, explains:

> In discovering, or creating his own political identify, the great leader also creates a political identity for his followers, that is, he makes

them into a group, however amorphous in actual structure. This explains why with great frequency, the leader-to-be appeals to previously unpolitical people, and brings them into the political arena. A Robespierre draws to him the sans-culottes, a Hitler, the non-voting, lower middle class German, a Mao Tse-tung, the Chinese peasants. Thus, leadership is a creative art, which, psychologically-grounded, brings forth a political identity for both the leader and the led.[95]

To further illustrate the advantage of group psychohistory, the Nazi era and World War II take center stage. Psychohistorians grapple with the bizarre and unusual occurrences in Nazi Germany. They deal with the concepts and issues of normality and pathology, and their application to Nazi leadership and the group behavior of the SS.[96] One work in particular, *L'Antisémitism nazi: Histoire d'une psychose collective* by Saul Friedländer, shows that the most ardent Nazis had authoritarian personalities, and that there was a correlation between emotional disorders and anti-Semitism. Friedländer also shows that traditional explanations of economic and political considerations to account for the rise of the Nazis and their conduct of the war are insufficient. Instead of following utilitarian motives, their behavior was irrational and self-defeating.[97]

Writing a decade later, George M. Kren also looks at the SS and raises the question of why these individuals, acting in organized groups, engaged in and rationalized the committing of mass murder. In "Psychohistory, Psychobiography and the Holocaust," Kren dovetails Friedländer's contributions, but he has a somewhat different perspective on the SS.[98] Kren does not disagree that many of these men had authoritarian personalities. He disagrees that an authoritarian personality, stemming from having received corporal punishment in childhood coupled with demands of compliance, or obedience, is sufficient to explain the death camps, because men of various personalities were in the SS. What was decisive, Kren says, was not personality, but membership in a group, even if many who engaged in murderous behavior were drawn to it for sadistic reasons.[99]

Kren extols psychohistory because it has provided an understanding of the Holocaust that conventional history has been limited in explaining. Kren considers whether lawful service to a state, or ideology, no matter how heinous, makes a person pathological, if it is part of the job or duty. He considers such pathology to be universal and not restricted to Germans.[100]

Kren has investigated concentration camp commanders, whom he describes as psychopaths and schizoid personalities. But, he says, "Seen within the context of the public definitions of normalcy these individuals were clearly not pathological. They fulfilled the role delegated them by their culture well, built during the Nazi period when the culture defined participation in mass murder as normal, and in the post war world when they held jobs, provided for their families and exhibited no behavior which would differentiate them from others."[101]

Kren notes that psychohistory has served to further our understanding of the nature of National Socialism, and the analysis of group behavior, "However, our understanding of the Holocaust has not caught up with the steadily increasing factual knowledge about it."[102] Kren concludes on a challenging note, pointing to a lacuna in theory, for he says "And above all, psychohistory must recognize that after the Holocaust no concept of human nature, no theory of human action which does not include the reality of Auschwitz can be considered legitimate."[103]

Fascism is also a reference point for other phenomena of group psychology, notably those bearing on women and the family. Marcia E. Bedard, in "Profamilism and the New Right: A Feminist Analysis of Fascist Ideology," examines how the ideology of fascism has impressed itself on the New Right in the United States.[104] Bedard, citing the work and contributions of George Kren, addresses herself to another aspect of Nazi ideology, namely women's role in society. What is called "profamilism," Bedard says, is really anti-feminism, and "a polite euphemism in fascist rhetoric."[105] The group most susceptible to this outlook tends to be, Bedard contends, "white, lower middle class or working class persons with little education beyond high school, and who are often devoutly religious."[106]

Fascism, and communism under Stalin, fostered the subordination of women to a male dominated family because it was advantageous to the state. The conformity learned in the family extended to conformity to the state. And, says Bedard, the ideology of the New Right, based on a conservative-fundamentalist alliance, is similar to the ideology and practices of totalitarian countries.[107] In this sense, the issues concern sexuality, reproduction, and gender socialization. Bedard qualifies her assertions in that persons or groups associated with the New Right are not outright fascists, who want to establish a fascist state. Nevertheless, many people "are ignorant of the implicitly fascistic principles which underly the profamilism ideology, masked as it is with reified symbols of patriotism, the family and religion."[108]

What the ideologies of the New Right desire is a male-dominated patriarchal family, supported solely by the father. Although such families are no longer the norm in the United States, the New Right would like to recreate the traditional family situation. Among the many complications mitigating against a return to the former structure is the fact that women have achieved a more equal role in society. The New Right drapes itself with the American flag, heralding its concern for the United States and designating itself the "Moral Majority."[109] By implication, Bedard says, feminists and those who do not approve their program are not only a minority, they are also called immoral. And as attempts at verbal persuasion have not been effective, there have been resorts to force, violence, and intimidation. This oppression manifests itself in many ways, but it is especially marked at family planning clinics, women's health centers, and at the offices of sympathetic elected officials.[110]

Bedard mentions many leaders of the New Right, notably Ronald Reagan.[111] Bedard argues that just as Hitler and Stalin sought to restore a sense of male dominance, so Ronald Reagan and other leaders of the New Right have sought "the same remedies."[112] The intention of such a program is to "Give men someone to look down on again so we can get back to business as usual."[113] Indirectly touching on the nature of the relationship between leader and led, Bedard says: "In Russia, Germany, and now the United States, we also see the profamilism anti-feminist movement led by charismatic male leaders who are extremely provincial and anti-intellectual in their outlook, who use emotion rather than reason in order to gain support from the easily manipulated uneducated segments of the population, and who present a simplistic formula for rebuilding national strength and pride: take away women's rights."[114]

In sum, Bedard objects to the New Right because she feels that their position fosters an "authoritarian, patriarchal family structure," which is "the fundamental building block of the fascist state."[115] Among its many goals and intentions is to serve male dominance, maintain rigid sex roles, and instill obedience and fear. This group will resort to force if necessary in order to ensure social control.[116]

In examining and defining groups, Mazlish addresses the issue of what constitutes a group. He makes general observations, the question of the methodology used to study groups, and the nature of the evidence available to the historian. He stipulates that a group may be a nationality, a race, or people sharing experiences that have shaped them into a group. The concept of group may be applied to religious or revolutionary movements, to the impact of slavery, or war on a group of people, or to national characteristics.[117] Although Mazlish expresses reservations about the use of psychoanalysis to study groups, as pioneered and applied by Freud, he does employ some of Freud's fundamental concepts in assessing a group. For example, in his study of "The American Psyche," he resorts to the Oedipus complex to explain, in part, the American Revolution and how the colonists saw themselves vis-a-vis Great Britain, their "mother country."[118] He notes that the language used by the colonists to break away was familial. At first they regarded themselves as "children" who were dependent on a nurturing king.[119] As the revolution began, they formed the "sons of liberty" organization to oppose George III, "'the father' who had betrayed them."[120] In becoming independent, the American colonists grew up, experienced a "new birth" and repudiated the values and traditions of the "parent" country.[121]

In his essay "Psychoanalytic Theory and History: Groups and Events," Mazlish concludes on a novel note, inviting psychohistorians to form groups themselves in order to facilitate studies of groups. He writes: "To explore the Promised Land, we need more than individual scouts, going forward in isolated forays. We need the collaboration of analysts and historians, working in sustained, connected, and continuing fashion. One analyst, one scholar may do well by one, individual subject. Large group phenoma, such as witchcraft movements, or mass conversions, require systematic and collaborative studies by many scholars. In short, much of the future work in group history will require group effort, a conclusion that seems to me altogether fitting. To this high as well as deep adventure, then, we are all invited."[122]

The Afro-American experience has also been studied by psychohistorians. The treatment of the movements, and their leaders have reflected the wide attention they have gained in the mass media. In the 1960s, the Black Panther Party, a well publicized group, had a meteoric-like career and existence. Its appeal and composition differed from the other more established Afro-American civil rights organizations. The Black Panther Party, begun in 1967, lasted only until 1973. Michael Tager, in "Looking into the Whirlwind: A Psychohistorical Study of the Black Panthers," examines the leaders as a group and their common denominators. He links them up with their followers and the wider historical condition in American.[123]

The leaders of this radical party, Huey Newton, Bobby Seale, and Eldridge Cleaver, drew their inspiration from Malcolm X, rather than Martin Luther King. This party was militant, used revolutionary language, and had a considerable success in organizing black inner city communities. What did these leaders have in common and what enabled them to resonate with their followers? All three leaders were born in the deep South and had moved to California in their youth with their families, as part of the black migration to other parts of the United States. California especially was appealing because of its well publicized and glamorized promise of opportunity, wealth and success. But, for many blacks, expectations of the better life were barely realized. California, symbolically had a special meaning because it seemed to be in the words of Cleaver the "last chance" at the "edge of the continent."[124]

Tager says that all three Panther leaders "experienced something akin to death immersion."[125] In their autobiographies, they describe the domestic violence they experienced or witnessed in families, the fights with knives and guns they saw in the streets, which led them to confront "the possibility of their

Psychohistory: Genre and Interpretations 195

own deaths."[126] In 1965, the assassination of Malcolm X, who had been a role model, not only made a deep impression on them, but galvanized them into organizing the radical Black Panther Party.[127]

Addressing himself to the criticism that Freudian concepts cannot be applied to understanding the African-American experience, Tager replies that "these objections do not seem to be borne out by the autobiographical material at hand."[128] He adds, "One looks in vain for a distinctively African world view or set of values. Instead, one finds the ambiguous mixture of materialism and idealism common to the American character."[129] In varying degrees, in all three leaders there are oedipal patterns of rebellion, as all of them had serious conflicts with their fathers. However, Tager also considers the issue of being black in a predominantly white society. He is well aware of the pioneering work by Frantz Fanon in *Black Skins, White Masks*, published in 1952, which deals with the trauma of black children educated in predominantly white societies.[130] All three leaders had internalized negative feelings about being black, and, in Fanon's view wanted alternative schools for blacks as therapy for the "black neurosis."[131] And, as in *Wretched of the Earth*, in which Fanon advocates revolutionary action against the white colonizers, the Black Panther leaders attempted to apply this injunction, stressing armed defense. The party adopted a uniform dress code, which included a black beret, black pants, a black leather jacket, black shoes, and guns. This posture, combined with a militant rhetoric aimed at the police, caused confrontations with them. As Tager points out, the membership of the party came "largely from young black males with a history of police confrontations."[132] However, the Black Panther Party also advocated improvements in the inner cities, especially housing and food, and control of their own communities.

The decline of the Black Panther Party in the 1970s, according to Tager, came about because white society accepted black individuality, and because of the splits which occurred in the Black Party membership.[133] With regard to the nature of groups, and the issue of leader and led, Tager concludes that: "despite the rapid decline of the Panthers, their rise to prominence in the late 1960s suggests that they successfully crystallized the psychological dilemma facing many urban blacks and placed it briefly in a political context. Many of the members underwent a death immersion similar to that of the founders. Violence was really endemic to the inner city, and the Panthers only channeled it into a more coherent form. Even if members did not experience an intensely neurotic situation in asserting their identity like the founders, they still felt as if these leaders spoke directly to their needs."[134]

An instance of collective trauma, but on a national scale, occurred in France in 1940. The unconscious group behavior of the French people between the two world wars contributed to what occurred in 1940. The military defeat, followed by invasion and occupation by German troops, caused wide-spread feelings of abandonment among the French people. The defeat was blamed on abandonment by the leadership of the country and by the allies of France.[135] Consequently, the aged Marshal Pétain, who himself had been abandoned as a child, was able to intuit the national mood, and initially on taking power was regarded as a national savior.[136]

The circumstances leading to the defeat of France in 1940 have been the object of enormous popular and scholarly attention. Because the quick defeat of France came as such a shock, the national group dynamic has been a subject of particular interest. The national group behavior of France in the 1930s reveals acquiescence to Hitlerian hostility, as exemplified by an essentially passive diplomacy. This passivity occurred despite Hitler's repeated provocations, and indicated self-destructive tendencies on the part of the French people. Not surprisingly, the entire period has been popularly labeled and accepted as one of "appeasement." The widespread unconscious demonstrations of these feelings were shown in many ways, in addition to the conduct of a passive foreign policy toward Germany. France was generally stronger militarily than Germany in the 1930s, and in combination with its allies dwarfed German power.[137] Yet, France was to stress the Maginot Line as its best defense. In the last two decades before 1940, but with increasing intensity in the 1930s, the Republican regime came under vehement attack by fascistic groups, thereby reducing national cohesion.[138] The violent expressions of opposition revealed an unresolved conflict over royalism, an issue which dated back to the French Revolution of 1789. Accordingly,

Hitler's charisma, characterized by his phallic aggressive qualities, set an example in Germany, which made him increasingly appealing in France. Pétain, who in 1940 intuited the unconscious group feelings, was himself a royalist, and Vichy was his attempt to re-establish the *ancien régime*.

An examination of the kinds of films that were popular in France in the interwar period further illuminates the collective unconscious fantasy of the French people. The psychohistorian Paul Monaco, in his book *Cinema and Society: France and Germany during the Twenties*, has made a contribution of signal importance to the understanding of group dynamics at this time. By analyzing the themes of these popular films, Monaco was able to provide insight into the concerns of the "group mind" following the trauma of World War I.[139]

A typical theme in French films is that of the child who is orphaned, or abandoned by his parents, and who later finds happiness and security. Another kind of popular film at this time was about the person who stands alone, who is isolated yet perseveres. Examples of this genre were Joan of Arc and Napoleon. Of the German films studied, forty out of sixty were concerned with the issue of betrayal. The French films differed from the German ones in their reflection of national experiences. As Monaco points out, the Germans felt that they would have been victorious in World War I if they had not been betrayed by traitors in their midst.[140] The popular metaphor used to explain their defeat was that they had been "stabbed in the back," and it is consistent with the theme in their movies.

Psychobiography and the study of groups complement each other, and they have common methodological and historiographical problems.[141] The psychohistorical approach to the study of groups has improved our understanding of collective psychology, but the work on theories of group history continues to concern psychohistorians.

3. Childhood

Along with the growth of psychohistory has come an interest in the history of childhood. Just as psychoanalysis is concerned with the formative period of the individual, so the psychohistorian is concerned with childhood for its historical significance. The history of childhood is a category of psychohistory, and much has been written about it.[142] For the psychohistorian, the dominant concern is with children's life experiences, considered from the perspective of their development rather than just with the attitudes toward them. The centrality of the oedipal situation and childrearing practices have enormous implications for society's political and social structures and on group behavior.

One person who stands out in the field of childhood history, and who has done pioneering work, is Lloyd deMause. He is the founder and first editor of *The Journal of Psychohistory: A Quarterly Journal of Childhood and Psychohistory*. DeMause has also founded a school and has stimulated studies on childhood history,[143] but his work is extremely controversial.

DeMause has formulated a novel evolutionary theory that he calls the "psychogenic theory of history." It is his contention that "the central force for change in history is neither technology nor economics, but the 'psychogenic' changes in personality occurring because of successive generations of parent-child interactions."[144] DeMause's interpretation is different indeed, as advanced in "The Evolution of Childhood." He posits that: "The history of childhood is a nightmare from which we have only recently begun to awaken. The further back in history one goes, the lower the level of child care, and the more likely children are to be killed, abandoned, beaten, terrorized, and sexually abused."[145] DeMause periodizes parent-child relations into six modes, which are summarized here. His schematic periodization of childrearing spans the various historical epochs. Each has a particular characteristic and leads to successive improvements in subsequent modes. The first, dating from antiquity to the fourth century A.D., is the "infanticidal mode," when parents "routinely resolved their anxieties about taking care of children by killing them."[146] The second, the "abandoning mode," from the fourth to the thirteenth centuries, is a period marked by children being commonly given away to wet nurses, or left in a monastery or nunnery. The third, from the fourteenth to the seventeenth centuries, is the "ambivalent mode," when children were provided with more personal attention than in previous periods. The fourth, occurring in the eighteenth century is the "intrusive mode," in which both parents take a more direct interest in the child, and are less punitive. It is a period in which pediatrics is introduced. The fifth, the nineteenth to the mid-twentieth century, is the "socializing mode," and is marked by still greater empathy for the child. At this time, the father is directly involved in childrearing. The sixth and final period is the "helping mode," beginning in the mid-twentieth century, and is noted for permissiveness. In dealing with children, according to DeMause, discussion and empathy are paramount. He points out that few parents indulge their children to such an extent, but where the "helping mode" is practiced "it results in a child who is gentle, sincere, never depressed, never imitative or group-oriented, strong willed, and unintimidated by authority."[147]

DeMause's schema are by and large not accepted by most psychohistorians. A representative of the counter position is Salvatore Prisco:

> What is highly questionable is the fact that deMause based his observation in large part, by his own admission, on *his* role as a parent and on his observations of *his* own son. The limited value of this data does not need further comment. Lloyd deMause may be the best parent in the world, but to project this self-serving evaluation as evidence of a new era of childrearing for mankind is unscientific.[148]

Overall, Prisco typically finds that: "While deMause's theories and hypotheses may have elements of truth in them his assertions and generalizations have gone far beyond the proof of evidence."[149] As for the psychogenic theory explaining historical causation, Prisco adds that it has "proved to be unprovable by contemporary standards."[150]

Whereas psychohistorians disagree with each other occasionally on matters of interpretation, most disagree with deMause in substance. Indeed, the differences may be described as a schism. Bruce Mazlish even goes so far as to say: "There is a man named Lloyd deMause who is helping discredit the field. He claims it [psychohistory] is a science, and he has a psychogenic explanation for everything."[151] In effect, although deMause has certainly helped to popularize childhood history and psychohistory, his work has not only been not well received but it has served to alienate many psychohistorians.

Two exhaustive studies in this category which support the position that childhood experiences must be considered in the development of the adult person are Elizabeth W. Marvick's

The Young Richelieu: A Psychoanalytic Approach to Leadership and *Louis XIII: The Making of a King*. Marvick has published a great deal in the field of childhood, including "Nature vs. Nurture: Trends and Patterns in Seventeenth Century French Childrearing."[152] Marvick's forte is the study of childhood.

These two books, *Young Richelieu* and *Louis XIII* complement each other well. Cardinal Richelieu became Louis XIII's chief minister and the preeminent statesman of his time. Armand-Jean Du Plessis de Richelieu is one of Europe's leading statebuilders, ranking in stature with Otto von Bismarck and Camillo di Cavour. In French history, Richelieu is often compared to such illustrious political leaders as Louis XIV, Napoleon and de Gaulle. However, each of these men had different styles of leadership and faced distinctive problems. Marvick's book, except for providing some highlights of Richelieu's years of greatest fame, concentrates on his formation and family constellation. Her view that childhood experiences must be considered in understanding the development of the adult is very much in line with the psychohistorical approach to the study of the individual. What further differentiates Marvick's work from conventional biographies of Richelieu is that she attempts to answer the fundamental question: What are the origins of his extraordinary reputation? The psychohistorical approach to the study of the individual is, after all, the search for motivations.

The strength of *The Young Richelieu* is its thorough documentation. Her sources include archival materials from France, Italy, Great Britain, the archives of the Richelieu family, and numerous other primary sources and memoirs. Furthermore, buttressed by psychoanalytic theory, Marvick uses her sources innovatively, thereby providing a more comprehensive and holistic portrait of Richelieu.[153]

Marvick's thesis is that Richelieu's drive for power, for mastery and control of the political process, stemmed from an idealized conception of his family dynamics. His familial introject was then projected onto the larger political arena. Like his father, Richelieu came to serve the king, but unlike his father, he served him as a cleric and not as a soldier. In regard to his choice of careers, Marvick points out that when Richelieu "assumed the feminine robes of a priest," he was motivated by a desire to "gratify a profoundly masculine ambition to surpass his own father,"[154] Richelieu, to use his own words, considered the church to be the "holy bride of the sovereign monarch of the world."[155]

In *Louis XIII*, Marvick describes the upbringing of the future King of France, and relates his childhood to his adult behavior. It is the story of a poor little rich boy. Marvick is alert to the nuances of personality development and to the various phases of childhood, applying psychoanalytic theories from Sigmund Freud to Margaret Mahler. This results in a psychodynamic portrait of Louis. Marvick's major source is the voluminous diary of Louis' physician, Jean Héroard, which he kept from Louis' birth on September 27, 1601, through his twenty-sixth year. Whereas the dynamic meaning of this diary has been largely neglected by historians, Marvick uses it to explain Louis' socialization; another historian, not untypically, dismissed the detailed diary because it consisted of volumes "in which you will find nothing except that at what time he (Louis) awakened, breakfasted, spat, pissed, crapped, etc."[156] But for psychohistorian Marvick, this information is grist for the mill.

Marvick raises a fundamental question about Louis XIII, a powerful ruler of the kind that still prevails today in totalitarian states: Was he a good man? Such a question leads immediately to issues of aggression and war, and Marvick notes that when Louis was almost seven, he said that he wanted to be at war all the time. And indeed he was at war longer than either his father, Henri IV, or his son, Louis XIV. Many contemporaries considered him cruel, for "he could on occasion take aim and fire upon a pair of rebellious peasants, killing them with the same apparent satisfaction he showed at bagging game birds or shooting a stag."[157] Other contemporaries considered Louis "a good man," although he had many men executed for questionable reasons.

Marvick discusses other members of Louis' household, such as his personal physician, and provides a detailed account of Héroard's influence and motivations. Héroard, a Protestant, was selected by Louis' father for his position because of his prominent reputation. But the account of Héroard's treatment of his young charge is shocking in the degree he was controlling, overly concerned, eager to exert his power, and sadistic.

Some of the practices Héroard engaged in were common at that time. For example, on the second day of Louis' life, Héroard perceived that his charge had difficulty in sucking, and had a surgeon cut the membranes at the base of the tongue to improve his ability to nurse. For us, it is appalling to learn that Louis, under the guise of being given the best and most pampered care of his day, was actually abused. As the narrative progresses, it became evident why Louis' relationship with Héroard was marked by frequent conflict, from the oral through the phallic phase of development. Héroard contributed to Louis XIII's rage. Not surprisingly, Louis developed a severe stutter, related according to Marvick, to cathexis of the anal zone. Despite these abuses, Héroard in time became a surrogate father and later Louis' confidant.[158]

Subtitled the "Making of a King," this study is actually the story of the rationalized destruction of a human being. Although given what passed for "royal" care, in reality Louis was alternatively abandoned, neglected, abused, seduced, betrayed, and manipulated. The marriage of his parents was arranged in order to produce a suitable heir to the throne. After Louis' birth, his mother and father took little direct interest in him, but they encouraged his genitality so that he in turn would eventually produce an heir, in effect raising the little boy merely to be a virile man. His mother, Marie de Medici, did not nurse him. This task was given to Madam Antoinette Joron, whose sole function was to nurse Louis, which she did until he was twenty five months old. Louis had a complicated and difficult family constellation. His father Henri IV, was called le *vert galant* (the gay blade) because of his many mistresses and numerous children. His favorite son was not Louis, but César de Vendôme, who was seven years older than Louis and the son of Henri's most beloved mistress, Gabrielle d'Estrées. Louis' relationship with his father was stormy and ambivalent. His father beat him frequently, and ordered other members of the household to whip him when he was away. Henry IV demanded submission from Louis to such an extent that he pushed the boy toward homosexuality. For example, Louis began to experience masochistic pleasure at being whipped. According to Marvick, it was fortunate for Louis that his father was absent frequently, which eased his depression and permitted him to resume his heterosexual interests. In 1610, when Louis was eight, his father was assassinated, and although Louis grieved for him, he was also reported to have become more sociable afterward.[159]

In October 1610, at the age of nine, Louis was crowned the King of France at Reims. Thereafter, he received greater public attention, which sometimes caused him difficulties, as some of his early negative experiences unconsciously manifested themselves. It was noted that he would easily become enraged and strike people. Louis himself said that he was not a happy person. He was often ill, and developed ulcerative colitis. Marvick points out that he frequently felt slighted, victimized or deceived. He generally distrusted the good intentions of those around him, when in actuality those who supervised him and were responsible for his welfare were rather permissive.

If, at nine years of age, Louis was the king, his mother was the regent, and the distance between them, established early in Louis' life, was now exacerbated by the political requirement of mutual cooperation. Marvick describes Marie de Medici as a cold and emotionally needy woman. The dominant feeling between mother and son was hostility and distrust. Their views diverged on many critical diplomatic, domestic, and religious issues. Indeed, the conflict between them was so serious that Louis "entertained thoughts of having her killed."[160] However, in the presentation of the clash between Louis and his mother, Marvick shows how this rift, as it was expressed in political terms, reflected their different backgrounds and personal animosities. Fundamentally, Louis stood for an anti-Spanish and anti-Austrian Habsburg policy, which by extension was also an anti-papal one. His mother, on the other hand, was an Italian who was raised in a convent. She came from a prominent family that included popes and was sympathetic to the Holy See and the Habsburgs.[161]

4. The Family

The institution of the family is a fundamental category of psychohistory and warrants separate attention. It is also a pivotal link between the individual and the group. From a psychohistorical point of view, as Mazlish notes, it is important because "Loving and hating, giving and receiving, obeying and commanding, controlling and being controlled all take their origin here."[162] The key development of transference and its vicissitudes originate in the family dynamics. Later, transference is the basis in adult life for patterns of behavior toward authority and other relationships.[163]

Just as family life affects history, so historical developments affect the family. There are many complexities in the study of the family, as its structure may be affected by revolution, war, religious belief, economic conditions, and medical advancements. These developments have demographic effects on the structure of the family. As for childrearing, practices vary according to class, region, nation, and whether they are in rural or urban settings.[164] In other words, the family is shaped by forces larger than itself.

In his assessment of family history, Mazlish notes that in comparison to the other genres of psychohistory "the family is not the prime actor in history."[165] Certainly, the family molds individuals, but it is not a historical group like a church, an army, or a class, nor does it behave like an individual leader who influences events. Therefore, historians, in contrast to sociologists, do not give primacy to family studies. Nevertheless, Mazlish affirms that: "Study of family history is entirely valid in its own right, and it can also be done psychohistorically. It is also absolutely essential as providing an intelligent and meaningful context for life histories, which otherwise exist in a timeless, mythical vacuum of the life of the 'hero.' With this said, however, family history cannot be expected to serve as a substitute for the oft-demanded treatment and analysis of 'group history.'"[166]

In most cases individuals are raised in families over a period of many years. The vicissitudes of family life vary, and conditions are related to historical and social changes as well as to internal emotional crises within a family. There may be a death or incapacitation of one or both parents, and there may be dislocation because of war or natural disaster. As E. James Anthony, in "The Family and the Psychoanalytic Process in Children" says, these formations, "Parts of this familial environment are gradually internalized into the conflictual spheres of the psyche, while other portions gain varying degrees of object representation."[167]

Freud pioneered studies of both the group and the family. Although the individual, rather than the family, was the focus of Freud's work, he nevertheless provided a conceptual framework for dealing with the technical problems of studying the family psychoanalytically. Even if a comprehensive theoretical system is not formed, Freud has advanced elements "that still need to be considered in dealing with either the psychology or the psychopathology of family life."[168]

Freud was well aware of the transmission of neuropathic tendencies within families. In his own extended family there was pathology. Two of his cousins, for example, had hereditary illnesses. One became psychotic at nineteen and another developed a psychosis in her 20's. Freud remarked that he and his sister Rosa had "a pronounced tendency to neurasthenia."[169] Freud recognized that the family environment could affect other members of a family, complicating intrapsychic and interpersonal developments. Freud also said that social conditions had to be considered as well in dealing with psychoanalytic case histories: "Above all, our interest will be directed towards their family circumstances."[170] In his theory of neurosis, which was familial, Freud noted the influence and responsibility of the father as well as that of the mother. For example, he said that pedophilic practices stemmed from paternal dysfunction.[171]

As Anthony points out, Freud dealt with the problem of incest in *Totem and Taboo*; he proposed three postulates that can be considered to be the foundation of psychoanalytic family theory and therapy. Anthony paraphrases Freud in arguing "that there was a family psyche whose psychological processes correspond fairly closely with those of the individual; that there was a continuity of emotional life in the family psyche from one generation to the next; and that the mysterious transmission of attitudes through the generations was the result of unconscious understanding that made the latent psychic life of one generation accessible to the succeeding one."[172] This means that neurosis can be transmitted from one generation to another, that there is a "collective psychological life of the family,"[173] which causes conflict for the individual.

From his study of groups, Freud extrapolated the dynamics which can be applied to understanding families. As in a group, the family depends on the "qualities of parental leadership," and this includes the "mechanism of identification" and "feelings of mutual empathy."[174] These qualities affect the individual's narcissism in relation to parents and family. Family life operates on three different levels: the leadership of parents, the child as a follower, and the psychological composition of the family as a group. Accordingly, the child's initial family background will continue to affect it intrapsychically into adult life.[175]

In studying neurosis, Freud assigned the Oedipus complex a central role, which he related to the "family complex." This complex was affected by parents whose behavior could range from support to aggression and seduction. Within the family, there is sibling rivalry, narcissistic injuries, and feelings of hostility, which could not be directed at the parents. Birth order also shaped personality development, as well as the death of a sibling especially when it came at a time of hostility toward a sibling—wishing a sibling dead.[176] In formulating the "family complex," Freud, as Anthony says, "compounded the intrapsychic events occurring in the family such as parental attitudes and behavior, sibling birth and rivalry; the exigencies of ordinal position, and finally such traumas as death, illness, and abuse in the family."[177]

Concerning the psychic development of the child, ambivalances toward its family and its fantasy life, Freud elaborated the concept of "family romance." In essence, the child's initial overevaluation of the parents, as it is accompanied by frustrations and disappointments, leads to a disparagement of the parents and to a fantasy of having aristocratic lineage.[178] This elevates the parents to nobility.

Anthony concludes that Freud laid the groundwork for the psychoanalytic understanding of the family, and that his work was continued by John C. Flugel, as in *The Psychoanalytic Study of the Family*, published in 1921,[179] and by Anna Freud's work in England. Anthony says that in psychoanalytic theory "we need to bring the family as a psychic phenomenon more fully and more frequently into our analytic work, to recognize the impact of the actual family on the analytic process, and to uncover the repressed unconscious elements relating to it."[180] On a broader scale, Anthony's final statement is that "this should provide us with the necessary experience to construct a more substantive theory than we presently have."[181]

Affecting the study of the family, in addition to the psychoanalytical, historical, and sociological factors is political orientation. For example, for several decades now, but cresting in the 1990's in the United States, the call for "family values" has become a shibboleth, whose discourse has entered presidential campaigns. This politicization, over the issue as to which party would best foster "family values," was a debate over strengthening families, curbing illegitimacy, and retaining the father in the household. This subject, which has turned into a major controversy, has interfaced political conservatism with the academic approach to the importance and the study of the family. The implication is that family life has declined, and in tandem with this issue, that the moral fabric of society is declining too. A general division in this matter ultimately can be traced back to the French Revolution of 1789, which became the fountainhead of modern democracy. David Hunt, in *Parents and Children in History: The Psychology of Family Life in Early Modern France*, has examined this question for the period prior to the revolution, focusing on seventeenth century France.[182] Hunt was influenced by the work of Philippe Ariés, *Centuries of Childhood: A Social History of Family Life*,[183] and guided by Eriksonian theory. Just as the historiography on the French Revolution is marked by political partisanship, so is the historiography on the family. As Hunt states, "For a long time family history in France was the special preserve of monarchist scholars. Mention of the topic was almost equivalent to a confession of conservative allegiance."[184] Certainly, the nostalgia and idealization of former family life by conservative historians have a reactionary intent, but Hunt himself expresses the view that the contemporary family is hardly in a healthy state, and that the left is also disillusioned with it.[185]

The idyllic view of the family of the past sees it as cohesive and stable. Each member had a sense of belonging and security, and the key component was paternal authority. In modern times, however, the pillars on which the family rested, such as religion, tradition, authority, and economic security, have been undermined. Instead, there is now disintegration of the family, and with it, its former benefits to the individual and to society.[186]

The institution of marriage has accordingly undergone changes. In modern times, companionship is considered to be the main reason for marriage and the sentiment which maintains the relationship. In the seventeenth century, the role of the parents was far more pronounced, as parents were expected to provide a dowry for their daughter, but the son-in-law would be expected to provide assistance to his in-laws if they were in economic need. As financial considerations were so important for both parties in affecting a marriage, many just could not afford to marry. Nevertheless, contrary to present belief, many couples cohabited, without being formally married by the church. Yet they were considered married by their communities.[187]

Companionship is the expected criterion in the modern marriage, but, as Hunt wonders, this ideal does "not always square with the reality of the situation; one has only to reflect on the extent to which the ideal of companionship is realized in the marriages of our own day to see that this is the case."[188]

Hunt finds that marriages were different in the seventeenth century, but he does not idealize them. With respect to the changes in attitudes, Hunt says that "they [marriages] were regarded with more cold calculating, more disillusioned cynicism, than they are today."[189] And overall, as to the fundamental purpose of marriage, from the seventeenth century to the present, the psychological meaning for the partners "has remained relatively stable through the years."[190]

Family conditions in New England, in roughly the same period as that considered by Hunt, bore some similarities to the French, but the physical setting of this Old Colony, made for significant differences in its family life. John Demos, in *A Little Commonwealth: Family Life in Plymouth Colony*, also applies an Eriksonian model to the study of this particular colonial society.[191] First of all, the family was basically nuclear, but it was much larger than today's family. The respective members of the family had their prescribed roles, the husband being the head of the family and, as Demos qualifies it, "at least in theory," and "the wife had her own sphere of competence and a corresponding measure of authority."[192]

The family in Plymouth, as elsewhere, fulfilled basic economic and emotional needs, but, as Demos says, the history of the family in America "has been a history of contraction and withdrawal; its central theme is the gradual surrender to other institutions of functions that once lay very much within the realm of family responsibility."[193] A characteristic of the Plymouth family was that it was a "business." All its members worked, and it was economically relatively self-sufficient. It was also a "school" because the parents were required by law to teach their children how to read, at least the Scriptures.[194] The family was also a "church," and it was expected to engage in "family worship." It was even a "house of correction," as criminals were sentenced by the court to live in the household of a respected citizen and perform servant's duties.[195] The family provided many of the social services now performed by the modern state, such as "welfare," hospital care, and taking in orphans. To ensure that the essential social fabric functioned well, the government could and did exert its supervisory powers over the household.[196] In the case of disputes, the "government was also empowered to determine *who* might head a household in the first place."[197]

If the Plymouth family resembled the European family to some extent, conditions in America gave it another dimension. Because of greater mobility, both geographic and social, as land was plentiful in America, the greater opportunities also allowed greater competition and made for more anxiety. Demos says that "men had reason to feel somewhat anxious and insecure in the world of work: here, indeed was the price they paid for the chance to better themselves—a whole darker side of the 'American Experiment'."[198] Unlike Europe, the ready availability of land made for a mobility which eroded traditions and authority. Finally, Demos concludes that "For while the family is now less important from a social standpoint, it may well be *more* important from a psychological one."[199]

Another look at family life, in the nineteenth century, and with a view of its limitations, is Stephen Kern's "Explosive Intimacy: Psychodynamics of the Victorian Family."[200] Kern's main contention is that the Victorian family, although commonly regarded as stable, nurturing, and an institution that provided comfort and safety for its members, was actually riddled with conflicts and anxiety.[201] This "other side" of the Victorian family was its difficulty accepting sexuality, its fear of venereal disease. The "explosive atmosphere that appears to have crept into so many Victorian families was a function of the excessive intimacy and interdependence that the family imposed upon its members."[202]

Kern's essay, although it concentrates on England in the nineteenth century, also has a bearing on the European family in general at this time. There was a spurt in medical discoveries and in popular medical literature, but this was accompanied by a fear of hereditary illness and sexually transmitted disease, especially syphillis. The proliferation of a self-help medical literature and marriage manuals even became detrimental. As Kern says, "the confusion tended to produce a conception of the family as a biological unit which the values, sex cells, and germs of parents worked in and upon the minds and bodies of children leaving little room for individuals development."[203] Such beliefs put more pressure on children, who came to feel "trapped" due to hereditary circumstances, a reflection of Lamarck's theory of the hereditary transmission of acquired characteristics.[204]

Kern, who examines European sources, including French, German, Russian, and of course British literature, argues that certain themes were especially pronounced at this time, namely oedipal issues, with emphasis on father and son conflicts. One representative novel, Fyodor Dostoevsky's *The Brothers Karamazov*, Kern considers and argues that its parricide portends the Russian Revolution and the fall of the Czar.[205] Father-daughter conflicts were depicted in literature too, but to a lesser extent than father-son conflicts. The roots of the conflicts, Kern says, is that "The severely restrictive sexual morality of the nineteenth century was imposed by the newly triumphant bourgeoisie."[206] As the bourgeois ethos emphasized thrift and the amassing of wealth, any "expenditure of energy" or what was considered "waste," whether financial or sexual, was considered to reveal a lack of self-restraint and was therefore immoral.[207]

In sum, whereas family life in the Victorian period was glorified and sanctified, and divorce disparaged, the Victorian family had a "stickiness" that made it "as unbearable as it was vital to its members who had become dependent on it."[208]

Psychohistorians who have studied the family have been guided or influenced by a theoretical framework for understanding its dynamics. From the perspective of today, they have raised the question of the nature of the changes that have occurred and whether or not they have been beneficial for family life and for the individual.[209] Vivian C. Fox and Martin Quitt, in *Loving, Parenting, and Dying: The Family circle in England and America, Past and Present*, a massive account, contend that in the Anglo-American family there have been vast changes in the roles of husband and wife.[210] They have became more egalitarian, and married women work outside the household in numbers approaching that of husbands. The state now has many more functions. The authors also believe that marriages are now more romantic, spouses expecting personal satisfaction from the relationship, but that these demands, as we now live longer, "appear to be more subject to psychological strain than those of the past."[211] In their concluding overview, Fox and Quitt take an optimistic position: "while the early modern centuries experienced profound transformation in economic, social, political, and cultural developments, the pace of change surely has accelerated in our own time with resulting strains and readjustments being forced upon contemporary family relationships that seem to us to be even more intense. Yet the continuing high rate of marriage and remarriage after divorce as well as the continued bearing of children within marriage suggest not only the resiliency of the family cycle but its capacity to evolve new relationships as it repeats itself across the generations."[212]

Christopher Lasch, however, the author of the acclaimed *The Culture of Narcissism: American Life in an Age of Diminishing Expectation*, takes an adverse view of the changes in the family, in the period from the late nineteenth century to the 1970s. What strikes Lasch is that in these decades the family became more unstable, demonstrated not only by the ever rising divorce rate, but also because so many people remained unmarried. Lasch contends that marriage is not working well. As for the celebrating of romantic love, Lasch says that this ideal is difficult to maintain, as adultery is widespread. By the 1960s, the youth culture in America specifically targeted the institution of the family.[213]

Lasch, who takes a psychoanalytic perspective on the direction of the family, argues that it is not properly achieving its main purpose, which is the socialization of the child. In this respect, Lasch says that child care has deteriorated and that among the negative influences causing this situation are the growth of feminism and the mass culture, especially television because it undermines parental authority.[214] And since the work of the parents, especially that of the father, is no longer centered in the home, the child sees the parents less, and is no longer able to adequately identify with and internalize the parents. Because of this minimal contact, oedipal issues are not resolved.[215]

What has occurred is that childrearing functions have been taken over by agencies, such as the state and private industry, now the surrogate parents. Lasch says that "in the course of bringing culture to the masses, the advertising industry, the mass media, the health and welfare services, and other agencies of mass tuition took over many of the socializing functions of the home and brought ones that remained under the direction of modern science and technology."[216] The abdication of the traditional parental authority has led to a permissiveness which "conceals a stringent system of controls, all the more effective because it avoids direct confrontations between authorities and the people on whom they seek to impose their will."[217]

Accordingly, parents turn to experts, such as physicians, psychiatrists, and even the child's own peers, to help them control the child. Lasch describes the length which parents will go to make the child conform: "If the child refuses to eat what his parents think he ought to eat, the parents appeal to medical authority. If he is unruly, they call in a psychiatrist to help the child with his own 'problem.' In this way, parents make their own problems—insubordination—the child's. Similarly at school, the child finds himself surrounded by authorities who wish only to help. If one of the students gets 'out of line' they send him to a counselor for guidance."[218] Further measures to achieve control are illustrated by Lasch as follows: "Thus if a teacher finds an unruly student smoking in the washroom, he should neither 'beat him calmly and coolly and with emotional restraint' or publicly humiliate him, on the one hand, nor ignore the offense, on the other hand, as a minor infraction that should not contribute to the student's reputation as a troublemaker. The teacher should refer him instead to the school psychiatrist. Beating him would make him more unmanageable than ever, in the student's view, whereas the psychiatric solution, in effect, enlists his own cooperation in the school's attempt to control him."[219]

Lasch's critique of American society and the family, which reads like a Jeremiad, does end on a hopeful note. He believes that the will to build a better society does survive, as the work ethic does endure, but "most of all in those who knew the old order . . ."[220]

In conclusion, all the genres of psychohistory can be characterized as being both more advanced than traditional historical studies, and in need of continuing methodological work. And they are of quintessential import in the effort to understand human beings who are simultaneously historical and psychological in nature.[221]

Notes

1. Alan Bullock, *Hitler, A Study in Tyranny*, Harper Torchbooks, 1966, p. 15.
2. *Ibid.*
3. *Ibid.*, p. 56.
4. Walter C. Langer, *The Mind of Adolf Hitler: The Secret Wartime Report*, Basic Books, 1972, p. 212.
5. *Ibid.*, p. 195.
6. *Ibid.*, p. 206.
7. Robert G. L. Waite, *The Psychopathic God: Adolf Hitler*, Basic Books, 1977, pp. 135-170.
8. *Ibid.*, p. 389.
9. Rudolph Binion, *Hitler Among the Germans*, Elsevier, 1976, pp. 14-23.
10. *Ibid.*, p. 127.
11. Helm Stierlin, *Adolf Hitler: A Family Perspective*, The Psychohistory Press, 1976, p. 15.
12. *Ibid.*, p. 16.
13. *Ibid.*, p. 39.
14. *Ibid.*
15. *Ibid.*, pp. 53-56.
16. *Ibid.*, p. 58.
17. *Ibid.*, p. 59.
18. *Ibid.*
19. *Ibid.*, p. 60.
20. *Ibid.*, p. 74.
21. *Ibid.*, p. 85.
22. *Ibid.*, p. 103.
23. *Ibid.*, p. 122.
24. *Ibid.*, p. 127.

25. *Ibid.*, For a lively and critical discussion of Stierlins's viewpoint of Hitler see his "Symposium Article," "Hitler as the Bound Delegate of His Mother," and the comments made by several scholars in *The Journal of Psychohistory*, Spring 1976, Vol. 3, pp. 463-507. For Stierlin's theoretical approach to family therapy, in which the author also pays attention to group fantasies, see his *Psychoanalysis and Family Therapy: Selected Papers*, Jason Aronson, 1977. A study that interprets Hitler in primarily clinical psychoanalytic terms and is explicitly diagnostic is by Norbert Bromberg, M.D., and Verna V. Small, *Hitler's Psychopathology*, International Universities Press, 1983. Thomas Kornblicher's book in German, *Adolf Hitler-Psychogramme*, Peter Lang, 1994, in addition to being biographical, encompasses the contributions on group psychology and fascism made by Freud, Wilhelm Reich, and Alfred Adler. Another work by Thomas Kornblicher, *Tiefenpsychologie und Biographik*, Peter Lang, 1989, provides an overview of the growth and acceptance of psychoanalysis and psychohistory in many countries. Published as the Cold War was coming to an end, Kornblicher also discusses the, course of psychoanalysis in the German Democratic Republic, Poland, and the Soviet Union.

26. Robert C. Tucker, *Stalin as Revolutionary, 1879-1929: A Study in History and Personality*, W. W. Norton, 1974, p. xviii.

27. *Ibid.*

28. *Ibid.*, pp. 69-75

29. *Ibid.*, p. 466.

30. *Ibid.*

31. *Ibid.*

32. *Ibid.*

33. *Ibid.*, pp. 466-467

34. *Ibid.*, p. 449.

35. Robert Robins, "Paranoid Ideation and Charismatic Leadership," *The Psychohistory Review*, Fall 1986, Vol. 5, No. 1, p. 37. In this article, the author compares Stalin with Hitler, noting their similarities.

36. Tucker, *Stalin*, p 450.

37. For an extensive discussion of Pétain's controversial role see Jacques Szaluta, "Apotheosis to Ignominy: The Martyrdom of Marshal Pétain," *The Journal of Psychohistory*, Spring 1980, Vol. 7, No. 4, pp. 415-453.

38. *Ibid.* pp. 435-447.

39. Cited in Jacques Szaluta, "Marshal Pétain and the French Army Mutiny of 1917: A Study in Military Leadership and Political Personal-

216 *Psychohistory: Genre and Interpretations*

ity," *Third Republic/Throisième République*, Fall 1978, No. 6, p. 210. For a Lacanian approach to the study of Pétain, see Gérard Miller, *Les pousse-au-jour du Maréchal Pétain*, Editions du Seuil, 1975.

40. Jacques Szaluta, "The Correspondence between Maréchal and Madame Pétain, 1913 to 1949: A Psychoanalytic Interpretation," *American Imago*, Summer 1990, Vol. 47, No. 2, pp. 170-178.

41. *Ibid.*, pp. 193-194.

42. Szaluta, "The Martyrdom of Pétain," p. 433.

43. *Ibid.*, pp. 435-445.

44. Philippe Pétain, "Les Lettres du Maréchal Pétain à son épouse, 1913-1949," Archives Nationale de France, 415 AP, 523 Microfilm, Paris.

45. *Ibid.*, Szaluta, "Correspondence," p. 194.

46. Szaluta, "The Martyrdom of Pétain," pp. 435-445.

47. *Ibid.*, p. 438.

48. *Ibid.*, p. 446

49. *Ibid.*

50. *Ibid.*, p. 445

51. *Ibid.*

52. Szaluta, "Correspondence," pp. 192-193.

53. Sigmund Freud and William C. Bullitt, *Thomas Woodrow Wilson, Twenty-eigth President of the United States: A Psychological Study*, Houghton Mifflin, 1966, pp. v-xvii.

54. *Ibid.*, p. 194

55. *Ibid.*, p. 61

56. *Ibid.*, p. 63.

57. Alexander L. George and Juliette L. George, *Woodrow Wilson and Colonel House: A Personality Study*, Dover Publications, 1964, pp. 302-315.

58. Edwin A. Weinstein, *Thomas Woodrow Wilson: A Medical and Psychological Biography*, Princeton University Press, 1981, p. ix.

59. Edwin A. Weinstein, "Bullitt, Freud and Wilson," *Journal of the American Academy of Psychoanalysis*, 1988, Vol. 16, no. 3, p. 352.

60. *Ibid.*, p. 355.

61. *Ibid.*, p. 356.

62. *Ibid.*

63. Silas L. Warner, "Fourteen Wilsonian Points for Freud and Bullitt," *Journal of the American Academy of Psychoanalysis*, 1988, Vol. 16, No. 4.

64. *Ibid.*, p. 479.

65. *Ibid.*, p. 481.

66. *Ibid.*, p. 488.

67. *Ibid.*

68. Joseph A. Bongiorno, "Woodrow Wilson Revisited: The Prepolitical Years," in *The Leaders: Psychohistorical Essays*, ed. by C. B. Strozier and D. Offer, Plenum Press, 1985, p. 134.

69. *Ibid.*, p. 173.

70. Dorothy Ross, "Review Essay/Woodrow Wilson and the Case for Psychohistory," *The Journal of American History*, December 1982, Vol. 69, No. 3, p. 661.

71. *Ibid.*

72. *Ibid.*, p. 668.

73. *Ibid.*, p. 666.

74. *Ibid.*, p. 668. For an assessment of the works on Wilson, the divergence between the medical and psychohistorical explanations of Wilson, see William Friedman, "'Woodrow Wilson and Colonel House' and Political Psychobiography," *Political Psychology: Journal of the International Society of Political Psychology*, March 1994, Vol. 15, No. 1, pp. 35–59.

75. James P. Johnson, "Nixon and the Psychohistorians," *The Psychohistory Review*, 1978, Vol. VII, No. 3, pp. 38–42.

76. *Ibid.*, p. 39.

77. *Ibid.* Although Nixon acknowledged that childhood experiences affected adult behavior, he disapproved of psychohistory, even specifying Freud's work on Wilson. He wrote, "I happen to think that most of the so-called new 'science' of psycho-biography is pure baloney. For example, in a book he coauthored with former Ambassador William Bullitt, Sigmund Freud suggested that Woodrow Wilson, who worshipped his father, subconsciously hated him and that this hatred contributed to his arbitrary rigidity in dealing with those who disagreed with him on foreign policy. This strikes me as so outlandish as to be downright silly." See Richard Nixon, *Leaders: Profiles and Reminiscences of Men Who Have Shaped the Modern World*, Warner, 1982, pp. 16–17.

78. Richard Nixon, *Six Crises*, Doubleday, 1962.

79. Richard Nixon, *RN: The Memoirs of Richard Nixon*, Grosset and Dunlap, 1978, pp. 969-981.

80. Johnson, *Nixon*, p. 39

81. *Ibid.*

82. *Ibid.* A little over a decade after his resignation, Jules Levey in "Richard Nixon as Elder Statesman," describes Nixon's attempt at achieving political rehabilitation; Levey too notes that Nixon's insecurities caused him to be particularly aggressive and unethical, the very tactics he accused the Communists of employing, *The Journal of Psychohistory*, Spring 1986, Vol. 13, No. 4, pp. 427-448. For another characterization of Nixon's personality, his "need for enemies," and his self-defeating tendencies, see Paul H. Elovitz, "Review Essay. Richard Milhous Nixon Revisited: The Haldeman Diaries," *The Psychohistory Review*, Fall 1995, Vol. 24, No. 1, pp. 99-111.

83. Bruce Mazlish, *The Leader, the Led, and the Psyche: Essays in Psychohistory*, Wesleyan University Press, 1990, p. 198.

84. *Ibid.*, p. 222.

85. *Ibid.*, p. 224.

86. *Ibid.*

87. *Ibid.*, p. 245.

88. *Ibid.*

89. *Ibid.*

90. Johnson, *Nixon*, p. 42. Other psychobiographical accounts are by a psychoanalyst, David Abrahamsen, *Nixon vs. Nixon: An Emotional Tragedy*, Farrar, Strauss and Giroux, 1977; and by a psychiatrist, Eli S. Chesen, *President Nixon's Psychiatric Profile: A Psychodynamic-Genetic Interpretation*, Wyden, 1973.

91. Sigmund Freud, Freud's personal *Prochaska calendar books, 1918*, Container B21, The Sigmund Freud Collection, The Sigmund Freud Archives, Inc., Manuscript Division, The Library of Congress, Washington, D.C.; See especially Sigmund Freud's two works of this period, "Civilization and its Discontents," *The Standard Edition*, Vol. 21, Hogarth Press, 1961 and "Moses and Monotheism," *The Standard Edition*, Vol. 23, Hogarth Press, 1964. For a discussion of the influences on Freud at this time, see Jacques Szaluta, "Sigmund Freud's Biblical Ego Ideals," *The Psychohistory Review*, Fall 1994, Vol. 23, No. 1, pp. 27-34.

92. Louise E. Hoffman, "Psychoanalytic Interpretations of Adolph Hitler and Nazism, 1933-1945: A Prelude to Psychohistory," *The Psychohistory Review*, Fall 1982, Vol. 11, No. 1, p. 70.

93. *Ibid.*, p. 80.

94. *Ibid.*, p. 82.

95. Bruce Mazlish, "The Next 'Next Assignment': Leader and Led, Individual and Group," *The Psychohistory Review*, Vol. 9, 1981, p. 219.

96. George M. Kren, "Psychohistorians Contra The Third Reich," *The Psychohistory Review*, Vol. 5, 1976, pp. 34-36.

97. Saul Friedländer, *L'Antisémitism nazi: Histoire d'une psychose collective*, Editions du Seuil, 1971, pp. 151-155. For a pioneering and important contribution on this subject, see Theodor W. Adorno, *et al*, *The Authoritarian Personality*, W.W. Norton, 1982.

98. George M. Kren, "Psychohistory, Psychobiography and the Holocaust," *The Psychohistory Review*, Fall 1984, Vol. 13, pp. 40-45.

99. *Ibid.*, pp. 40-41.

100. *Ibid.*, p. 43.

101. *Ibid.*

102. *Ibid.*, p. 66.

103. *Ibid.*

104. Marcia E. Bedard, "Profamilism and the New Right: A Feminist Analyst of Fascist Ideology," *The Psychohistory Review*, Winter 1987, Vol. 15, No. 2.

105. *Ibid.*, p. 77.

106. *Ibid.*, p. 80.

107. *Ibid.*, p. 78.

108. *Ibid.*, p. 79.

109. *Ibid.*, p. 81.

110. *Ibid.*, p. 87.

111. *Ibid.*, pp. 96-97.

112. *Ibid.*, p. 96.

113. *Ibid.*

114. *Ibid.*, pp. 96-97.

115. *Ibid.*, p. 97.

116. *Ibid.*, p. 98. Feminism and gender issues have also been studied psychohistorically, and have been marked by controversy and critiques of psychoanalysis. For an examination of these issues, see Nancy J. Chodorow, *Feminism and Psychoanalytic Theory*, Yale University Press, 1989; Judith M. Wellman, "Some Thoughts on the Psychohistorical Study of Women," *The Psychohistory Review*, Fall 1978, Vol. 7, pp. 20-24; Naomi Rosenthal, "The Psychology of Women," *The Psychohistory Review*, Spring 1980, Vol. 8, pp. 32-36; Ann Schofield, "'To Do and To Be': Mary Dreier, Pauline Newman, and the Psychology of Feminist Activism," *The Psychohistory Review*, Fall 1989, Vol. 18, pp. 33-55.

117. Mazlish, "Psychoanalytic Theory and History: Groups and Events," *The Annual of Psychoanalysis*, 1978, Vol. 7, p. 47.

118. Mazlish, *The Leader*, p. 279.

119. *Ibid.*

120. *Ibid.*

121. *Ibid.*

122. Mazlish, "Psychoanalytic Theory and History: Groups and Events," *The Annual of Psychoanalysis*, 1978, Vol. 6, p. 57. Even though there is a paucity of available dream material by historical figures, psychohistorians are interested in this source. For example, see the exploratory work by Paul H. Elovitz, "Psychohistorical Dreamwork: A New Methodology Applied to a Dream of Sir Humphrey Davy;" and J. Donald Hughes, "Psychohistorical Dreamwork: Dreams from the Ancient World," in *The Variety of Dream Experience*, ed. by M. Ullman and C. Limmer, Continuum Publishing Comps., 1987, pp. 253-265, 266-279. See also Jacques Szaluta, "Freud on Bismark: Hanns Sachs' *Interpretation of a Dream*," *American Imago*, 1980, Vol. 37, pp. 215-244.

123. Michael Tager, "Looking into the Whirlwind: A Psychohistorical Study of the Black Panthers," *The Psychohistory Review*, Winter 1984, Vol. 12, No. 2/3, pp. 61-62.

124. *Ibid.*, p. 62. Eldridge Cleaver's ringing manifesto, very critical of American white society, and written when he was in prison, is *Soul on Ice*, McGraw-Hill, 1968.

125. Tager, "Whirlwind," p. 62.

126. *Ibid.*

127. *Ibid.*, p. 63.

128. *Ibid.*, p. 64.

129. *Ibid.*

130. Frantz Fanon, *Black Skins, White Masks*, trans. by C. M. Markman, Grove Press, 1967.

131. Tager, "Whirlwind," p. 67.

132. *Ibid.*, p. 68.

133. *Ibid.*, p. 6. For a discursive essay of the historical, literary, and social issues dealt with by contemporary Afro-American women writers, and the growth of black feminism, see Linda S. Beard, "Daughters of Clio and Calliope: Contemporary Afro-American and Revisionist Herstorians," *The Psychohistory Review*, Spring 1989, Vol. 17, No. 3. pp. 301-343.

134. *Ibid.*, p. 69. See also Louis Corsino, "Malcolm X and the Black Muslim Movement: A Social Psychology of Charisma," *The Psychohistory Review*, Spring/Summer 1982, Vol. 10, No. 3/4, pp. 165-184. For both a Marxist and Freudian approach to the development of African-American militancy, see Victor Wolfenstein, *The Victims of Democracy: Malcom X and the Black Revolution*, University of California Press, 1981. On the preoccupation with virility and manliness by the Black Panther leaders see Bruce Perry, "Malcom X and the Politics of Masculinity," *The Psychohistory Review*, Winter 1985, Vol. 13, No. 2-3, pp. 18-25. An example of continuing interest on a popular level, on the issue of this radicalism, two popular films, seen by mass audiences, are *Malcolm X*, released in 1993, produced and directed by Spike Lee, and *Panther*, released in 1995, a fictionalized account directed by Melvin Van Peebles. For a critique of the film *Malcom X*, see Jonathan Scott Lee, "Spike Lee's *Malcolm X* as Transformational Object," *American Imago*, Vol. 52, No. 2, Summer 1995, pp. 155-167.

135. Rudolph Binion, *Introduction à la psychohistoire*, Presses Universitaires de France, 1982, p. 61.

136. Szaluta, "Pétain," *Journal of Psychohistory*, 1980, p. 438-442.

137. Jacques Szaluta, book review of Robert J. Young's *In Command of France: French Foreign Policy and Military Planning, 1933-1940*, *The Psychohistory Review*, Winter 1981, Vol. 10, pp. 130-135.

138. On this aspect, see Robert Soucy, *French Fascism: The First Wave, 1924-1933*, Yale University Press, 1986.

139. Paul Monaco, *Cinema and Society: France and Germany during the Twenties*, Elsevier, 1976, pp. 4-5.

140. *Ibid.*, pp. 84-133.

141. Bruce Mazlish, "What is Psychohistory?" in *The Varieties of Psychohistory*, edited by George M. Kren and Leon H. Rappoport, Springer, 1976, p. 19.

142. On childhood development and its complexities, see Margaret S. Mahler, *The Psychological Birth of the Human Infant: Symbioses and Individuation*, Basic Books, 1975; Alice Miller, *For Your Own Good: Hidden Cruelty in Child-Rearing and the Roots of Violence*, trans. H. and H. Hannum, Farrar Strauss, Giroux, 1983; and Charles B. Strozier, Review Essay, "Suffer the Children," *The Psychohistorical Review*, Spring 1993, Vol. 21, pp. 319–327.

143. See Glenn Davis, *Childhood and History in America*, The Psychohistory Press, 1976. Another work which provides a survey of the field, but tilted in favor of the works published in the de Mause camp and dismissive of the critics, is by Henry Lawton, *The Psychohistorian's Handbook*, The Psychohistory Press, 1988. Of the opposition, Lawton says, "Some of our more traditional and timid critics and colleagues have made de Mause the lighting rod for all of their anxiety about psychohistory—if only Lloyd de Mause would keep quiet and stop producing those outrageous ideas, then psychohistory could become respectable" (p. 237). Charles B. Strozier and Daniel Offer, in "The Growth of Psychohistory," *The Leader*, take an extremely dim view of de Mause's work and that of his followers, calling them "abusers of the field and engaging in 'exaggeration'" (p. 63). Strozier and Offer argue that "Finally there is the basic problem that De Mause and his followers have an insecure grasp of both psychoanalytic and historical methodology" (p. 64).

144. Lloyd deMause, "The Evolution of Childhood," *The History of Childhood*, Lloyd deMause, Editor, The Psychohistory Press, 1974, p. 3.

145. *Ibid.*, p. 1.

146. *Ibid.*, p. 51.

147. *Ibid.*, p. 54.

148. Salvatore Prisco III, *An Introduction to Psychohistory: Theories and Case Studies*, University Press of America, 1980, p. 37.

149. *Ibid.*

150. *Ibid.*

151. Bruce Mazlish, "Psychohistory and Politics," *The Center Magazine*, Vol. x, September/October 1977, p. 13.

152. Elizabeth W. Marvick, *The Young Richelieu: A Psychoanalytic Approach to Leadership*, University of Chicago Press, 1983; Marvick "Nature vs. Nurture: Trends and Patterns in Seventeenth Century French Childrearing," *The History of Childhood*, ed. Lloyd deMause, The Psychohistory Press, 1974.

153. Marvick, *Richelieu*, pp. 1–29.

154. *Ibid.*, p. 162.

155. *Ibid.* For a further discussion, see Jacques Szaluta, book review of Elizabeth W. Marvick's *The Young Richelieu, The Psychohistory Review, The Psychoanalytic Quarterly*, Fall 1985, Vol, 14, No. 1, pp. 47-49.

156. Elizabeth W. Marvick, *Louis XIII: The Making of a King*, Yale University Press, 1986, p. xvii.

157. *Ibid.*, p. 1.

158. *Ibid.*, pp. 17-18.

159. *Ibid.*, pp. 88-89.

160. *Ibid.*, p. 208.

161. *Ibid.*, p. 6. See also the book review by Jacques Szaluta of Elizabeth W. Marvick's *Louis XIII: The Making of a King*, 1988, Vol. 57, No. 3, pp. 453-457.

162. Mazlish, "Psychohistory," *Varieties*, p. 26.

163. Vivian C. Fox and Martin H. Quitt, editors, *Loving, Parenting and Dying: The Family Cycle in England and America, Past and Present*, The Psychohistory Press, 1980.

164. Mazlish, "Psychohistory," *Varieties*, pp. 26-27.

165. Bruce Mazlish, "Reflections on the State of Psychohistory," *The Psychohistory Review*, Vol. 5, 1977, p. 8.

166. *Ibid.*

167. E. James Anthony, "The Family and the Psychoanalytic Process in Children," *The Psychoanalytic Study of the Child*, 1980, Vol. 35, p. 3.

168. *Ibid.*, p. 6.

169. *Ibid.*

170. *Ibid.*, p. 7.

171. *Ibid.*

172. *Ibid.*

173. *Ibid.*

174. *Ibid.*, p. 8.

175. *Ibid.*

176. *Ibid.*, pp. 8-9.

177. *Ibid.*, p. 9.

178. *Ibid.*

179. John C. Flugel, *The Psycho-Analytic Study of the Family*, The International Psycho-Analytic Press, 1921.

180. Anthony, "The Family," p. 33.

181. *Ibid.*

182. David Hunt, *Parents and Children in History: The Psychology of Family Life in Early Modern France*, Basic Books, 1970, pp. 27-31.

183. Phillipe Ariès, *Centuries of Childhood: A Social History of Family Life*, Knopf, 1962.

184. Hunt, *Parents and Children*, p. 27.

185. *Ibid.*, pp. 30-31.

186. *Ibid.*, pp. 28-29.

187. *Ibid.*, pp. 58-58.

188. *Ibid.*, p. 79.

189. *Ibid.*

190. *Ibid.* See also by Lynn Hunt, *The Family Romance of the French Revolution*, University of California Press, 1992.

191. John Demos, *A Little Commonwealth: Family Life in Plymouth Colony*, Oxford, 1970. Demos has written other works on the family, *Entertaining Satan: Witchcraft and the Culture of Early New England*, Oxford, 1982; *The Unredeemed Captive: A Family Story from Early America*, Knopf, 1994.

192. Demos, *Plymouth Colony*, p. 81.

193. *Ibid.*

194. *Ibid.*, p. 183.

195. *Ibid.*

196. *Ibid.*, p. 184.

197. *Ibid.*, p. 186.

198. *Ibid.*, p. 187.

199. *Ibid.*, p. 186. For a discussion of the work by Hunt and Demos, and the use of theories from other disciplines to sensitize scholars in studying the family, see Tamara K. Hareven, "The History of the Family as an Interdisciplinary Field," *The Family in History: Interdisciplinary Essays*, ed. T. K. Rabb and Robert I. Rotberg, Harper, 1971, pp. 211-226.

200. Stephen Kern, "Explosive Intimacy: Psychodynamics of the Victorian Family," *The New Psychohistory*, ed. Lloyd de Mause, The Psychohistory Press, 1975.

201. *Ibid.*, p. 30.

202. *Ibid.*

203. *Ibid.*, p. 31.

204. *Ibid.*

205. *Ibid.*, p. 42.

206. *Ibid.*, p. 44.

207. *Ibid.*

208. *Ibid.*, p. 50.

209. Fox and Quitt, *Parenting*, pp. 4-7.

210. *Ibid.*, pp. 62-64.

211. *Ibid.*, p. 64.

212. *Ibid.*

213. Christopher Lasch, "The Family as a Haven in a Heartless World," *Salmagundi: A Quarterly of the Humanities and Social Sciences*, Fall 1976, No. 35, pp. 42-55.

214. Lasch, 'The Waning of Private Life," *Salmagundi*, Winter 1977, No. 36, pp. 3-15.

215. *Ibid.*

216. Lasch, *The Culture of Narcissism: American Life in An Age of Diminishing Expectations*, Warner Books, 1979, p. 268.

217. *Ibid.*, p. 310.

218. *Ibid.*, p. 311.

219. *Ibid.*, p. 311-312.

220. *Ibid.*, p. 397.

221. Mazlish, "Psychohistory Varieties," p. 36. For broad treatments of changes of family life, see Edward Shorter, *The Making of the Modern Family*, Basic Books, 1975; and the "Special Issue: Psychohistorical Study of the American Family," *The Psychohistory Review*, Vol. VI, Nos. 2-3, Combined Issue: Fall-Winter, 1977-78, pp. 4-101.

Chapter 7

Conclusion: The Future of Psychohistory

1. Toward a New Understanding of the Past

After the above discussion of the field of psychohistory, one is led to conclude that good history is psychohistory. Psychohistory has grown enormously in the last several decades, despite the opposition to it, because it offers a more profound and fuller understanding of man and his past. Behaviorism, however, with its notion that evidence be based on what is measurable and on statistical data, is still entrenched in many psychology departments. Such empiricism in the historical profession is trotted out to oppose psychohistory. This position is akin to opposing quantum theory in physics or the theory of evolution because they cannot be observed. The departure from traditional history was psychohistory's initial promise, and this has been realized. The blending of the two disciples has been a methodological breakthrough. This has been a significant development in the understanding of human affairs. Its ever-increasing success to date points to a brighter future for psychohistory. Psychohistory both needs and fosters a democratic political climate because it recognizes man's complexity and his need for free expression.

Another reason for optimism about psychohistory is that the developments which have occurred in the field of history have also occurred in the humanities and in the social sciences in general. The impact of psychoanalysis is felt in literature, art, history, anthropology, sociology, philosophy, economics, and political science and is fueled by the burgeoning field of mental health and its allied fields.[1] A wholly new climate of opinion is being created, as is evident in various cultural expressions, including film and television.[2] This new view of man, which is concerned with his unconscious motivation, his feelings, his relationships with individuals and society, is receiving a revolutionary interpretation, one that is based on his psychological and historical conditions.

It does not suffice, however, to declare that combining history and psychoanalysis necessarily produces good history; the practitioner of the craft must also be included in the formulation. The critical *desideratum* in this new field is ultimately a psychohistorian, trained in psychoanalysis as well as in history. Although there is no established academic curriculum for training psychohistorians, there is a recognition that a knowledge of psychoanalytic literature is a basic requirement. But the degree of training and expertise among psychohistorians varies, some are self-taught, others take courses in psychoanalytic institutes, and still others undergo a personal analysis. Nevertheless, an optimum standard is emerging, even if it is not yet formally established. And the ideal is to become a fully trained psychoanalyst, including clinical training in an institute and academic training as a historian. Such a combination of professions for the psychohistorian has become a growing practice since the 1970s. However, even though it is more common now, it is the exception because completed training in a psychoanalytic institute is lengthy, costly, and very arduous. Although training in psychoanalytic institutes is the direction many historians are taking, others contend that this training need not be a requirement for doing psychohistory. The approaches are eclectic. Nevertheless, a compelling case can be made for psychoanalytic training. Most psychohistorical works are written by scholars who initially were trained as historians or in the social sciences, although psychoanalysts also occasionally write psychohistorial works. This preponderance of historians writing psychohistory is a natural outgrowth of their scholarly training, with its concomitant intention to 'tell a story'. Psychoanalysts and many psychohistorians advocate clinical training because they consider it indispensable for competent utilization of psychoanalytic theory. The noted psychoanalyst Kurt R. Eissler considers not only training in, but also the practicing of psychoanalysis essential for applying psychoanalytic concepts to other fields.[3] In his renowned address given in

1957, William L. Langer admonished historians to attend psychoanalytic institutes. Already, at the time, he reminded his audience of historians that scholars in other fields—anthropology, sociology, religion, literature, education, and so forth—had availed themselves of such training. And what he predicted in 1957 has at least been partially realized, for he said "I have no doubt, that modern psychology is bound to play an ever greater role in historical interpretation."[4]

More recently, Robert A. Pois, in "The Case for Clinical Training and Challenges to Psychohistory," categorically argues for clinical experience.[5] Indeed, the case for clinical training is compelling. Pois says that the acquisition of such knowledge, which brings with it greater empathic understanding, also enhances self-analytical abilities. The tools and insights thus acquired will provide the historian with "a methodological sharpness."[6]

Alongside his advocacy of psychoanalytic training, Pois observes that psychoanalysis has come in for much opposition, which itself bears on psychohistory. Of the adverse contemporary climate, Pois says: "Yet, one cannot gainsay the fact that psychoanalysis now seems to be under a sustained attack that it has not had to endure for some time."[7] The challenges, he recognizes, are serious, and among the many charges leveled at psychoanalysis is the perennial one, that it is not scientific. However, Pois replies, it is precisely those with just such training who are best able to counter this kind of opposition, even if some opponents remain unconvinced or indifferent to psychoanalysis. Again, those best able to respond to the attacks on the field are those "individuals whose empathic and analytic abilities have been honed by clinical experience."[8]

Clinical psychoanalytic training enhances the historian's ability to interpret historical events and personages. Yet, this need not obviate the diversity of approaches that has existed in the historical profession. There are many mansions in the psychohistorical domain.

2. Psychoanalysis and Psychohistory

Even if there is reason for optimism about the future of psychohistory, there are also grounds for concern. The continuing growth and vitality of psychohistory is tied to psychoanalysis remaining a vibrant and viable field. Psychoanalysis has come in for serious attacks in the last several decades, certainly since the 1980's, in the United States. The problems confronting psychoanalysts are both internal and external. For one, as was noted in Chapter 5, there has been a growing fragmentation in opposition to mainstream Freudian psychoanalysis. For another, there is a large literature now devoted to debunking Freud, which has produced a climate of Freud bashing. Other sources of opposition can be attributed to the cultural climate in which people seek instant gratification and quick "cures". And, paradoxically, as more people have sought help with emotional problems, it has become more difficult to receive financial assistance for psychotherapy. The proliferation of medical Health Maintenance Organizations (HMO), which offer what is known as managed care, discourage prolonged mental health treatment. And a key barometer to this climate is a decline in the number of candidates applying to psychoanalytic institutes.

There is a multitude of reasons for the crises now facing psychoanalysis, but a leading one is the criticism that psychoanalysis is a treatment of long duration, and therefore too expensive and time-consuming. In effect, this has contributed to financial considerations being in the forefront in driving the opposition to psychoanalysis. The issues concerning psychoanalysis are not just the contentious deliberations of academics, but have also spilled over into public awareness. They have received wide media attention. Indeed, the nature of medical and psychological treatment has received such wide coverage that it has become something of a national crisis. The twin targets of attack are Freud, and by extension, the merit of psychoanalysis itself. In this intense debate, as reflected in the mass circulation publications, there have been stinging rejoinders to the critics. Indicative of the strident controversy, and to list just a few of the leading publications in which articles have appeared, they are the *New York Times, Newsday, The Los Angeles Times, The Wall Street Journal, Time,* and the *New Republic*.[9] These issues have also been aired on television.[10] To be sure, objections to the views of the opponents have also been voiced in professional journals.

Conclusion: The Future of Psychohistory 231

One article, which appeared in the *New York Times* on December 10, 1995, exemplifies the essence of the contemporary furor over Freud. Entitled "Freud May Be Dead, But His Critics Still Kick," Dinitia Smith writes that the "battle in a culture war" has "been raging around Freud for nearly one hundred years."[11] She also says that despite the criticisms leveled at Freud, "Freud is far from dead."[12] Her irony stems from the fact that a planned exhibit on Freud by the Library of Congress in Washington, D.C. was canceled, or at least postponed, because of opposition to it. Critics petitioned for a "full spectrum of informed opinion"[13] on Freud, which meant that they considered the planned exhibit too favorable to Freud. Such reactions caused Smith to wonder "why an exhibit on Freud arouses such wrath."[14] Her report goes to the core of the present crises and is stated in a few pithy sentences. She says "After all, it isn't as if psychoanalysis is on the rise. The number of people going into training institutes to become analysts is declining. Prozac has been adopted as the quick cure for depression. And, in the age of managed care, insurance companies are, to say the least, unenthusiastic about psychoanalysis."[15] Smith asks: "why is it necessary to suppress" Freud's ideas?[16] In still another rhetorical question, she asks: "so why is everyone working so hard to crush a movement that may be dying on its own?"[17]

A lead article, of December 1, 1995, in *The Wall Street Journal* discusses this trend in a series of articles devoted to "The New Economics of Mental Health."[18] Just the title and subtitles indicate the concerns: "Managed Care's Focus on Psychiatric Drugs Alarms Many Doctors. They Say Effort to Cut Cost Leads to Overuse, Misuse of Pills for Mental Illness. Talk Therapy is Discouraged." The "alarms" discussed in this article are that managed care is leading to the widespread use of drugs because of the "mandate to cut costs,"[19] to the detriment of the people who should be receiving psychotherapy. This new direction has "transformed the mental health field," and even children are given drugs, to their detriment, because the alternative, "talk therapy," is the "most costly option."[20] The article states that children are prescribed drugs "even though little research has been done on the effects of drugs on the very young."[21] One physician is cited as saying that use of drugs—and the most widely used ones are Prozac, Zoloft, and Paxil—actually may be "covering up the problems."[22] The pressure from the managed care companies on physicians ranges from "subtle" to the "explicit", which compromises them.[23] This practice of economizing leads to creating a "torturous ethical situation."[24] Although some people are helped, many are very badly affected by the too ready prescription of drug therapy.

In another article, of December 2, 1991, in *The Wall Street Journal*, there is not only a vigorous defense of Freud—because of the widespread "debunking" going on—and a synopsis of Freud's enormous contributions to present society and culture, but an explanation of reasons why Freud's thought is so controversial.[25] Although serious in content, the article is notable for its humor and irony. Entitled "Head Doctor: Doubted and Resisted, Freud's Daring Map of the Mind Endures."[26] The subtitle is "Even Today's Modern Drugs Don't Unseat the Master of Murky Unconscious."[27] The article, by Michael Waldholz, goes to the core of the resistance to Freud's ideas as the author states: "what troubled Freud's contemporaries and still riles many today—was Freud's initial explanation that the unconscious was filled with repressed sexual wishes and fantasies that people experience when they are young children."[28] The author credits Freud with laying the foundation on which most psychotherapy is based and "used for treating millions of people."[29] Waldholz notes that contemporary attitudes of child rearing originate from Freud's theories. Regarding the ongoing opposition to Freud, the author says that "it is a tribute to Freud's lasting influence that his ideas can still arouse controversy as fiery as when he was alive."[30]

Another central concept which Waldholz says, "to this day can arouse near-violent reaction from people,"[31] is the Oedipus complex. But, it is in therapy that many "discover it in their own lives."[32] However, even as psychoanalysis is under attack, the author notes that in academia Freud's thought has been increasing in popularity and that in many colleges and universities professors utilize the "Freudian vision to teach critical thinking."[33]

Waldholz gives Freud the last word. In what is an apocryphal story, the question is how Freud would view the current climate of hostility to his ideas. The reporter concludes with a humorous anecdote. When Sandor Firenczi, a colleague, complained about the vituperation of critics, Freud replied: "Don't worry so much, Sandor. Surely our opponents deride our theories by day, but they dream according to them at night."[34]

Jonathan Lear's "The Shrink Is In: A Counterblast in the War on Freud,"[35] examines the attacks on Freud from a psychoanalytic point of view. Lear's critique adds still another perspective as he contends that "psychoanalysis is crucial for a truly democratic culture to thrive."[36] According to Lear, the present unfavorable climate is due to the mind-altering drugs, such as Prozac, which seem to render psychoanalysis unnecessary. Consumers have turned to HMOs and insurance companies, which prefer relatively inexpensive pharmacological treatment over expensive and lengthy psychotherapy. Lear also notes that in the 1950's and 1960's psychoanalysts made exaggerated claims about the possibilities of psychoanalysis. And the medicalization of the profession, and its guild-like restrictions against non-physicians, created a situation ripe for revisionist criticism and opposition to the dominant American Psychoanalytic Association.[37]

Among Lear's survey of the anti-Freud literature is his critique of Jeffrey Masson's notorious *The Assault on Truth*. Masson, who has accused Freud of suppressing and minimizing evidence about childhood seductions, and who has thereby made a name for himself, is himself accused by Lear of "suppressing the evidence in order to advance his career."[38] The real issue, according to Lear is the fantasy of abuse. Lear writes that "In realizing that one could not take all memory-claims at face value, Freud effectively discovered that the *mind* [Lear's italic] is active and imaginative in the organization of its own experience. This is one of the crucial moments in the founding of psychoanalysis."[39] Freud argued that "imaginative activity fantasy,"[40] which is unconscious, plays a major role in shaping a person's experience. Accordingly, Lear posits a significant interpretation: "This, surely, contains the seeds of a profound insight into the human condition; it is the central insight of psychoanalysis, yet in the heated debate over child abuse, it is largely ignored."[41]

Yet, the most significant contribution in Lear's article is his understanding of psychoanalysis. He credits Freud with establishing a therapeutic "procedure which genuinely avoids suggestion."[42] The intention of psychoanalysis is therefore to set "*freedom* rather than some specific image of human *happiness*"[43] [Lear's italics]. Psychoanalysis is a therapy which leaves it to the analysand to determine his or her goals for personal change, rather than receiving advice for some particular outcome, such as improving self-esteem or inspiration for feeling better.[44]

Lear compares history and the social sciences in general with the physical sciences. He notes that if there is a crisis in political affairs, or if we need answers to particular problems, we turn to historical or economic studies for explanations. However, even if all explanations regarding causality in human affairs are subject to disagreement or changing interpretations, we do not seriously entertain doing away with these fields. To expect the same kind of validation as exists for physics is specious, because "if psychoanalysis *were* [Lear's italics] to imitate the methods of physical science, it would be useless for interpreting people."[45] Psychoanalysis deals with people's fears, desires, hopes, and beliefs, it seeks to understand their unconscious motivations, their wishes and fantasies. What seems to be a weakness is really a strength. In Lear's view: "In fact, it is a sign of psychoanalysis' *success* [Lear's italics] as an interpretive science that its causal claims cannot be validated in the same way as those of the physical sciences."[46]

After evaluating the merits of psychoanalysis, Lear turns to the meaning of the personal attacks on Freud, which he refers to as a "gangup."[47] Indeed, he says, the real intention of attacking Freud is to dismiss his theory of the unconscious. Lear takes to task the so called "self-help publications" that stress "muscle tone," diet, exercise, job success, and other programs claiming to bring shortcuts to "human happiness."[48] These directions in our culture, which promote physical and pharmacological panaceas really reveal "a culture that wishes to ignore the complexity, depth and darkness of human life."[49] And, if Freud can be dismissed as a charlatan, then one can also dismiss the enigmatic nature of mankind. Pharmacological interventions, though they are of value, cannot solve "the problems posed in and by human life,"[50] says Lear. And, he situates Freud alongside other great thinkers who grappled with the complex conditions of human existence, namely Socrates, Plato, Shakespeare, Proust, and Nietzsche. In other words, the opponents of Freud fail to address the problems of life, whereas psychoanalysis does just that. Lear considers the attacks on Freud reminiscent of the oedipal situation. He says: "Isn't the attack on Freud itself a repetition and re-enactment of Oedipus's complex, less an attack on the father than an attack on the very idea of repressed, unconscious meaning?"[51] It is indeed the "pervasive manifestations of human irrationality"[52] which the detractors of Freud ignore.

Although the opponents of psychoanalysis also deride it by saying that it is available to, and a luxury for, very few people, in fact, Lear says of Freud: "no thinker has made creativity and imagination more democratically available than Freud."[53] Lear recommends psychoanalysis for what it promises and provides, for he writes: "creativity is no longer the exclusive preserve of the divinely inspired, or the few great poets. From a psychoanalytic point of view, everyone is poetic; everyone dreams in metaphor and generates symbolic meaning in the process of living. Even in their prose, people have unwittingly been speaking poetry all along."[54]

Lear cites many publications and authors who attack Freud, but one that he mentions and which warrants particular attention is the article "The Assault on Freud," which appeared in the mass circulation magazine *Time* on November 29, 1993. This article is especially hostile. Lear notes that on the cover page of the magazine there is a full page photograph of Freud, but the top of his head is blown off, with parts of his missing skull falling in pieces of a jigsaw puzzle around his face. Looking at this arresting picture, the viewer will see that *"there is nothing there"*[55] [Lear's italics]. The caption on the cover, in large bold letters, asks a question, "Is Freud Dead?"[56] Whereas Lear and Paul Gray, the author of the *Time* article cite similar sources on psychoanalysis, Gray denigrates the field.

Gray's deriding of Freud's thought is clever indeed. He attacks Freud for disingenuously protecting his ideas from any criticism, for when it occurs, Freud regards it as a form of "resistance."[57] In effect, Gray claims, you either accept Freud's dogmas or it means you are opposed to self-knowledge. And, since psychoanalysis is not scientific, Gray suggests that psychoanalysis is really like astrology.[58] He cites the many critics of Freud who argue that Freud treated patients ineptly, that he was not scientifically objective, and that he made incorrect diagnoses. Gray spuriously cites a statistic of approximately 10 million Americans on medication for mental disorders as evidence of success for this method of treatment, therefore obviating "the domain originally claimed for psychoanalytic treatment."[59] In a different context, however, Gray provides another statistical count, that of between 10 to 15 million Americans being treated by "some kind of talking therapy."[60] In sum, Gray proclaims that "Psychoanalysis and all of its offshoots may in the final analysis turn out to be no more reliable than phrenology or mesmerism or any of the countless other pseudosciences that once offered unsubstantiated answers or false claims."[61]

A detailed look, based on personal experience, of how managed care intrudes on the confidential analyst/analysand relationship is discussed by Joel Gavriele-Gold, "Managed Care and the Dissolution of the Therapeutic Alliance in Psychoanalysis."[62] Gavriele-Gold, a psychoanalyst and psychologist in private practice, cites his encounters with this system and the obstacles it creates in maintaining uninterrupted treatment. In essence, Gavriele-Gold provides evidence for the way managed care impairs the "therapeutic alliance," which depends on the patient's trust in the analyst so that he can speak freely, and that all such communications between them remain confidential. It is imperative that in the "working alliance" the transference, with all its thoughts, feelings and hostilities, that the patient has for the therapist, not be revealed and thereby eroded.[63]

Gavriele-Gold argues that since insurance companies are not yet regulated by federal and state laws, and the companies are in fierce competition with each other, the companies make their profit by cutting benefits and reducing services. The companies hired by the insurance industry, as it pertains to mental health care, put these practices into effect by carefully limiting the amounts of psychotherapeutic sessions.[64]

After reviewing the conditions for successful therapy, Gavriele-Gold shows how these organizations frustrate the therapist in his dealings with them. First of all, they require vast amounts of paper work on the part of the therapist, such as the "On-going Patient Treatment Reports," and secondly, the therapist has to call the companies to request additional sessions for patients.[65]

Gavriele-Gold's descriptions of his phone calls to one particular organization, Empire Blue Cross Mental Health Choice, is daunting indeed. On the one hand, it is difficult to reach the clinical case manager, because the phones are busy, and on the other hand, when contact is made, the therapist is expected to provide information about the patient which violates confidentiality. Patients are referred to by name, rather than by an identification number. The information requested is tantamount to an invasion of privacy, and it is computerized. And what is so pernicious is that, as Gavriele-Gold says, "whenever possible, managed care prefers for patients to be medicated!"[66] With so many obstacles and intrusions, aimed at limiting the amount of sessions and complicating the patient-analyst relationship, the analyst is compelled to resolve the quandary by refusing the sparse insurance reimbursement, thus lowering his/her fees. The resulting severance is what the insurance companies really want.[67]

Gavriele-Gold condemns managed care companies and wonders what they do with all the information they collect. He rhetorically asks: "Is this process different from the work of the KGB in Stalin's era or the Orwellian Big Brother?"[68]

In other observations, relevant to psychohistory, Gavriele-Gold deprecates behaviorist psychology for its reactionary role. Behaviorist psychology rejects psychoanalysis because it deals with phenomena that cannot be observed or measured, and is therefore pronounced invalid. For the managed care companies, acceptance of behaviorism fits in well with its needs. Gavriele-Gold accuses these companies of foisting a model of therapy that reverts back to the early part of the twentieth century, thereby obviating the advances that psychoanalysis has made since that time. Gavriele-Gold recognizes that behavior therapy can be helpful in treating phobias and addictions, but he notes that psychoanalysis is more humanistic. He strongly denounces the negation of psychoanalysis and declares: "For managed care to kick this knowledge under the table and disregard it in order to save the insurance company money is a travesty—not unlike the book-burning orgies of the National Socialist Movement."[69]

Another reflective statement on the current state of psychoanalysis is by Richard A. Friedman, "Psychoanalysis and Managed Health Care," published in *NAAP News*, the newsletter of the National Association for the Advancement of Psychoanalysis.[70] Friedman expresses the same concerns as Gavriele-Gold, and is alarmed that the private practice of psychoanalysis is threatened in the United States as never before. Friedman makes recommendations for countering the threats by offering alternatives to the present unfavorable trends. He remarks that "a collective squall of pain can be heard from psychoanalysts who worry that their profession is about to be taken away and the discipline to which they have devoted their professional lives is about to be rendered irrelevant."[71] Friedman feels that the opposition by the insurance companies is not that they are "our enemies in the sense that they hate psychoanalysis,"[72] but rather that they just don't care about psychoanalysis and don't want the financial burden of paying for lengthy therapy. Friedman is of the opinion that insurance companies are aware that psychoanalysis is a therapy "that perhaps could be appropriately prescribed for the majority of the population"[73] and that could perhaps make it prohibitively expensive for them.

Since the managed care approach to mental health is inappropriate, steps must be taken to reverse the tendencies of the last several decades. Among Friedman's suggestions is that the psychoanalytic establishment resort to professional public relations forums—"the best we can find"[74] and educate the public about the benefits of therapy. Friedman notes that other professions have resorted to such methods, and it has benefited them. Still another recommendation is to make psychotherapy tax deductible. Friedman argues that affordable psychoanalytic treatment should be "a desirable social ideal."[75] And he cites precedents, as society subsidizes charities and religions by allowing contributions made to be tax deductible. Such changes would end the dependence of psychotherapy on insurance companies and the compromising of the therapeutic situation, which would permit psychoanalysis to continue in this country.[76]

Conclusion: The Future of Psychohistory

To close on a more hopeful tone, and rounding out the decade of the 1990's and a century of psychoanalysis, there is a strong re-emergence of psychoanalysis in Russia and Eastern Europe. On December 11, 1996, *The New York Times* printed an article "Freud in Russia: Return of the Repressed" on the front page.[77] After having experienced variable fortunes, psychoanalysis was recognized and encouraged by the initial Bolshevik Soviet government, but then was banned by Stalin. It has again been recognized, by President Boris Yeltsin, as a legitimate form of treatment. The article notes that psychotherapy is flourishing there. Significantly, the present tendency in Russia is to depart from the past dependence on drug therapy so marked during the Soviet regime. As Alessandra Stanley reports, "Russian therapists are shaking free of 70 years of drug based Soviet psychiatry to explore the id and the ego just as many of their western counterparts—spurred by advances in biochemistry and the rise of managed care—are turning away from such long-term talk therapies in favor of drugs like Prozac."[78]

Indeed, Russia's Freudians have high expectations for the future of psychoanalysis, for the reporter quotes a leading Russian analyst, the president of the Moscow Psychoanalytic Society, who says "Psychoanalysis is one weapon with which we can restore some order in our society."[79]

As evidence of its new found official support, psychoanalysis is even taught at the Military University of the Ministry of Defense of the Russian Federation and is in the curriculum for psychology students. Although Russian analysts have not yet reached the level of standards set in western psychoanalytic institutes, many have gone abroad to be trained—to the United States, France, and the Czech Republic. The reporter finds that there are now numerous institutes in Russia, some located in St. Petersburg and Moscow. Psychoanalysis in Russia is largely classical Freudian, but there are Jungians and Lacanians as well. And with a nod to psychohistory, one Russian psychoanalyst is even writing a book on Nikita Khrushev in order to examine his "unconscious motivation in taking Crimea from Russia and giving it to Ukraine in 1954."[80]

Psychohistory is a field in ferment, in which different approaches flourish, and it is in the vanguard of historical thought. It has been instrumental in providing a new conceptual framework and in advancing the scientific method in the study of historical events. The psychohistorical vision demonstrates that it is more insightful, more empathic, more encompassing, and more humane than other previous approaches to the study of man and society. During its brief existence psychohistory has shown its creative potential and has generated a rich literature. A new era in historical studies has been established and is now well underway.

Notes

1. For a monograph with interdisciplinary essays in painting, sculpture, literature, history, anthropology, and philosophy, see Laurie Adams and Jacques Szaluta, editors, *Psychoanalysis and the Humanities*, Brunner/Mazel, 1996. See also, by Laurie Adams, *Art and Psychoanalysis*, Harper Collins, 1993.

2. See *Freud on Broadway: A History of Psychoanalysis and the American Drama*, by W. David Silvers, Hermitage House, 1955. At the annual meeting of the American Historical Association, when Robert B. Toplin, the chair, introduced filmmaker Oliver Stone, before a capacity audience, he said matter-of-factly that Stone's film *Nixon*, released in 1995, was "psychohistorical." For the listing of this session and the panelists, see "Historians Film Committee: The film *Nixon* as History and Commentary on American Civilization," Program of the *American Historical Association's One-Hundred Eleventh Annual Meeting*, January 2-5, 1997, New York City, p. 37.

3. Kurt R. Eissler, *Medical Orthodoxy and the Future of Psychoanalysis*, International Universities Press, 1965, pp. 164-165. Eissler bolsters his contention by noting that Freud was stimulated by his clinical work with patients. This led Freud to write on Leonardo's childhood. In the same work, in part of a chapter entitled "Psychoanalysis and History," Eissler explores the possible causes of the fall of the Roman Empire. Eissler applies his clinical experience in his major studies of noted geniuses, as in his *Leonardo da Vinci*, International Universities Press, 1961; and *Goethe: A Psychoanalytic Study, 1775-1786*, 2 vols., Wayne State University Press, 1963. In this debate, some historians have expressed concern that having patients may lead them to "go over the line" and become primarily psychoanalysts rather than being historians. See Paul H. Elovitz "A Conversation with Charles B. Strozier," *Clio's Psyche*, Vol. 3, No. 4, March 1997, pp. 121-122.

4. William L. Langer, "The Next Assignment," *Psychoanalysis and History*, ed. Bruce Mazlish, Grosset and Dunlap, 1971, p. 106.

5. Robert A. Pois, "The Case for Clinical Training and Challenges to Psychohistory," *The Psychohistory Review*, Vol. 18, No 2, Winter 1990, pp. 169-187.

6. *Ibid.*, p. 178.

7. *Ibid.*, p. 182.

8. *Ibid.*, p. 186. Although the practice of psychoanalysis for the historian is certainly desirable, the profession of psychoanalysis poses possible

dilemmas for the practitioner. For example, Peter Loewenberg in "Psychoanalysis, Sexual Morality and the Clinical Situation," discusses not only the difficulties in overcoming resistances on the part of the analysand, but the nature of the patient's problems, which may be anti-social behavior, may be in conflict with state law, and may embroil the analyst in legal problems and litigation. This essay is in *Rediscovering History: Culture, Politics and the Psyche*, ed. by Michael S. Roth, Stanford University Press, 1994, pp. 61-82. For the gravity and counteractions to psychotherapy in the United States and In Europe, see the issue devoted to this subject, pertinently entitled "Backlash Against Psychotherapy," *The Journal of Psychohistory*, Vol. 22, No. 3, Winter 1995. Another issue faced by the psychohistorian is the appropriate language to be used when combining history and psychoanalysis. Should it be expository, as preferred by historians, or technical scientific, as preferred by clinicians? This subject is addressed by David J. Fisher, "The Question of Psychohistory," in *Cultural Theory and Psychoanalytic Tradition*, Transaction Publishers, 1991, pp. 227-235.

9. There has been a constant stream of articles, in the nature of exposes, in the press. For criticisms of HMO's, such as complaints against them by physicians, the too ready prescription of Prozac, the inadequacy of mental health care, patients' complaints about general health coverage, violations in maintaining confidential information, to name but a few of the concerns expressed in these articles, see the series in *The Los Angeles Times*, August 27, 28, 29, and 30, 1995; *Newsday*, October 29, 1995, January 25 and 30, February 18, and April 1, 1996; *The New York Times*, September 21, October 13, and November 24; and a special twenty-two page section of *The Wall Street Journal*, entitled "Health and Medicine," which contains the article "Shrinking Coverage: Has managed care hurt mental health? It depends on whom you ask," October 24, 1996.

10. The public has further been alerted to the crisis by leading television broadcasts. Ted Koppel on *ABC's Nightline* devoted an entire program to "The Tension Between Mental Health and Managed Care," October 17, 1996; and *CBS*, "60 Minutes," had a segment on the difficulties created by managed care on January 5, 1997.

11. Dinitia Smith, "Freud May Be Dead, But His Critics Still Kick," *New York Times*, December 10, 1995, p. 14.

12. *Ibid.*

13. *Ibid.*

14. *Ibid.*

15. *Ibid.*

16. *Ibid.*

17. *Ibid.*
18. Ellen Joan Pollack, "Managed Care's Focus on Psychiatric Drugs Alarms Many Doctors. They Say Effort to Cut Costs Leads to Overuse, Misuse of Pills for Mental Illness. Talk Therapy is Discouraged, *Wall Street Journal*, December 1, 1995, p. 1.
19. *Ibid.*
20. *Ibid.*
21. *Ibid.*, p. 11
22. *Ibid.*
23. *Ibid.*
24. *Ibid.*
25. *Ibid.*
26. Michael Waldholtz, "Head Doctor: Doubted and Resisted, Freud's Daring Map of the Mind Endures," *Wall Street Journal*, December 2, 1995, p. 1.
27. *Ibid.*
28. *Ibid.*
29. *Ibid.*
30. *Ibid.*
31. *Ibid.*
32. *Ibid.*, p. 8.
33. *Ibid.*
34. *Ibid.*
35. Jonathan Lear, "The Shrink Is In: A Counterblast in the War on Freud," *The New Republic*, December 25, 1995.
36. *Ibid.*, p. 20.
37. *Ibid.*, p. 18.
38. *Ibid.*
39. *Ibid.*, p. 20
40. *Ibid.*
41. *Ibid.*
42. *Ibid.*, p. 21.

43. *Ibid.*
44. *Ibid.*
45. *Ibid.*, p. 22.
46. *Ibid.*
47. *Ibid.*, p. 24.
48. *Ibid.*
49. *Ibid.*
50. *Ibid.*
51. *Ibid.*, p. 25.
52. *Ibid.*
53. *Ibid.*
54. *Ibid.*, p. 18
55. *Ibid.*
56. *Ibid.*
57. Paul Gray, "The Assault on Freud: He invented psychoanalysis and revolutionized 20th century ideas about the life of the mind. And this is the thanks he gets?" *Time*, November 29, 1993, p. 49.
58. *Ibid.*, p. 47.
59. *Ibid.*
60. *Ibid.*, p. 51.
61. *Ibid.*
62. Joel Gavriele-Gold, "Managed Care and the Dissolution of the Therapeutic Alliance in Psychoanalysis," paper presented at the *Third International Conference on Social Values*, "Changing Ethics in the Professions," University of Oxford, England, July 1995.
63. *Ibid.*, pp. 1-3.
64. *Ibid.*, p. 6.
65. *Ibid.*, pp. 6-7.
66. *Ibid.*, p. 8.
67. *Ibid.*, p. 19.
68. *Ibid.*, p. 14.
69. *Ibid.*, p. 22.

70. Richard A. Friedman, "Psychoanalysis and Managed Health Care," *NAAP News*, Vol. 16, No. 2, Spring 1994.
71. *Ibid.*, p. 5.
72. *Ibid.*
73. *Ibid.*
74. *Ibid.*
75. *Ibid.*
76. *Ibid.*
77. Alessandra Stanley, "Freud in Russia: Return of the Repressed," *New York Times*, December 11, 1996.
78. *Ibid.*, p. 1.
79. *Ibid.*
80. *Ibid.*, p. 10.

Bibliography

Abramson, David. *Nixon vs. Nixon: An Emotional Tragedy*. Farrar, Strauss and Giroux, 1977.

Adams, Laurie. *Art and Psychoanalysis*. Harper Collins, 1993.

―――― and Szaluta, Jacques, eds. *Psychoanalysis and the Humanities*. Brunner/Mazel, 1996.

Albin, Mel, ed. *New Directions in Psychohistory, The Adelphi University Papers in Honor of Erik H. Erikson*. Lexington Books, 1980.

Altman, Leon L. *The Dream in Psychoanalysis*. International Universities Press, 1975.

American Historical Association. *Program of the One Hundred Third Annual Meeting*, 1988, Session 138, "Psychohistory and Psychohistorians: The First Fifty Years."

American Historical Association. *Program of the One Hundred Seventh Annual Meeting*, 1992, Session 85, "Sigmund Freud and Historians: New Interpretations and Directions."

Andersen, David C. "Beyond Rumor and Reductionism: A Textual Dialogue with Erik H. Erikson," *The Psychohistory Review*, Fall 1993, Vol. 22, No. 1, pp. 35–68.

Anthony, James E. "The Family and the Psychoanalytic Process in Children," *The Psychoanalytic Study of the Child*, 1980, Vol. 35, pp. 3–34.

Ariès, Phillipe. *Centuries of Childhood: A Social History of Family Life*. Knopf, 1962.

Baron, Salo W. "Book Review of Moses and Monotheism" in *Psychoanalysis and History*, ed. Bruce Mazlish. Grosset and Dunlap, 1971.

―――. *The Contemporary Relevance of History: A Study in Approaches and Methods*. Columbia University Press, 1986.

Barzun, Jacques. "History: The Muse and Her Doctors," *American Historical Review*, 1972, Vol. 77, pp. 36-64.

―――. *Clio and the Doctors: Psycho-History, Quanto-History, and History*. University of Chicago Press, 1974.

Beard, Linda S. "Daughters of Clio and Calliope: Contemporary Afro-American and Revisionist Herstorians," *The Psychohistory Review*, Spring 1989, Vol. 17, No. 3, pp. 301-343.

Bedard, Marcia E. "Profamilism and the New Right: A Feminist Analysis of Fascist Ideology," *The Psychohistory Review*, Winter 1987, Vol. 15, No 2, pp. 77-108.

Bernfeld, Suzanne C. "Freud and Archeology," *American Imago*, 1951, Vol. 8, pp. 107-128.

Bernstein, Anne E. and Warner, Gloria M. *An Introduction to Contemporary Psychoanalysis*. Jason Aronson, 1981.

Binion, Rudolph. *Hitler Among the Germans*. Elsevier, 1976.

―――. *Soundings: Psychohistorical and Psycholiterary*. Psychohistory Press, 1981.

―――. *Introduction à la psychohistoire*. Presses Universitaires de France, 1982.

Bischler, W. "Schopenhauer and Freud: A Comparison," in *Sigmund Freud: Critical Assessments*, ed. L. Spurling, Vol. 1, *Freud and the Origins of Psychoanalysis*. Rutledge, 1989.

Bizière, Jean-Maurice. "'Before and After.' Essai de psychohistoire," *Revue d'histoire moderne et contemporaire*, April-June 1980, Vol. XXVII, pp. 177-207.

Blanck, Gertrude and Rubin. *Ego Psychology: Theory and Practice*. Columbia University Press, 1974.

Bibliography

Boehlich, Walter, ed. *The Letters of Sigmund Freud to Eduard Silberstein, 1871-1881*, trans. by A. J. Pomerans. Cambridge, 1990.

Bongiorno, Joseph A. "Woodrow Wilson Revisited: The Prepolitical Years," in *The Leader: Psychohistorical Essays*, ed. by C.B. Strozier and D. Offer. Plenum Press, 1985.

Brenner, Charles. *An Elementary Textbook of Psychoanalysis*. Anchor, 1974.

Breuer, Joseph and Freud, Sigmund. *Studies on Hysteria*, Standard Edition, Vol. 2. Hogarth Press, 1955.

Bromberg, Norbert and Small, Verna V. *Hitler's Psychopathology*. International Universities Press, 1983.

Bulletin de la Societé d'Histoire Moderne, Sixteenth Series, 1980, No. 6, pp. 12-15.

Bullock, Alan. *Hitler: A Study in Tyranny*. Harper Torchbooks, 1966.

Chesen, Eli S. *President Nixon's Psychiatric Profile: A Psychodynamic-Genetic Interpretation*. Wyden, 1973.

Chodorow, Nancy J. *Feminism and Psychoanalytic Theory*. Yale University Press, 1989.

Cleaver, Eldridge. *Soul on Ice*. McGraw-Hill, 1968.

Cocks, Geoffrey C. *Psychoanalysis in the Third Reich: The Göring Institute*. Oxford University Press, 1985

Coles, Robert. *Erik H. Erikson: The Growth of His Work*. Little, Brown, 1970

———. and Fitzpatrick, John J. "The Writings of Erik H. Erikson," *The Psychohistory Review*, 1976, Vol. 5, No. III, pp. 42-46.

Columbia Broadcasting System. (CBS) "Sixty Minutes," January, 5, 1997.

Corsino, Louis. "Malcolm X and the Black Muslim Movement: A Social Psychology of Charisma," *The Psychohistory Review*, Spring/Summer 1982, Vol. 10, No. 3/4, pp. 165-184.

Cremerius Johannes, ed. *Die Rezeption der Psychoanalyse in der Soziologie, Psychologie und Theologie in deutschsprächigen Raum bis 1940*. Suhrkamp Verlag, 1981.

Das Comité für die Glückwunsch-Addresse an Prof. Sigmund Freud. Series E. Carton 4, The Sigmund Freud Collection, Library of Congress, Washington, D.C.

Davis, Glenn. *Childhood and History in America*. The Psychohistory Press, 1976.

DeMause, Lloyd. "The Evolution of Childhood," *The History of Childhood*, L. deMause ed. The Psychohistory Press, 1974.

DeMijolla, Alain. "La Psychanalyse en France (1893-1965)," *Histoire de la Psychanalyse*, Vol. II, ed. by Roland Jacard. Hachette, 1982.

Demos, John. *A Little Commonwealth: Family Life in Plymouth Colony*. Oxford University Press, 1970

———. *Entertaining Satan: Witchcraft and the Culture of Early New England*. Oxford, 1982.

———. *Past, Present, and Personal: The Family and the Life Course in American History*. Oxford University Press, 1986.

———. *The Unredeemed Captive: A Family Story from Early America*. Knopf, 1994.

Diagnostic and Statistical Manual of Mental Disorders. Fourth Edition, *DSM-IV* Published by the American Psychiatric Association, 1994.

Eissler, Kurt R. *Leonardo da Vinci*. International Universities Press. 1961.

———. *Goethe: A Psychoanalytic Study, 1775-1786*, 2 Vols. Wayne State University Press, 1963.

———. *Medical Oxthodoxy and the Future of Psychoanalysis*. International Universities Press, 1965.

Elovitz, Paul H. "Psychohistorical Dreamwork: A New Methodology Applied of a Dream of Sir Humphrey Davy." *The Variety of Dream Experience*, ed. by M. Ullman and C. Limmer. Continuum Publishing Comps. 1987, pp. 253-265.

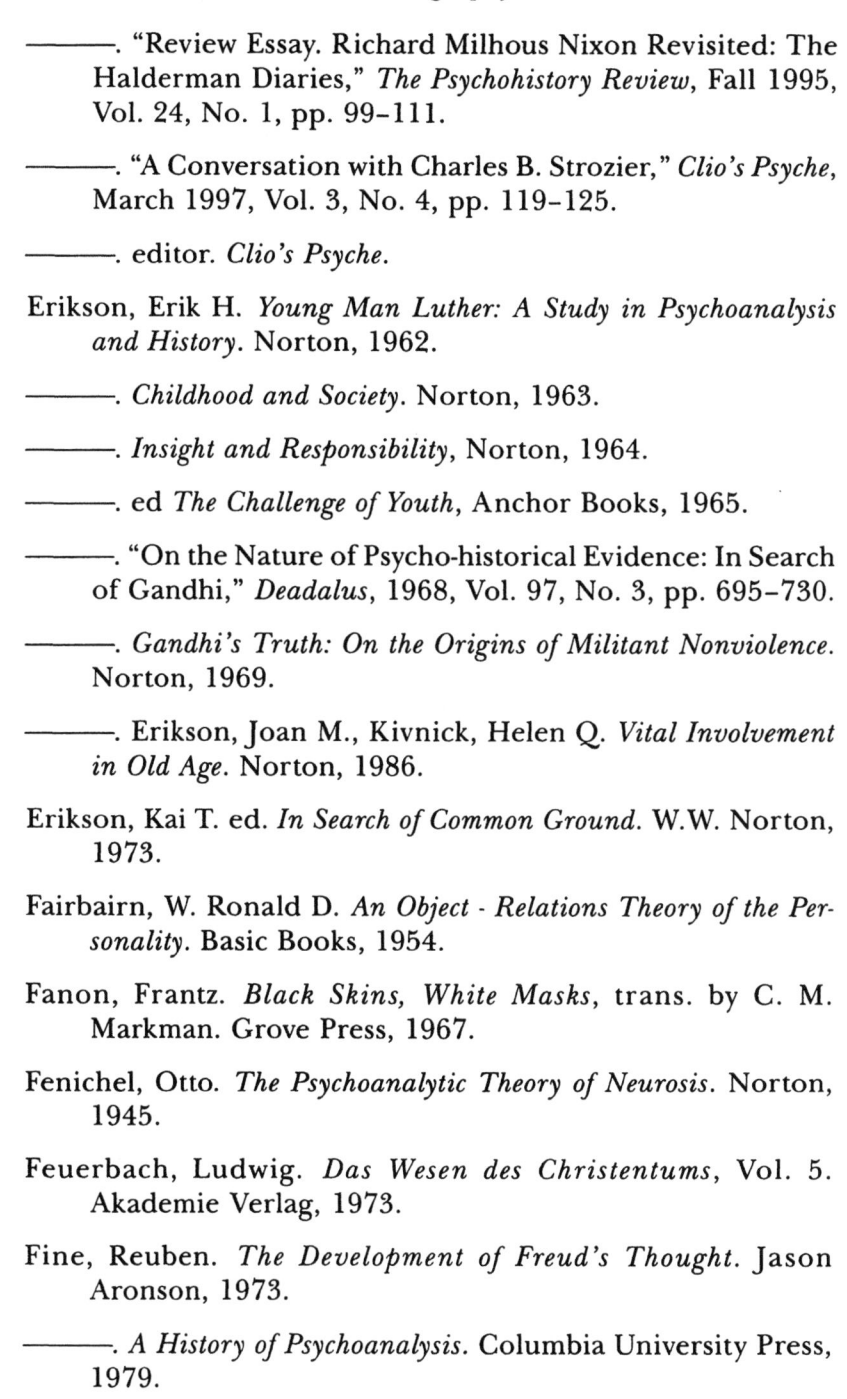

———. "Review Essay. Richard Milhous Nixon Revisited: The Halderman Diaries," *The Psychohistory Review*, Fall 1995, Vol. 24, No. 1, pp. 99-111.

———. "A Conversation with Charles B. Strozier," *Clio's Psyche*, March 1997, Vol. 3, No. 4, pp. 119-125.

———. editor. *Clio's Psyche*.

Erikson, Erik H. *Young Man Luther: A Study in Psychoanalysis and History*. Norton, 1962.

———. *Childhood and Society*. Norton, 1963.

———. *Insight and Responsibility*, Norton, 1964.

———. ed *The Challenge of Youth*, Anchor Books, 1965.

———. "On the Nature of Psycho-historical Evidence: In Search of Gandhi," *Deadalus*, 1968, Vol. 97, No. 3, pp. 695-730.

———. *Gandhi's Truth: On the Origins of Militant Nonviolence*. Norton, 1969.

———. Erikson, Joan M., Kivnick, Helen Q. *Vital Involvement in Old Age*. Norton, 1986.

Erikson, Kai T. ed. *In Search of Common Ground*. W.W. Norton, 1973.

Fairbairn, W. Ronald D. *An Object - Relations Theory of the Personality*. Basic Books, 1954.

Fanon, Frantz. *Black Skins, White Masks*, trans. by C. M. Markman. Grove Press, 1967.

Fenichel, Otto. *The Psychoanalytic Theory of Neurosis*. Norton, 1945.

Feuerbach, Ludwig. *Das Wesen des Christentums*, Vol. 5. Akademie Verlag, 1973.

Fine, Reuben. *The Development of Freud's Thought*. Jason Aronson, 1973.

———. *A History of Psychoanalysis*. Columbia University Press, 1979.

———. *The Psychoanalytic Vision*. The Free Press, 1981.

———. *The Logic of Psychology: A Dynamic Approach.* University Press of America, 1983.

Fisher, David J. *Cultural Theory and Psychoanalytic Tradition.* Transaction Publishers, 1991.

———. Book Review of *Jacques Lacan & Co.: A History of Psychoanalysis in France, 1925-1985*, by Elizabeth Roudinesco *Psychoanalytic Books*, 1994, Vol. 5, pp. 365-377.

Fisher, Seymour and Greenberg, Roger P. *The Scientific Credibility of Freud's Theories and Therapy.* Basic Books, 1977.

Fitzpatrick, John J. "Some Problematic Features of Erik H. Erikson's Psychohistory," *The Psychohistory Review*, 1976, Vol. V, No. III, pp. 16-27.

Flugel, John C. *The Psycho-Analytic Study of the Family.* The International Psycho-Analytic Press, 1921.

Fox, Vivian C. and Quitt, Martin H. eds. *Loving, Parenting and Dying: The Family Circle in England and America, Past and Present.* The Psychohistory Press, 1980.

Freud, Anna and Burlingham, Dorothy. *War and Children.* Medical War Books, 1943.

———. *The Ego and the Mechanisms of Defence*, trans. by C. Baines. International Universities Press, 1946.

———. *Introduction to Psychoanalysis: Lectures for Child Analysts and Teachers, 1922-1935.* International Universities Press, 1974.

Freud, Sigmund. *The Interpretations of Dreams, Standard Edition*, Vol. 4. Hogarth Press, 1953.

———. *Three Essays on Sexuality, Standard Edition*, Vol. 7. Hogarth Press, 1953.

———. *Totem and Taboo, Standard Edition*, Vol. 13. Hogarth Press, 1953.

———. *On Narcissism: An Introduction, Standard Edition*, Vol. 14. Hogarth Press, 1956.

———. *Group Psychology and the Analysis of the Ego*, Standard Edition, Vol. 18. Hogarth Press. 1957.

———. *Civilization and Its Discontents*, Standard Edition, Vol. 21. Hogarth Press 1991.

———. *The Future of an Illusion*, Standard Edition, Vol. 21. Hogarth Press, 1961.

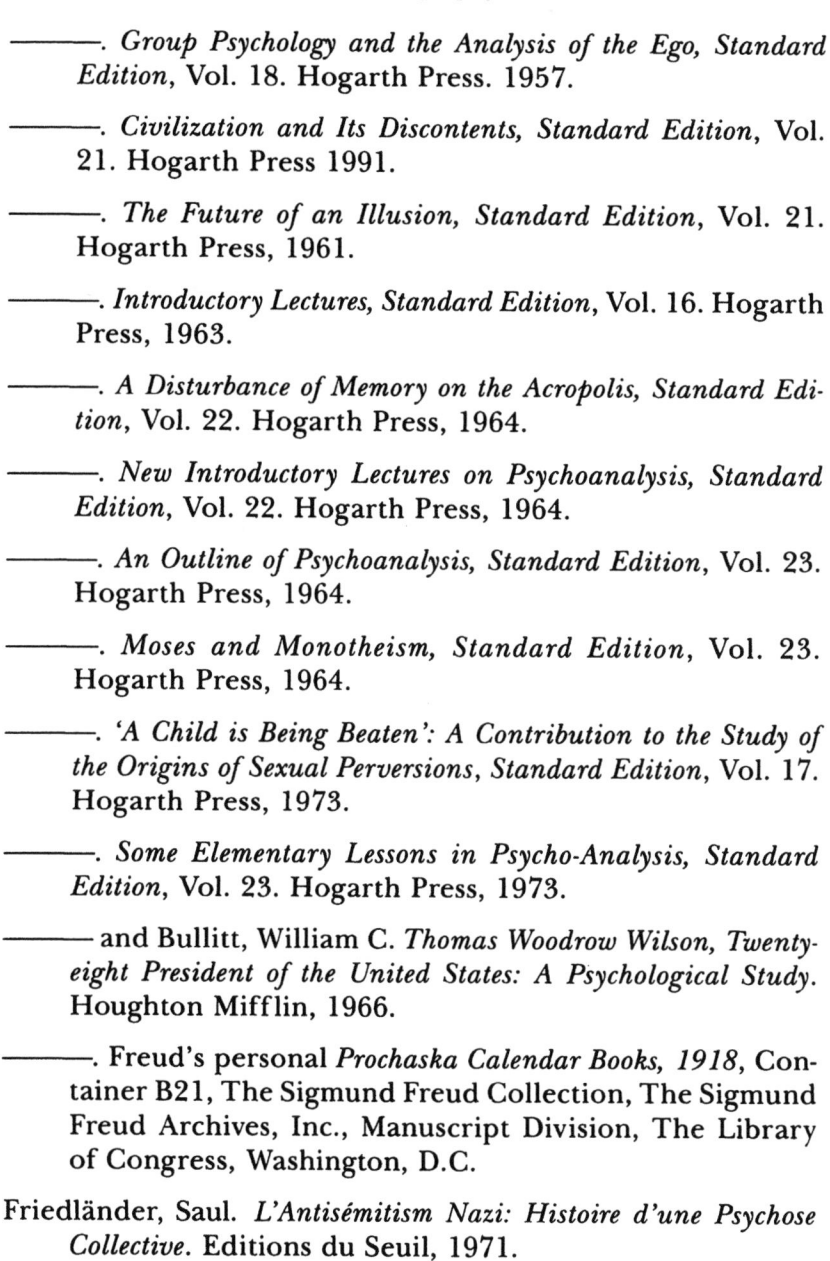

———. *Introductory Lectures*, Standard Edition, Vol. 16. Hogarth Press, 1963.

———. *A Disturbance of Memory on the Acropolis*, Standard Edition, Vol. 22. Hogarth Press, 1964.

———. *New Introductory Lectures on Psychoanalysis*, Standard Edition, Vol. 22. Hogarth Press, 1964.

———. *An Outline of Psychoanalysis*, Standard Edition, Vol. 23. Hogarth Press, 1964.

———. *Moses and Monotheism*, Standard Edition, Vol. 23. Hogarth Press, 1964.

———. *'A Child is Being Beaten': A Contribution to the Study of the Origins of Sexual Perversions*, Standard Edition, Vol. 17. Hogarth Press, 1973.

———. *Some Elementary Lessons in Psycho-Analysis*, Standard Edition, Vol. 23. Hogarth Press, 1973.

——— and Bullitt, William C. *Thomas Woodrow Wilson, Twenty-eight President of the United States: A Psychological Study*. Houghton Mifflin, 1966.

———. Freud's personal *Prochaska Calendar Books, 1918*, Container B21, The Sigmund Freud Collection, The Sigmund Freud Archives, Inc., Manuscript Division, The Library of Congress, Washington, D.C.

Friedländer, Saul. *L'Antisémitism Nazi: Histoire d'une Psychose Collective*. Editions du Seuil, 1971.

———. *History and Psychoanalysis: An Inquiry into the Possibilities and Limits of Psychohistory*, trans. by Susan Suleiman. Holmes and Meier, 1978.

Friedman, Richard A. "Psychoanalysis and Managed Health Care," NAAP News, Spring 1994, Vol. 16, No. 2, p. 5.

Friedman, William. "'Woodrow Wilson and Colonel House' and Political Psychobiography," *Political Psychology: Journal of the International Society of Political Psychology*, March 1994, Vol. 15, No. 1, pp. 35-59.

Gavriele-Gold, Joel. "Managed Care and the Dissolution of the Therapeutic Alliance in Psychoanalysis," paper presented at the *Third International Conference on Social Values*, "Changing Ethics in the Professions." University of Oxford, England, July 1995.

Gay, Peter. *Freud for Historians*. Oxford University Press, 1985.

———. *The Bourgeois Experience: Victoria to Freud*, 4 vols. W.W. Norton, 1984-1995.

George, Alexander L. and Juliette L. *Woodrow Wilson and Colonel House: A Personality Study*. Dover Publications, 1964.

Gilmore, William J. *Psychohistorical Inquiry: A Comprehensive Research Bibliography*. Garland Publishing, 1984.

Gray, Paul. "The Assault on Freud: He invented psychoanalysis and revolutionized 20th century ideas about the life of the mind. And this is the thanks he gets?" *Time*, November 29, 1993.

Greenberg, Jay R. and Mitchell, Stephen A. *Object Relations in Psychoanalytic Theory*. Harvard University Press, 1983.

Greene, Marshall A. "The Self Psychology of Heinz Kohut," *Bulletin of the Menninger Clinic*," 1984, Vol. 48, No. 1, 1984, pp. 37-53.

Grinberg, Leon, et al. *New Introduction to the Work of Bion*. Jason Aronson, 1993.

Grinstein, Alexander. *Freud's Rules of Dream Interpretation*. International Universities Press, 1983.

Grosskurth, Phyllis. *Melanie Klein: Her World and Her Work*. Alfred A. Knopf, 1986.

Hareven, Tamara K. "The History of the Family as an Interdisciplinary Field," *The Family in History: Interdisciplinary Essays*, eds. T.K. Rabb and R.I. Rotberg. Harper, 1971.

Hartmann, Heinz. *Ego Psychology and the Problem of Adaptation*. International Universities Press, 1958.

Heller, Peter. "Erikson on Luther," *The Psychohistory Review*, Fall 1993, Vol. 22, No. 1, pp. 87-99.

Himmelfarb, Gertrude. "The 'New History,'" *Commentary*, January 1975. Vol. 59. pp. 72-78.

Hinshelwood, R. D. *A Dictionary of Kleinan Thought*. Free Association Books, 1989.

Hoffman, Louise E. "Psychoanalytic Interpretations of Adolph Hitler and Nazism, 1933-1945: A Prelude to Psychohistory," *The Psychohistory Review*, Fall 1982, Vol. 11, No 1, pp. 68-87.

———. "Object-relations Theory and Psychohistory," *Bulletin of the Menninger Clinic*, 1985, Vol. 49, No. 2, pp. 113-123.

———. "Erikson on Hitler: The Origins of 'Hitler's Imagery and German Youth'," *The Psychohistory Review*, Fall 1993, Vol. 22, No. 1, pp. 69-86.

Holt, Robert R. "Freud's Adolescent Reading: Some Possible Effects on His Work," in *Freud: Appraisals and Reappraisals*, Vol. 3, ed. Paul E. Stepansky. The Analytic Press, 1988.

Hopkins Brooke. "Keats' 'Negative Capability' and Winnicott's Creative Play," *American Imago*, Spring 1984, Vol. 41, pp. 85-100.

Hughes, H. Stuart. *History as Art and Science*. Harper and Row, 1964.

———. *The Obstructed Path: French Social Thought in the Years of Desperation, 1930-1960*. Harper and Row, 1968.

Hughes, J. Donald. "Psychohistorical Dreamwork: Dreams from the Ancient World," *The Variety of Dream Experience*, ed. by M. Ullman and C. Limmer. Continuum Publishing Camps., 1987.

Hughes, Judith M. *Emotion and High Politics: Personal Relations at the Summit in Late Nineteenth Century-Century Britain and Germany.* University of California Press, 1983

———. *Reshaping the Psychoanalytic Domain: The Work of Melanie Klein, W.R.D. Fairbairn, and D.W. Winnicott.* University of California Press, 1989.

Hunt, David. *Parents and Children in History: The Psychology of Family Life in Early Modern France.* Basic Books, 1970.

Hunt, Lynn. *The Family Romance of the French Revolution.* University of California Press, 1992.

Hutton, Patrick H. "The Psychohistory of Erik Erikson from the Perspective of Collective Mentalities," *The Psychohistory Review,* 1983, Vol. 12, No 1, pp. 18-25.

Jobe, Thomas and Muslin, Hyman L. *Lyndon Johnson: The Tragic Self.* Plenum Press, 1991.

Johnson, James P. "Nixon and the Psychohistorians," *The Psychohistory Review,* 1978, Vol. VII, No. 3, pp. 38-42.

Jones, Ernest. *The Life and Work of Sigmund Freud,* 3 Vols. Basic Books, 1956.

Keniston, Kenneth. *The Young Radicals.* Harcourt, Brace and World. 1968.

———. *Youth and Dissent.* Harcourt Brace Jovanovich, 1971.

———. "Psychological Developments and Historical Change," *Explorations in Psychohistory: The Wellfleet Papers.* Simon and Schuster, 1974.

———. "Revolution or Counterrevolution?" in *Explorations in Psychohistory. The Wellfleet Papers.* Simon and Schuster, 1974.

Kern, Stephen. "Explosive Intimacy: Psychodynamics of the Victorian Family," *The New Psychohistory,* ed. L.de Mause. The Psychohistory Press, 1975.

Kernberg, Otto F. *Borderline Conditions and Pathological Narcissism.* James Aronson, 1975.

Klaf, Franklin S. "Napoleon and the Grand Army of 1812: A Study of Group Psychology," *The Psychoanalytic Review*, 1960, Vol. 47, pp. 68-73.

Klein, Melanie. *Envy and Gratitude: A Study of Unconscious Sources*. Tavistock Publications, 1954.

Kohut, Heinz. *The Analysis of the Self: A Systematic Approach to the Psychoanalytic Treatment of Narcissistic Personality Disorders*. International Universities Press, 1971.

———. "The Self in History," A Symposium Discussion, *Newsletter of the Group for the Use of Psychology in History*, 1975, Vol. 3, No. 4, pp. 3-10.

———. "Creativeness, Charisma, Group Psychology: Reflections on the Self-Analysis of Freud," in *Freud: The Fusion of Science and Humanism*, eds. John E. Gedo and George H. Pollock, *Psychological Issues*, Monograph 34/35. International Universities Press, 1976.

———. *The Restoration of the Self*. International Universities Press, 1977.

———. *How Does Analysis Cure?* Ed. by Arnold Goldberg, with the collaboration of Paul Stepansky. University of Chicago Press, 1984.

———. "Self Psychology and the Sciences of Man," *Self Psychology and the Humanities: Reflections on a New Psychoanalytic Approach*, ed. by C. B. Strozier. W. W. Norton, 1985.

Kohut, Thomas A. "Psychohistory as History," *The American Historical Review*, Vol. 91, No. 2, April 1986, pp. 336-354.

Koppel, Ted. *ABC's Nightline*, "The Tension Between Mental Health and Managed Care," October 17, 1996.

Kornblicher, Thomas. *Tiefenpsychologie und Biographik*. Peter Lang, 1989.

———. *Adolf Hitler-Psychogramme*. Peter Lang, 1994.

Kovel, Joel "Erik Erikson's Psychohistory," *Social Policy*, 1974, Vol. 4, pp. 59-66.

Kren, George M. "Psychohistorians Contra The Third Reich," *The Psychohistory Review*, 1976, Vol. 5, No. 1, pp. 34-40.

———. "Psychohistory, Psychobiography and the Holocaust," *The Psychohistory Review*, Fall 1984, Vol. 13, pp. 42-45.

Kurzweil, Edith. *The Freudians: A Comparative Perspective.* Yale University Press, 1989.

Kushner, Howard I. "Taking Erikson's Identity Seriously: Psychoanalyzing the Psychohistorian," *The Psychohistory Review*, Fall 1993, Vol. 22, No. 1, pp. 7-34.

Lacan, Jacques. *Le Séminaire de Jacques Lacan*, Livre I, ed. Jacques-Alain Miller. *Les Ecrits Techniques de Freud.* Editions du Seuil, 1975.

———. *Television: A Challenge to the Psychoanalytic Establishment*, trans. by J. Mehlman, ed. by J. Copjec. W.W. Norton, 1990.

Lagache, Daniel. *La psychanalyse. Que Sais-Je?* Presses Universitaires de France, 1979.

Langer, William L. "The Next Assignment," *Psychoanalysis and History*, ed. B. Mazlish. Grosset and Dunlap, 1971.

———. *The Mind of Adolf Hitler: The Secret Wartime Report.* Basic Books, 1972. Laplanche, Jean and Pontalis, J.B. *Vocabulaire de la Psychanalyse.* Presses Universitaires de France, 1967.

Lasch, Christopher. "The Family as a Haven in a Heartless World," *Salmagundi: A Quarterly of the Humanities and Social Sciences*, Fall 1976, No. 35, pp. 42-55.

———. "The Waning of Private Life," *Salmagundi*, Winter 1977, No, pp. 3-15.

———. *The Culture of Narcissism: American Life in an Age of Diminishing Expectations.* Warner Books, 1979.

Lawton, Henry. *The Psychohistorian's Handbook.* The Psychohistory Press, 1988.

Lear, Jonathan. "The Shrink Is In: A Counterblast in the War on Freud," *The New Republic*, December 25, 1995, pp. 18-25.

Lee, Jonathan Scott. "Spike Lee's *Malcolm X* as Transformational Object", *American Imago*, Summer 1995, Vol. 52, No. 2, pp. 155-167.

Lee, Spike. Director of film *Malcolm X*. 1993.

Lefebvre, Georges. *Napoleon*, trans. by H. F. Stockhold. Columbia University Press, 1969.

Levey, Jules. "Richard Nixon as Elder Statesman," *The Journal of Psychohistory*, Spring 1986, Vol. 13, No. 4, pp. 427-448.

Lifton, Robert J. *Death in Life: Survivors of Hiroshima*. Random House, 1968.

———. *Revolutionary Immortality: Mao Tse-Tung and the Chinese Cultural Revolution*. Vintage Books, 1968.

——— and Olson, Eric, eds. *Explorations in Psychohistory: The Wellfleet Papers*. Simon and Schuster, 1974.

———. *Living and Dying*. Prager, 1974.

———. *The Nazi Doctors: Medical Killing and the Psychology of Genocide*. Basic Books, 1986.

Liris, Robert, editor. *Or le temp: Revue Française de Psychohistoire*.

Loewenberg, Peter. *Decoding the Past*. Knopf, 1983.

———. Book Review, "Expanding History. Shrinking History: On Freud and the Failure of Psychohistory," *Partisan Review*, 1984, Vol. 51, No. 1, pp. 133-137.

———. "Why Psychoanalysis Needs the Social Scientist and the Historian" in *Psycho/History: Readings in the Method of Psychology, Psychoanalysis and History*, ed. by G. Cocks and T.L. Crosby. Yale University Press, 1987.

———. "Psychoanalytic Models of History: Freud and After," in *Psychology and Historical Interpretation*, ed. William M. Runyan. Oxford University Press, 1988.

———. "Psychoanalysis, Sexual Morality, and the Clinical Situation," *Rediscovering History: Culture, Politics and the Psyche*, ed. M. S. Roth. Stanford University Press, 1994

Lynn, Kenneth S. "History's Reckless Psychologizing," *Chronicle of Higher Education*, January 1978, Vol. 15, Number 18, p. 45.

Mahler, Margaret S. *The Psychological Birth of the Human Infant: Symbioses and Individuation*. Basic Books, 1975.

Manuel, Frank E. "The Use and Abuse of Psychology in History," *Daedalus*, Winter, 1971, Vol. 100, pp. 187-213.

Marcuse, Herbert. *Eros and Civilization: A Philosophical Inquiry into Freud*. Bacon Press, 1955.

———. *One-Dimension Man*. Beacon Press, 1964.

Marvick, Elizabeth W. "Nature vs. Nurture: Trends and Patterns in Seventeenth Century French Childrearing," *The History of Childhood*, ed. L. deMause. The Psychohistory Press, 1974.

———. *The Young Richelieu: A Psychoanalytic Approach to Leadership*. University of Chicago Press, 1983.

———. *Louis XIII: The Making of a King*. Yale University Press, 1986.

Mazlish, Bruce. "What is Psychohistory?" in *The Varieties of Psychohistory*, ed. George Kren and Leon H. Rappoport. Springer, 1976.

———. "Reflections on the State of Psychohistory," *The Psychohistory Review*, March 1977, Vol. 5, pp. 3-11.

———. "Psychohistory and Politics," *The Center Magazine*, 1977, Vol. X, September/October, pp. 5-14.

———. "Psychoanalytic Theory and History: Groups and Events," *The Annual of Psychoanalysis*, 1978, Vol. 6, pp. 41-57.

———. "The Next 'Next Assignment': Leader and Led, Individual and Group," *The Psychohistory Review*, 1981, Vol. 9, pp. 214-237.

———. *The Leader, the Led and the Psyche: Essays in Psychohistory*. Wesleyan University Press, 1990.

———. "Some observations on the Psychology of Political Leadership," *Political Psychology: Journal of the International Society of Political Psychology*, December 1994, Vol. 15, No. 4, pp. 745-753.

McGrath, William J. *Freud's Discovery of Psychoanalysis: The Politics of Hysteria*. Cornell University Press, 1986.

Merlan, Philip. "Brentano and Freud," *Journal of the History of Ideas*. Vol. 6, 1945, pp. 375-377.

———. "Brentano and Freud," *Journal of the History of Ideas*, Vol. 10, 1949, p. 451

Meyerhoff, Hans. "On Psychoanalysis as History," in *Psycho/History: Reading in the Method of Psychology, Psychoanalysis and History*, ed. G. Cocks and T.L. Crosby. Yale University Press, 1987.

Miller, Alice. *For Your Own Good: Hidden Cruelty in Child Rearing and the Roots of Violence*, trans. H. and H. Hannum. Farrar Strauss, Giroux, 1983.

Miller, Gerard. *Les pousse-au-jour du Maréchal Pétain*. Editions du Seuil, 1975.

Mohacsy, Ildiko. "The Legend of the Unicorn: An Illumination of the Maternal Split," *Journal of the American Academy of Psychoanalysis*, 1984, Vol. 12, No. 3, pp. 387-412.

———. "The Medieval Unicorn: Historical and Iconographic Applications of Psychoanalysis," *The Journal of the American Academy of Psychoanalysis*, 1988, Vol. 16, No. 1, pp. 83-106.

Monaco, Paul. *Cinema and Society: France and Germany during the Twenties*. Elsevier, 1976.

Moore, Burness E. and Fine, Bernard D. eds. *Psychoanalytic Terms and Concepts*. Yale University Press, 1990.

Muller, John P. and Richardson, William J. *Lacan and Language: A Reader's Guide to Ecrits*. International Universities Press, 1982.

Muslin, Hyman L. "Shakespeare and Psychology of the Self: The Case of Othello," in *Kohut's Legacy: Contributions to Self Psychology*, ed. P.E. Stepansky and A. Goldberg. The Analytic Press, 1984.

———in collaboration with Val, Eduardo R. *The Psychotherapy of the Self*, Brunner/Mazel, 1987.

Newsday, 1995-1996.

Nixon, Richard. *Six Crises*. Doubleday, 1962.

———. *RN: The Memoirs of Richard Nixon*. Grosset and Dunlap, 1978.

———. *Leaders: Profiles and Reminiscences of Men Who Have Shaped the Modern World*. Warner, 1982.

Oliner, Marion M. *Cultivating Freud's Garden in France*. Jason Aronson, 1988.

Olinick, Stanley L. "Psychoanalysis and Language," *Journal of the American Psychoanalytic Association*, 1984, Vol. 21, pp. 617-653.

Parker, Harold T. "The Formation of Napoleon's Personality: An Exploratory Essay," *French Historical Studies*, 1971, Vol. II, pp. 21-32.

Perry, Bruce. "Malcolm X and the Politics of Masculinity," *The Psychohistory Review*, Winter 1985, Vol. 13, No. 2-3, pp. 18-25.

Pétain, Philippe. "Les Lettres du Maréchal Pétain à son épouse, 1913-1949." Archives Nationale de France, 415 A P, 523 Microfilm, Paris.

Pois, Robert A. "The Case for Clinical Training and Challenges to Psychohistory," *The Psychohistory Review*, 1990, Vol. 18, No. 2, pp. 169-187.

Pollock, Ellen Joan. "Managed Care's Focus on Psychiatric Drugs Alarms Many Doctors. They say effort to cut costs leads to overuse, misuse of pills for Mental Illness, Talk Therapy is Discouraged," *The Wall Street Journal*, December 1, 1995.

Pomper, Philip. *The Structure of Mind in History: Five Major Figures in Psychohistory.* Columbia University Press, 1985.

Prisco III, Salvatore. *An Introduction to Psychohistory: Theories and Case Studies.* University Press of America, 1980.

Quinn, Susan. "Oedipus vs. Narcissus," *The New York Times Magazine,* 1980, No. 9, pp. 120-131.

Roazen, Paul. *Erik H. Erikson, The Power and Limits of a Vision.* The Free Press, 1976.

Robins, Robert. "Paranoid Ideation and Charismatic Leadership," *The Psychohistory Review,* Fall 1986, Vol. 5, No. 1, pp. 15-68.

Roland, Aland. ed. *Psychoanalysis, Creativity and Literature: A French-American Inquiry.* Columbia University Press, 1978.

Rosenthal, Naomi, "The Psychology of Women," *The Psychohistory Review,* Spring 1980, Vol. 8, pp. 32-36.

Ross, Dorothy. "Review Essay/Woodrow Wilson and the Case for Psychohistory," *The Journal of American History,* December 1982, Vol. 69, No. 3, pp. 659-668.

Rothstein, Arnold. ed. *Models of the Mind: Their Relationships to Clinical Work.* International Universities Press, 1985.

Roudinesco, Elisabeth. *Jacques Lacan & Co.: A History of Psychoanalysis in France, 1925-1985,* trans. with a Foreword by Jeffrey Mehlman. University of Chicago Press, 1990.

Roustang, François. *The Lacanian Delusion,* trans. by Greg Sims. Oxford University Press, 1990.

Runyan, William M. "A Historical and Conceptual Background to Psychohistory," in *Psychology and Historical Interpretation,* ed. W.M. Runyan. Oxford University Press, 1988.

———. "Alternatives to Psychoanalytic Psychobiography," *Psychology and Historical Interpretation.* Oxford University Press, 1988.

Saffady, William. "Manuscripts and Psychohistory," *The American Archivist,* 1974, Vol. 37, pp. 55-564.

Schneiderman, Stuart. Jacques Lacan: *The Death of an Intellectual Hero*. Harvard University Press, 1983.

Schoenwald, Richard L. "Historians and the Challenge of Freud," *Western Humanities Review*, 1956, Vol. X, pp. 102–109.

———. "Using Psychology in History: A Review Essay," *Historical Methods Newsletter*, 1973, Vol. 7, pp. 10–15.

———. "The Problem of Erikson," *The Psychohistory Review*, 1977, Vol VI, No. 1, pp. 76–87.

———. "The Psychological Study of History," in *International Handbook of Historical Studies: Contemporary Research and Theory*, eds. G.G. Iggers and H.T. Parker, Greenwood Press, 1979.

Schofield, Ann. "'To Do and To Be': Mary Dreier, Pauline Newman, and the Psychology of Feminist Activism," *The Psychohistory Review*, Fall 1989, Vol. 18 pp. 33–55.

Schopenhauer, Arthur. *Die Welt als Wille und Vorstellung*, Vol. 3. Brockhaus, 1891.

Searles, Harold F. "Countertransference and Theoretical Model," in *Countertransference and Related Subjects*. International Universities Press, 1979.

Shiner, Larry, editor. "Introduction: Psychohistory in France and England," *The Psychohistory Review*, Fall 1992, Vol. 21, No. 1, pp. 1–2.

———. Review Essay, "The History of Psychoanalysis, "*The Psychohistory Review*, Fall 1992, Vol. 21, No. 1, pp. 107–117.

———. "Special Issue: Psychohistorical Study of the American Family," *The Psychohistory Review*, Winter 1977–78, Vol. VI, Nos. 2–3, Combined Issue: Fall-Winter, pp. 4–101.

Shorter, Edward. *The Making of the Modern Family*. Basic Books, 1975.

Sievers, W. David. *Freud on Broadway: A History of Psychoanalysis and the American Drama*. Hermitage House, 1955.

Sinofsky, Faye et al. "A Bibliography of Psychohistory," *History of Childhood Quarterly*, Spring 1975, Vol. 2, No. 4, pp. 517-562.

Smith, Dinitia. "Freud May Be Dead, But His Critics Still Kick," *The New York Times*, December 10, 1995.

Soucy, Robert. *French Fascism: The First Wave, 1924-1933.* Yale University Press, 1986.

"Special Issue, *Backlash Against Psychotheraphy*," *The Journal of Psychohistory*, Winter 1995, Vol. 22, No. 3.

"Special Issue: Erik H. Erikson," *The Psychohistory Review*, Fall 1993, Vol. 22. No. 1,

Spence, Donald P. *Narrative Truth and Historical Truth: Meaning and Interpretation in Psychoanalysis.* Norton, 1982.

Spitz, Lewis W. "Psychohistory and History: The Case of Young Man Luther," *Soundings*, 1973, Vol. 56, pp. 182-209.

Stanley, Alessandra. "Freud in Russia: Return of the Repressed," *The New York Times*, December 11, 1996.

Stannard, David E. *Skrinking History: On Freud and the Failure of Psychohistory.* Oxford University Press, 1980.

Stierlin, Helm. *Adolf Hitler: A Family Perspective.* The Psychohistory Press, 1976.

———. *Psychoanalysis and Family Therapy: Selected Papers.* Jason Aronson, 1977.

Strout, Cushing. "Ego Psychology and the Historian," *History and Theory: Studies in the Philosophy of History*, 1968, Vol. 7, No. 3, pp. 281-297.

Strozier, Charles B. "Disciplined Subjectivity and the Psychohistorian: A Critical Look at the Work of Erik H. Erikson," *The Psychohistory Review*, 1976, Vol. V, No. III, pp. 28-31.

———. "Heinz Kohut and the Historical Imagination," *The Psychohistory Review*, Fall 1978, Vol. 7, No. 2, pp. 36-39.

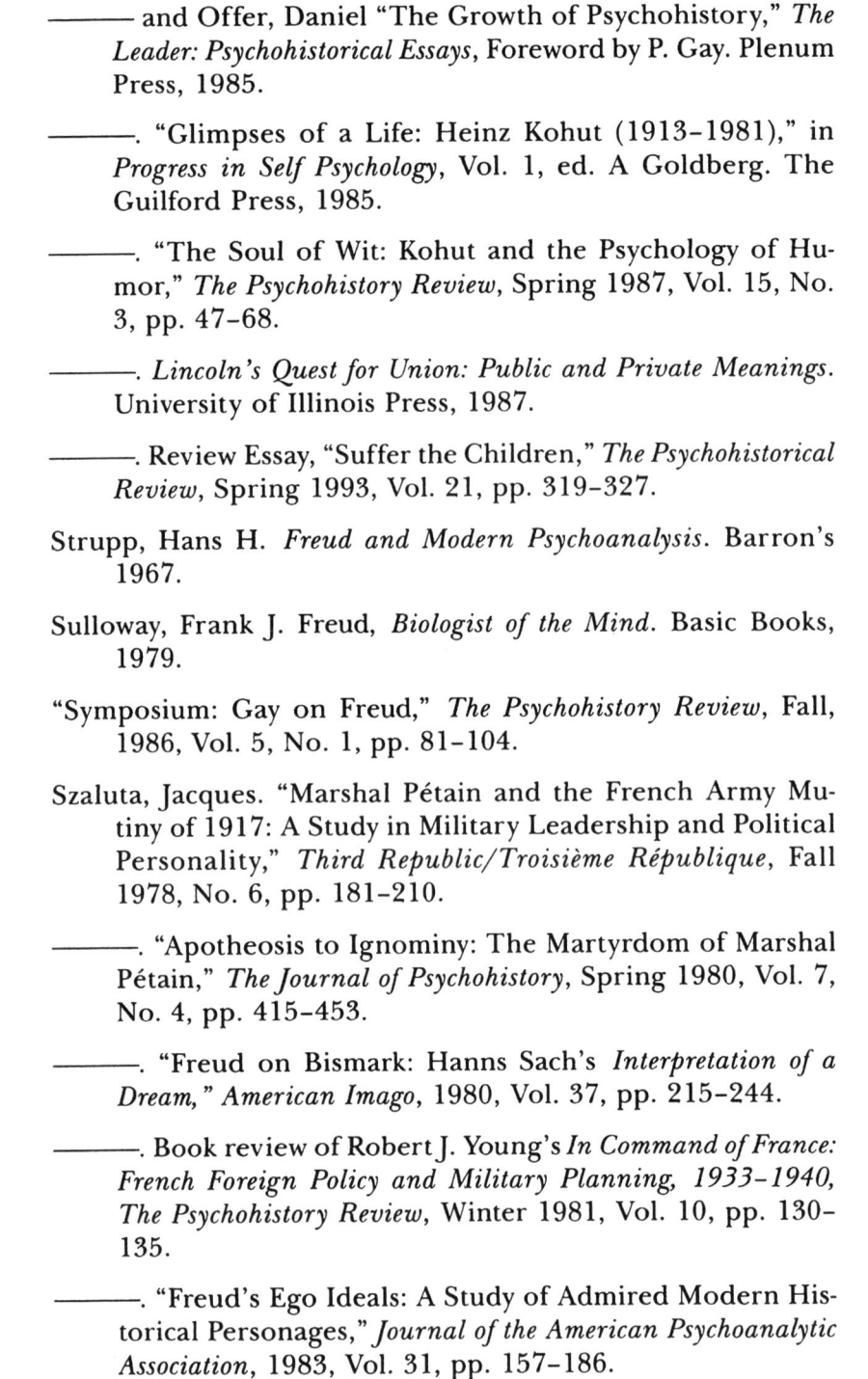

———and Offer, Daniel "The Growth of Psychohistory," *The Leader: Psychohistorical Essays*, Foreword by P. Gay. Plenum Press, 1985.

———. "Glimpses of a Life: Heinz Kohut (1913-1981)," in *Progress in Self Psychology*, Vol. 1, ed. A Goldberg. The Guilford Press, 1985.

———. "The Soul of Wit: Kohut and the Psychology of Humor," *The Psychohistory Review*, Spring 1987, Vol. 15, No. 3, pp. 47-68.

———. *Lincoln's Quest for Union: Public and Private Meanings*. University of Illinois Press, 1987.

———. Review Essay, "Suffer the Children," *The Psychohistorical Review*, Spring 1993, Vol. 21, pp. 319-327.

Strupp, Hans H. *Freud and Modern Psychoanalysis*. Barron's 1967.

Sulloway, Frank J. Freud, *Biologist of the Mind*. Basic Books, 1979.

"Symposium: Gay on Freud," *The Psychohistory Review*, Fall, 1986, Vol. 5, No. 1, pp. 81-104.

Szaluta, Jacques. "Marshal Pétain and the French Army Mutiny of 1917: A Study in Military Leadership and Political Personality," *Third Republic/Troisième République*, Fall 1978, No. 6, pp. 181-210.

———. "Apotheosis to Ignominy: The Martyrdom of Marshal Pétain," *The Journal of Psychohistory*, Spring 1980, Vol. 7, No. 4, pp. 415-453.

———. "Freud on Bismark: Hanns Sach's *Interpretation of a Dream*," *American Imago*, 1980, Vol. 37, pp. 215-244.

———. Book review of Robert J. Young's *In Command of France: French Foreign Policy and Military Planning, 1933-1940*, *The Psychohistory Review*, Winter 1981, Vol. 10, pp. 130-135.

———. "Freud's Ego Ideals: A Study of Admired Modern Historical Personages," *Journal of the American Psychoanalytic Association*, 1983, Vol. 31, pp. 157-186.

———. Book Review of Elizabeth W. Marvick's *The Young Richelieu, The Psychohistory Review*, Fall 1985, Vol. 14, No. 1, pp. 47–49.

———. Book Review of Elizabeth W. Marvick's *Louis XIII: The Making of a King, The Psychoanalytic Quarterly*, 1988, Vol. 57, No. 3, pp. 453–457.

———. "The Correspondence Between Maréchal and Madame Pétain, 1913 to 1949: A Psychoanalytic Interpretation," *American Imago*, Summer 1990, Vol. 47, No. 2, pp. 169–196.

———. "Sigmund Freud's Biblical Ego Ideals," *The Psychohistory Review*, Fall 1994, Vol. 23, No. 1, pp. 11–46.

Tager, Michael, "Looking into the Whirlwind: A Psychohistorical Study of the Black Panthers," *The Psychohistory Review*, Winter 1984, Vol, 12, No. 2/3, pp. 61–70.

The Freud-Silberstein Letters. Container B12, The Sigmund Freud Collection, Library of Congress, Washington, D. C.

The Los Angeles Times, 1995.

The National Psychological Association for Psychoanalysis. "Erik H. Erikson and Otto Rank: Clinical and Cultural Implications for Today," *Symposium*. November 20, 1982, New York City.

The New York Times, 1988, 1994, and 1996.

The Wall Street Journal, 1996.

Tuchman, Barbara W. "Can History Use Freud? The Case of Woodrow Wilson," *The Atlantic Monthly*, February 1967, Vol. 219, pp. 39–44.

Tucker, Robert C. *Stalin as Revolutionary, 1879–1929: A Study in History and Personality*. W. W. Norton, 1974.

Turkle, Sherry. *Psychoanalytic Politics: Freud's French Revolution*. Basic Books, 1976.

Van Peebles, Melvin. Director of film *Panther*, 1995.

Vitz, Paul C. *Sigmund Freud's Christian Unconscious*. Guilford Press, 1988.

Volosinov, V. N. *Freudianism: A Marxist Critique*, trans. by I. R. Titunik. Academic Press, 1976.

Waite, Robert G. L. *The Psychopathic God: Adolf Hitler*. Basic Books, 1977.

Waldholtz, Michael. "Head Doctor: Doubted and Resisted, Freud's Daring Map of the Mind Endures," *The Wall Street Journal*, December 2, 1995.

Warner, Silas L. "Fourteen Wilsonian Points for Freud and Bullitt," *Journal of the American Academy of Psychoanalysis*, 1988, Vol. 16, No. 4, pp. 479-489.

Wartofsky, Marx W. *Feuerbach*. Cambridge University Press, 1977.

Webb, Eugene. *The Self Between: From Freud to the New Social Psychology of France*. University of Washington Press, 1993.

Wehler, Hans-Ulrich. "Zum Verhältnis von Geschichtswissenschaft und Psychoanalyse," *Historische Zeitschrift*, 1969, Vol. 208, pp. 529-554.

Weinstein, Edwin A. *Thomas Woodrow Wilson: Medical and Psychological Biography*, Princeton University Press, 1981.

———. "Bullitt, Freud and Wilson," *Journal of the American Academy of Psychoanalysis*, 1988, Vol. 16, No. 3, pp. 349-357.

Weinstein, Fred and Platt, Gerald M. *Psychoanalytic Sociology: An Essay on the Interpretation of Historical Data and the Phenomenon of Collective Behavior*. The Johns Hopkins Press, 1973.

———. "The Coming Crisis in Psychohistory," *The Journal of Modern History*, June 1975, Vol. 47, pp. 202-228.

———. "The Transference Model in Psychohistory: A Critique," *The Psychohistory Review*, March 1977, Vol. V. No. 4, pp. 12-17.

Wellman, Judith M. "Some Thoughts on the Psychohistorical Study of Women," *The Psychohistory Review* Fall 1978, Vol. 7, pp. 20-24.

Winnicott, Donald W. *The Child and the Outside World: Studies in Developing Relationships*. Basic Books, 1957.

Wolf, Ernest S. "Psychoanalytic Selfobject Psychology and Psychohistory," in *New Directions in Psychohistory: The Adelphi Papers in Honor of Erik H. Erikson*, ed. Mel Albin. D. C. Heath, 1980.

Wolfenstein, Victor. *The Victims of Democracy: Malcolm X and the Black Revolution*. University of California Press, 1980.

Index

A

abandoning mode, childhood, 198
Abraham, Karl, 130
Action Française, 141-142
adaptation, concept of, 118-119
Address to the Christian Nobility of the German Nation, 95
adolescents, Erikson stage, 89-90
Adolf Hitler: A Family Perspective, 175
Against the Robbing and Murdering Hordes of Peasants, 96
aggression
  anal stage, 28
  Marxist view of, 37
aggressive drives, 34-35, 37
Aichhorn, August, 87, 148
"Alternatives to Psychoanalytic Psychobiography," 72
Althusser, Louis, 141
altruistic surrender, A. Freud on, 129
ambivalent mode, childhood, 198
American Historical Association, 9, 10, 59
  H. Kohut at, 148
American Historical Review, 8
American Imago, 12
"American Psyche, The," 193
American Psychoanalytic Association, 233
American Revolution, psychohistorical view, 193
Anabaptists, Luther's opposition to, 96
anal-erotic hypothesis, Stannard's attack on, 55
anal stage
  Freud on, 28-29
  psychosexual development, 26-27, 28-29
Analysis of a Phobia in a Five Year Old Boy, 55
Analysis of the Self, The, 151
Anderson, David C., Erikson critique, 84, 104-106
Anthony, E. James, 204-206
anti-Semitism, 35
  Hitler's, 173, 174-175, 177
  Luther's, 96
  National Socialist Germany, 190
Anzieu, Didier, 141, 142
"appeasement," 196
Ariés, Philippe, 207
"Assault on Freud, The," 235-236
Assault on Truth, The, 233
astrology, psychoanalysis compared to, 55
Austro-Prussian War, 18
autobiographies, historical evidence, 65
autonomous cognitive factors, 119
autonomy
  apparatuses of, 118
  emotional maturity and, 32
  vs. shame and doubt, Erikson stage, 88

"average expectable," environment, 119

B
Balfour, Arthur J., 135
Baron, Salo W., opposition to psychohistory, 56-58
Barzun, Jacques, 8-9, 10
  arguments against psychohistory, 49-52
basic trust
  Martin Luther and, 93, 96
  parental role, 105
  vs. basic mistrust, Erikson stage, 87-88
Bedard, Marcia E., 191-193
Behaviorist psychology, criticism of, 237
Berdyav, Nicolas, 42
Bernstein, Anne E., 131
"Beyond Rumor and Reductionism: A Textual Dialogue with Erik H. Erikson," 104-105
Beyond the Pleasure Principle, 34
bibliography, value of, 66
Binion, Rudolph
  on Hitler, 174-175
  psychohistory advocate, 3, 66-67
biography, psychohistory genre, 171-188
biological essentialism, 104
bipolar self, self-psychology, 159
Bismarck, Otto von, 18, 135, 136, 138, 172
Black Death, 61
Black Panther Party, 103, 194-196
Black Skins, White Masks, 195
Bloch, Eduard, 174
Blum, Leon, transference and, 122, 124-125
Bonaparte, Marie, 141, 142
Bonaparte, Napoleon, 66-67
  leadership of, 6-7, 51-52
  reforms of, 18
Bongiorno, Joseph A., 184-185

Booth, John Wilkes, 176
boys, phallic stage, 29-30
Brentano, Franz, 40-41
Breuer, Joseph, 21-22
British Psycho-Analytic Society, 134
British school, 127, 129-134
  impact on psychohistory, 134-134
Brodie, Fawn, 122-123
Brothers Karamazov, The, oedipal conflict in, 210
Brücke, Ernst, 19-20
Bullitt, William C., 182-183, 184, 185
Bullock, Alan, 172-173
Bülow, Bernhard von, 135
Burlingham, Dorothy T., 128

C
"Case for Clinical Training and Challenges to Psychohistory, The," 229
case study
  Little Hans, 55
  Miss Anna O, 21-22
castration, 29, 30
"castration complex," Erikson, 89
causation, nature of historical, 1-2
Cavour, Camillo di, 200
celibacy, Luther's rejection of, 95
Center for Psychosocial Studies, 148
Centuries of Childhood: A Social History of Family Life, 207
Challenge of Youth, The, 102
Chamberlain, Joseph, 135
character defense, 9. *See also* defense mechanism
character traits, anal stage, 28
Charcot, Jean-Martin, 20-21, 140
Chasseguet-Smirgel, Janine, 141
"Checkers Speech," 187
child abuse, reality of, 233
child rearing, Erikson, 91
childhood

Erikson stages, 88-89
psychohistory genre, 171, 197-203
psychosexual development, 26-31
self-psychology and, 159
six modes of, 198-199
Childhood and Society, 86, 87-91
children, psychoanalysis with, 127-128, 135
Churchill, Winston, 154
Cinema and Society: France and Germany during the Twenties, 197
civil disobedience, Luther on, 95-96
Civilization and Its Discontents, 35, 43
class struggle, 37
Cleaver, Eldridge, 194
Clemenceau, Georges, 183
Clio and the Doctor: Psycho-History, Quanto-History, and History, 8, 49
"collective mentality," study of, 61
Colton, Joel, 124-125
"Coming Crisis in Psychohistory, The," 120
common sense, historians and, 1, 7, 52, 172
Comte, Auguste, 41
concentration camps, study of, 190-191
condensation and displacement, dream work, 24
"conflict-free sphere," 118
Consulate and Empire, 18
Contemporary Relevance of History, The: A Study in Approaches and Methods, 57
"Contribution to the Psychogenesis of Manic-Depressive States, A," 130-131
Copernicus, 2
countertransference
definition, 124
psychohistory and, 122-126

Creativeness, Charisma, Group Psychology: Reflections on the Self-Analysis of Freud, 156
Cromwell, Oliver, 19
"crucial adaption," development, 118
cultural revolution (France), psychoanalytic acceptance, 139-140, 147
Culture of Narcissism, The: American Life in an Age of Diminishing Expectation, 211-213

D

Darwin, Charles, 2, 42
Das Wesen des Christentums, 42]
Da Vinci, Leonardo, 58, 72
day residue, dreams, 23
Death in Life: Survivors of Hiroshima, 108
death instinct, 36
death wish, Lacan's rejection of, 142
defense mechanisms, 33, 45n.39, 88
A. Freud on, 128
DeGaulle, Charles, 125
DeMause, Lloyd, 198-199
Demos, John
Plymouth family, 208-209
psychohistorian, 108, 151, 152-153
denial, A. Freud on, 129
depression, Klein on, 131
depth psychology, 75-76
Derrida, Jacques, 141
Descartes, René, 40
d'Estrées, Gabrielle, 202
development
normal human, 118-119
psychoanalysis and, 67-68
developmental tasks, Erikson, 87-91
diaries, historical evidence, 65
Die Welt als Wille und Vorstellung, 42

"Difficulty in the Path of Psychoanalysis, A," 42
"disciplined subjectivity," 98-99
displacement, dream work, 24-25
doctoral dissertations, psychohistory, 12
dowry, 207-208
dreams
  ancient view of, 22-23
  components of, 24
  Erikson on, 86
  Feuerbach on, 42
  Freud theory of, 22-25, 86
"Dream Specimen of Psychoanalysis, The,"
dream work, 24
drive theory, limitations of, 120
Dunkirk, 124
dynamic physiology, 20

E

Ecole Freudienne, 143
economic ethos, childhood, 89
ego
  concept of, 31
  development of, 32
  Fairbairn on, 132
  neurotic conflict, 33
  psychosis, 33
  Stannard's attack on, 55
Ego and the Mechanisms of Defense, The, 128
ego-drives, 121
ego ideals, 18-19
ego instincts, 119
ego integrity vs. despair, 90-91
ego psychology, 75-76
  development of theory, 117-126
  Erikson's use of, 101, 103, 104
  Lacan's rejection of, 146
  Loewenberg on, 122-123
Ego Psychology and the Problem of Adaptation, 118
ego-splitting, Guntrip, 132
"Eight Ages of Man," Erikson, 87
Eissler, Kurt R., 228

Emotion and High Politics: Personal Relations at the Summit in Late Nineteenth-Century Britain and Germany, 135, 138
empathy, 4-5
  H. Kohut on, 150, 151, 154, 159
  T. Kohut on, 157-158
  Wolf on, 153, 154
Empire Blue Cross Mental Health Choice, 237
Engels, Friedrich, 42
Enlightenment ideas, 34
Entertaining Satan: Witchcraft and the Culture of Early New England, 108
epileptic convulsions, study of, 20
Erik Erikson Center, 83-84
Erikson, Erik H., 13, 53, 72, 177
  background of, 83, 86-87, 102-104, 107
  career of, 83-84
  contributions to psychoanalytic theory, 87-91
  Friedländer on, 68
  relationship with Freud, 83, 86-87
  theological interests, 105
  works of, 86, 87-93, 98, 102, 103, 105, 106, 116n.123
Erikson, Joan Serson, 83, 86
"Erikson on Hitler: The Origins of Hitler's Imagery and German Youth," 106
"Erikson on Luther," 106
erotogenic zone, 27
Eulenburg, Philipp, 135, 158
evidence. *See also* records
  Barzun on, 50-51
  Himmelfarb on, 52-53
  Runyan on, 72-73
  T. Kohut on, 157
"Evolution of Childhood, The," 198
experience, ego and, 31

Explorations in Psychohistory: The Wellfleet Papers, 108-109
"Explosive Intimacy: Psychodynamics of the Victorian Family," 209-210

F

Fairbairn, W. Ronald, British school, 129, 132
family
  Plymouth colony, 108, 208-209
  political institution of, 206-207
  psychohistory genre, 171, 203-213
  role of, 120
  Victorian, 209-210
"Family and the Psychoanalytic Process in Children, The," 204
"family complex," 206
"family romance," 206
family values, 207
Fanon, Frantz, 195
fascism, psychohistorians on, 189, 191
father
  Freud's, relationship to his, 30, 31, 37, 205
  Hitler's relationship with his, 173, 174, 175, 177
  superego as, 32
  Wilson's relationship with his, 183, 185
fatherhood
  Hoffman on, 138-139
  prehistoric role of, 35-36
  Winnicott on, 134
female genitalia, dream symbols of, 25
female psychology, Erikson on, 105
feminists, Erikson critique, 103
Ferenczi, Sandor, 130, 233
Feuerbach, Ludwig, 40, 41-42
Fine, Reuben, 119

Fisher, David J., 144-145
Fitzpatrick, John J., 9, 99
Flugel, John C., 206
Foucault, Michel, 141
Fourteen Points, Wilson, 183
"Fourteen Wilsonian Points for Freud and Bullitt," 184
Fox, Vivian C., 211
France
  films viewed in, 197
  1940 defeat, 196
  psychoanalysis, acceptance of, 139-140, 147-148
  psychotherapy, resistance to, 139-141
Franco-Prussian War, 18
free association, 3
  children and, 129
  dream work and, 24
free conscience, Luther, 95, 96
Free French movement, 125
French Revolution, 18, 171, 196
Freud, Anna, 86-87, 127-129, 135, 206
Freud for Historians, 69-71
"Freud in Russia: Return of the Repressed," 239
Freud: Living and Dying, 57
"Freud May Be Dead, But His Critics Still Kick," 231
Freud, Sigmund
  background of, 18
  contemporary attacks on, 230-231
  education of, 17-22, 40
  ego ideals of, 18-19
  ego psychology, 117-118
  family pathology of, 205
  philosophical interests, 40-43
  philosophy of history, 34-37
  prizes received by, 17
  psychohistory role, 2-3
  self-criticism, 75
  settlement in England, 127
  works of, 2, 7, 12, 18, 22, 34-36, 42, 43, 57, 117-118, 205

Freud, Sigmund, critiques of:
  by Erikson, 97
  by Friedländer, 68
  by H. Kohut, 148-149, 154, 156
  by Lacan, 145-146
  by Lear, 235
Freud, Sigmund, theories of:
  dreams, 22-25
  personality, 25-31
  personality structure, 31-34, 159
  transference, 121
Freud, Sigmund, views on:
  family, 204-206
  groups, 205-206
  Marxism, 37-39
  religion, 39-40
  Russian Revolution, 39
  Woodrow Wilson, 182-183, 184, 185
Friedländer, Saul, 190
  psychohistory advocate, 67-69
Friedman, Lawrence J., Erikson critique, 100
Friedman, Richard A., 238
frugality, anal stage, 28
Future of Illusion, The, 35, 42

G

"Galilean Sayings and the Sense of 'I,' The," 105
Gandhi, Mahatma, Erikson on, 101, 105, 188
Gandhi's Truth, 86
Garibaldi, Giuseppe, 19
Gavriele-Gold, Joel, 236-238
Gay, Peter, psychohistory advocate, 69-72
gender
  Erikson on, 87
  Hoffman on, 138-139
  phallic stage differentiation, 29
generativity vs. stagnation, 90
generosity, anal stage, 28
genetic approach, 4
genital stage, 27, 30-31

George, Alexander, 183
George, Juliette, 183
George III, 193
Germany
  childrearing in, 135-136
  films viewed in, 197
  Hitler's appeal, 173-174, 175, 177
  National Socialist period, 190
Gestalt psychology, origin of, 41
Gilligan, Carol, Erikson critique, 105
Gilmore, William J., 10-11
girls, phallic stage, 29, 30
Gladstone, William E., 135
Goethe, Johann Wolfgang, 19, 42
Goethe Prize for Literature, 17
Gomperz, Theodor, 41
Gray, Paul, 235-236
great man, role of, 39
Green, Marshall A., 158-159
Greenacre, Phyllis, 72-73
Greenberg, Jay R., 131-132
Grosskurth, Phyllis, 130-131
group behavior, study of, 2, 11, 188
group psychology, 6
  Napoleon Bonaparte and, 6-7
Group for the Use of Psychology in History (GUPH), 148
Group Psychology and the Analysis of the Ego, 7, 34-35, 117-118
groups
  Freud on, 205-206
  psychohistory genre, 171
Guntrip, Harry, British school, 129, 132

H

Hamlet, nature of crisis, 154-155
Hampstead Child Therapy Clinic, 127-128
Harriman, Averell, 178-179
Hartmann, Heinz, 87, 118-119
"Head Doctor: Doubted and Resisted, Freud's Daring

Map of the Mind Endures," 232
Health Maintenance Organization, 230, 232
Heidegger, Martin, 42
Heller, Peter, Erikson critique, 84, 106-107
helping mode, childhood, 199
Henri IV, 201-202
Herbart, Johann, 40
heredity
　id influence, 31
　Lamarckian theory, 210
Héroard, Jean, 201-202
Herodotus, 2
Himmelfarb, Gertrude, antipsychohistory, 52-53
Himmler, Heinrich, 136-137, 172
"Historians and the Challenge of Freud," 62
"Historical and Conceptual Background to Psychohistory, A," 11, 12
historical craft, Himmelfarb on, 53
"historical truth," 75
history
　Barzun's criteria of, 8
　as science, 51-52, 54
History and Psychoanalysis: An Inquiry into the Possibilities and Limits of Psychohistory, 67
History as Art and as Science, 5
"History: The Muse and Her Doctors," 8, 9
Hitler, Adolf
　Binion on, 174-175
　Bullock on, 172-173
　Erikson on, 101, 105, 106
　L. Hoffman on, 189
　Loewenberg on, 123-124
　Stierlin on, 175-177
　transference and, 122
　W. C. Langer on, 173-174
　Waite on, 101-102, 174
　Wolf on, 155, 156
Hitler Among the Germans, 174
Hitler, A Study in Tyranny, 172-173
Hoffman, Louise E.
　Erikson critique, 84, 106
　on National Socialism, 189
　psychohistory critique, 136-139
Holocaust, 190-192
Holstein, Friedrich von, 135
Homburger, Theodor, 86, 102
Hughes, H. Stuart, psychohistory advocate, 5, 63-64, 140
Hughes, Judith M., 134-136
　Hoffman critique, 138-139
human development, Erikson, 85
Hume, David, 40
Hunt, David, 207-208
hypnosis, Miss Anna O, 22
hysteria
　Miss Anna O, 22
　study of, 20-21
"hysterical crisis," 20

I

id
　concept of, 31-32
　neurotic conflict, 33
　shift from, 117
　Stannard's attack on, 55
identification, 9
　psychosexual development, 31
　with the aggressor, A. Freud on, 129
identity crisis
　critique of concept, 101, 102
　Erikson, 87, 89
"identity salad," 99-100
identity vs. role confusion, Erikson stage, 89-90
"imaginative activity fantasy," 233
Imperiled Union, The: Essays on the Civil War, 123-126
In Search of Common Ground, 103
incest, 205
independence, emotional maturity, 32

individual, impact on history, 38
industry vs. inferiority, Erikson stage, 89
infancy, Erikson stage, 87-88
infanticidal mode, childhood, 198
infantile sexuality, Erikson, 91
initiative vs. guilt, Erikson stage, 88-89
Insight and Responsibility, 86, 98
instinct, id as, 31
internalization, 33
International Psychoanalytic Association, Lacan expulsion, 143
Interpretation of Dreams, The, 22, 86
intimacy vs. isolation, Erikson stage, 90
Introduction á la Psychohistoire, 3
introjection
  A. Freud on, 129
  Klein, 129
introspection
  Erikson, 97-98
  H. Kohut, 154
intrusive mode, childhood, 198-199
"iron curtain," historical conservativism, 60-61
irrationality, 4, 33, 72
isolation, A. Freud on, 129
Isorni, Jacques, 181

J

Jacques Lacan: The Death of an Intellectual Hero, 143
James, William, 10
Jesus of Nazareth, Erikson on, 105
Johnson, James P., 186-187, 188
Jones, Ernest, 42, 127, 132, 189
  relationship with Klein, 129, 130
Joron, Antoinette, 202
Joseph, 23
Journal of Psychohistory, The: A Quarterly Journal of Childhood and Psychohistory, 12, 198
Journal of the American Psychoanalytic Association, 86
Jung, Carl, Friedländer on, 68

K

Kant, Immanuel, 42
Keniston, Kenneth, psychohistorian, 108-109
Kern, Stephen, 209-210
Kernberg, Otto, 150, 177
Khrushev, Nikita, 239
Kierkegaard, Søren, 42
Kivnick, Helen Q., 86
Klaf, Franklin S., 7
Klein, Melanie, British school, 127-131
Kohut, Heinz
  background of, 148-149
  evaluation of, 158-159
  theoretical views of, 149-151
Kohut, Thomas, 156-157
Kovel, Joel, Erikson critique, 99-100
Kren, George M., 190-191
Kushner, Howard I., Erikson critique, 84, 100-104

L

Lacan, Jacques
  background of, 141-142
  evaluation of, 145, 146-147
  psychoanalysis and, 142-144
  theoretical contributions of, 145, 146
Lagache, Daniel, 141
Langer, Walter C., 50, 173-174
Langer, William L., 9-10, 59-62, 228-229
language
  Lacan on, 144, 145
  outside of conflict, 118
L'Antisémitism nazi: Histoire d'une psychose collective, 190
Laplanche, Jean, 141
Lasalle, Ferdinand, 19

Lasch, Christopher, 211
latent dream content, 24
Leader, the Led, and the Psyche, The: Essays on Psychohistory, 107
leadership, 38-39
League of Nations, Wilson and the, 183
Lear, Jonathan, 233-235
Leçons sur les maladies du système nerveux, 21
Lefebvre, Georges, 6, 7, 72
Lenin, V. I., 178
Leon Blum: Humanist in Politics, 124
Les Ecrits Techniques de Freud, 145
letters, historical evidence, 65
libido theory
    Fairbairn on, 132
    Freud, 3, 27, 122, 135
"Lieben und arbeiten," 90
life cycle, Erikson, 85, 87, 91
Life History and the Historical Moment, 86
Lifton, Robert J., psychohistorian, 108
Lincoln, Abraham, 172
Little Commonwealth, A: Family Life in Plymouth Colony, 108, 208-209
Little Hans, case study, 55
Living and Dying, 108
Lloyd George, David, 183
Loewenberg, Peter, 4, 5, 10, 122-126
    Hoffman critique of, 136-138
Loewenstein, Rudolf, 142
"Looking into the Whirlwind: A Psychohistorical Study of the Black Panthers," 194
Louis XIII, 200-203
Louis XIV, 200-201
Louis XIII: The Making of a King, 200, 201-203
Loving, Parenting, and Dying: The Family Circle in England and America, 211

Luther, Martin
    Erikson on, 61, 72, 87, 91-98, 101, 105, 106-107, 188
    William Langer on, 61-62

M

Mahler, Margaret, 20
Malcolm X, 194
"Managed Care and the Dissolution of the Therapeutic Alliance in Psychoanalysis," 236-238
managed care, psychoanalytic practice and, 238-238
manifest dream, 24
Mann, Thomas, birthday committee, 43
Mannoni, Octave, 141
Manuel, Frank E., 60
"Manuscripts and Psychohistory," 64
marriage, changing function of, 207-208, 211
Marvick, Elizabeth W., 199-203
Marx, Karl, Feuerbach's influence on, 42
Marxism
    ideas of, 37-39
    view of analytic tradition, 141
mass hysteria, study of, 188
Masséna, André, 18
Masson, Jeffrey, 233
Maurras, Charles, 142
Mazlish, Bruce
    on deMause, 199
    on family impact, 203-204
    group behavior, 189-190, 193-194
    on Nixon, 187-188
    psychohistorian, 13, 57, 107
McCarthyism, 83
Medici, Marie de, 202, 203
Melanie Klein: Her World and Her Work, 130
memory, 67-68
mental illness, origin of, 30
method

Barzun on historical, 50
Himmelfarb on historical, 53
Meyerhoff, Hans, 5
middle age, Erikson stage, 90
Mill, John Stuart, 41
Mind of Adolf Hitler, The: The Secret Wartime Report, 50, 173-174
Miss Anna O, case study, 21-22
Mitchell, Stephen A., 131
Monaco, Paul, 197
moralistes tradition, 140
"Moral Majority," 192
moratorium, adolescent, 89
Moscow Psychoanalytic Society, 239
Moses, 56-57, 58
Moses and Monotheism, 57, 117
mother
  Freud's relationship with his, 27, 29-30, 31, 205
  Hitler's relationship with his, 173, 174, 175-177
  Wilson's relationship with his, 185
mothering
  "good enough," 135-136
  Guntrip on, 133
  Hoffman on, 138-139
  Klein on, 131
  Winnicott on, 133, 134
motivation, psychohistory and, 2
motor development, outside of conflict, 118
"myth-making," 176

N

Napoleon, 6-7, 51
narcissism
  H. Kohut on 151-152
  unconscious and, 26
narcissistic character disorders, 149-150, 159
narrative
  Himmelfarb on, 52
  historical requirement, 2
  "narrative truth," 75

Narrative Truth and History Truth: Meaning and Interpretation in Psychoanalysis, 75
National Association for the Advancement of Psychoanalysis, 238
National Socialism, 189, 190-191
  attraction of, 137-138, 189
Nature vs. Nurture: Trends and Patterns in Seventeenth Century French Childrearing," 200
Nazi Doctors, The; Medical Killing and the *Psychology of Genocide*, 108
nervous system, study of, 20
Neue Vorlesungen über die Krankheiten des Nervensystems insbesondere über Hysterie, 21
neurosis, 3, 22
  Klein, 131
  origin of, 30
neurotic conflict, 33
"new history," objection to, 52
New Right, 191-193
New York Times
  attack on Freud, 230, 231
  Erikson article, 84-85
  Erikson obituary, 83-84
  psychoanalytic practice in Russia, 239
New York Times Magazine, H. Kohut, 149
Newton, Huey P., 103, 104, 194
"Next Assignment, The," 9, 59, 62
Nietzsche, Friedrich, 42, 235
"Nine Ages of Man," 97
"Nixon and the Psychohistorians," 186
Nixon, Richard M.
  psychohistory and, 186-188
  transference, 122-123
nurture, superego influence, 31

O

objective relations school, 129, 132

Object Relations in Psychoanalytic Theory, 131-132
object relations, phallic stage, 29
object relations theory, 104, 117, 119, 121, 122
    Guntrip on, 132
    Klein role in, 131-132
    psychohistory and, 136-139
"Object Relations Theory and Psychohistory," 136
Oedipal Complex, 17-18, 36-37, 119, 138, 206
    attack on Freud, 235
    H. Kohut rejection of, 150
    modern resistance to, 232
    Stannard's attack on, 55
Oedipal stage, psychosexual development, 26-27, 29-30
Oedipus vs. Narcissus," 149-150
old age, Erikson stage, 90-91
old old age, Erikson, 85, 91
omission, dream work, 24
"On-going Patient Treatment Reports," 237
"On Narcisissism: An Introduction," 18
"On Psychoanalysis as History," 5
"On the Nature of Psycho-Historical Evidence: In Search of Gandhi," 98
oral stage, psychosexual development, 26-28
"outer goodness," 88
"outside of conflict," 118
overdetermined, dream work, 24

P

parables, 105
paranoia, Klein, 131
Parents and Children in History: The Psychology of Family in Early Modern France, 207-208
parents, dream symbols of, 25
Paris Peace Conference, Wilson at, 184
Parker, Harold T., 6, 7
Parsons, Talcott, 119
Past, Present, and Personal: The Family and the Life Course in American History, 108
Pasteur, Louis, 20
Paxil, use of, 232
Peasant's War, 96
penis, dream symbols of, 25
penis envy, Klein on, 135
personality
    Freud's theory of, 25-31
    structure of, 31
    Wolf rejection of, 153
Pétain, Henri Philippe, 172, 179-182, 196-197
Peter the Great, 172
phallic stage, psychosexual development, 26-27, 29-30
phenomenology, origin of, 41
Physiology Institute, University of Vienna, 19, 21
Plato, 235
Platt, Gerald N., 101, 119-122, 139
pleasure principle, 32
    Stannard's attack on, 55
Plymouth family, 208-209
Pois, Robert A., 229
Political Psychology: Journal of the International Society of Political Psychology, 12
Pontalis, Jean-Baptiste, 141
pre-oedipal period, Klein, 129-130, 131
priesthood of all believers, 95
primal horde, 34
Principles of Psychology, The, 10
Prisco, Salvatore, 199
productivity, outside of conflict, 118
"profamilism," 191-192
"Profamilism and the New Right: A Feminist Analysis of Fascist Ideology," 191
projection

A. Freud on, 129
Klein on, 129
Prozac, use of, 231, 232, 233
Proust, Marcel, 235
"Psychical Mechanism of Hysterical Phenomena,The," 22
"psychical provinces," 31
psychoanalysis
  British school, 127, 129-134
  contemporary attacks on, 230-232
  definition of, 2, 25
  goal of, 159
  investigative method, 3
  managed care impact, 236-238
  Soviet rejection of, 39
  Stannard's attack on, 54-56
Psychoanalysis and History, 57
"Psychoanalysis and Managed Health Care," 238
Psychoanalysis for Teachers and Parents, 128
psychoanalytic clinical practice, psychohistory and, 121-122
"Psychoanalytic Interpretations of Adolf Hitler and Nazism, 1933-1945: A Prelude to Psychohistory," 189
"Psychoanalytic Models of History: Freud and After," 122
Psychoanalytic Politics: Freud's French Revolution, 144
"Psychoanalytic Selfobject Psychology and Psychohistory," 153
Psychoanalytic Sociology: An Essay on the *Interpretation of Historical Data and the Phenomena of Collective Behavior*, 119, 120
  critique of, 120
Psychoanalytic Study of the Family, The, 206
psychoanalytic theory, French interpreters, 139-148

"Psychoanalytic Theory and History: Groups and Events," 193-194
Psychoanalytic Treatment of Children, The, 128
psychobiography, 11. *See also* biography
"psychogenic theory of history," 198
psychohistorians
  educational requirements, 228-229
  Erikson's influence on, 107-110
  T. Kohut critique of traditional, 156-157
Psychohistorical Inquiry: A Comprehensive Research Bibliography, 10-11
Psychohistorical Origins of the Nazi Youth Cohort, The, 137-138
psychohistory, 1
  British school's impact, 134-139
  case for, 59-76, 227-228
  college courses in, 13
  definition of, 1
  Erikson's contribution to, 84, 85-86, 98
  journals of, 12, 63
  literature in field of, 12
  opposition to, 7-8, 49-59
  three feature of, 4
  wings of, 11
"Psychohistory and Psychohistorians: The First Fifty Years," 10
"Psychohistory as History," AHR, 156-157
"Psychohistory, Psychobiography and the Holocaust," 190
Psychohistory Review, 12, 69
  Erikson issues, 84, 98, 100
psychological determinism, dreams, 23
"Psychological Development and Historical Change," 109

Psychology and Historical Interpretation, 11
Psychology from an Empirical Standpoint, 41
psychopathic personality, 33
Psychopathic God, The: Adolf Hitler, 174
psychosis, 3, 33
   Klein on, 131
   origin of, 30
punishments, use of, 33

Q

Quinn, Susan, 149-150
Quitt, Martin, 211

R

Ranke, Leopold von, 2, 75
reaction formation, 9
   A. Freud on, 129
Reagan, Ronald, 192
reality principle, 32
recall-phenomena, outside of conflict, 118
records, psychohistorians and, 64-66. *See also* evidence
Reformation, origin of, 94-95
regression, A. Freud on, 129
Reich, Wilhelm, 189
rejection, Napoleon Bonaparte, 6
religion
   Erikson on, 88
   Freud on, 39-40
repressed ego, Guntrip, 132-133
repression
   A. Freud on, 128-129
   dreams, 23-24
Reshaping the Psychoanalytic Domain: The Works of Melanie Klein, W.R.D. Fairbairn, and D.W. Winnicott, 134-135
resistance, 33, 235
Restoration of Self, The, 150
reversal, A. Freud on, 129
"Review Essay/Woodrow Wilson and the Case for Psychohistory," 185

Revolutionary Immortality: Mao Tse-Tung and the Chinese Cultural Revolution, 108
"Revolution or Counterrevolution," 109
rewards, use of, 33
Richard Nixon: The Shaping of His Character, 122
Richelieu, Armand-Jean Du Plessis de, 200-201
Ricoeur, Paul, 141
RN: The Memoirs of Richard Nixon, 186
Robespierre, Maximilien, 172
Rolland, Romain, birthday committee, 43
Romains, Jules, birthday committee, 43
Roosevelt, Theodore, drawings of, 73
Ross, Dorothy, 185
Rostand, Edmond, 90
Roudinesco, Elisabeth, 142
Rulers, role of, 36
Runyan, William M., advocate, 11, 12, 13, 72-74
Russia, psychoanalytic resurgence in, 239
Russian Revolution, 39

S

Sachs, Hanns, 12
sadism, anal stage, 28
Saffady, William, advocate, 64-66
Salisbury, Robert G., 135, 138
Salpêtrière medical complex, 20
salvation by faith, 95
Sartre, Jean-Paul, 141
Saussure, Raymond de, 189
Schneiderman, Stuart, 143
Schoenwald, Richard L.
   advocate, 62-63, 120
   Erikson critique, 99
Schopenhauer, Arthur, 40, 42-43
Schur, Max, 57
Schweinitz, George de, 184
Seale, Bobby, 194

Searles, Harold, 124
Second World War, 171
self, Lacan on the, 146
"Self in History, The," AHA, 148, 151-153
self psychology
　evaluation of, 159
　H. Kohut, 149, 154-156, 158-159
"Self Psychology and the Sciences of Man," 154-156
Self Psychology of Heinz Kohut, The: A Symposium, 158-159
self-esteem, superego, 32
sexuality
　Freud-Breuer split, 21
　role of, 3
　Schopenhauer on, 42, 43
Shakespeare, William, 235
Shrinking History: On Freud and the Failure of Psychohistory, 53-54
"Shrink is In, The: A Counterblast in the War on Freud," 233-235
Silberstein, Eduard, correspondence with, 40, 41, 42
Six Crises, 186
Smith, Dinitia, 231
Social and Religious History of the Jews, A, 56
social conflict, 121
socializing mode, childhood, 199
Social Policy, Erikson critique, 99
social psychology, 35
social psychopathology, 72
social roles, Erikson, 87
Socrates, 235
"Some Character Types Met With in Psychoanalytic Work," 126
Soundings: Psychohistorical and Psycholiterary, 66
sources, Baron on, 57-58. *See also* evidence, records
"specialism," 50
Spence, Donald P., 75

Spinoza, Baruch, 40
splitting, Klein, 130
"stagecrafting," 176
Stalin as Revolutionary, 1879-1929: A Study in History and Personality, 177-179
Stalin, Joseph, 172, 177-179
Stalingrad, 124
Stampp, Kenneth, 125-126
Standard Edition, 42
Stanley, Alessandra, 239
Stannard, David E., arguments against psychohistory, 53-56, 67
Stierlin, Helm, 175-177
Strozier, Charles B., 98, 99, 149
stubbornness, anal stage, 28
Studies on Hysteria, 22
subjectivity, individual, 4
sublimation, 9
　A. Freud on, 129
suicidal drive, Hitler and his, 173, 176
superego
　concept of, 31, 32
　development of, 32-33
　Stannard's attack on, 55
Surrealists, psychoanalytic tradition and, 140
symbolization, dream work, 25

T

Tager, Michael, 194-196
"Taking Erikson's Identity Seriously: Psychoanalyzing the Psychohistorian," 100-101
"technical jargon," 9, 50
technique of observation, 92, 97-98
Ten Commandments, 35
theology, Erikson interest in, 105
therapeutic alliance, managed care impact on, 236
Thiers, Adolph, 18
thinking, outside of conflict, 118

Thomas Woodrow Wilson: A Medical and Psychological Biography, 183-184
Thomas Woodrow Wilson, Freud/Bullitt, 182-183
"Those Wrecked by Success," 126
time, psychoanalysis and, 67-68
Time magazine, attack on Freud, 230, 235-236
toilet training, anal stage, 28
Toole, James, 184
totalitarianism, psychohistorians on, 189
Totem and Taboo, 2, 34, 35-36, 117, 205
transference, 105, 121
"Transference Model in Psychohistory, The: A Critique," 121
transitional objects, Winnicott, 133-134
traumatic paralysis, study of, 20
treatment, psychoanalytical, 3
Treaty of Versailles, 183, 185
"Tricky Dick," 186
Troeltsch, Ernst, 42
Tucker, Robert C., 177-179
Turkle, Sherry, 144

U

unconscious
  attack on theory of, 234
  Freud theory of, 25-26
  relation to conscious mind, 26
  Schopenhauer influence on concept of, 42-43
unconscious behavior, 3, 4
unconscious motivation, historians and, 63
United States, psychoanalytic acceptance, 140
"Unsuccessful Adolescence of Heinrich Himmler, The," 136-137

V

values, superego, 32
venereal disease, fear of, 209-210
verification, Friedländer on, 68
Vichy regime, 125, 179, 181, 197
Vital Involvement in Old Age, 86
Voltaire, 42

W

Wagner, Richard, 176
Waite, Robert G. L., 101, 174
Waldholtz, Michael, 232-233
Wall Street Journal
  mental health economics, 230, 231-232
  Sigmund Freud defense, 232
War and Children, 128
Warner, Gloria M., 131
Warner, Silas L., 184
Watergate scandal, 123, 186
Weimar Germany, Wolf on, 155-156
Weinstein, Edwin A., 183-184, 185
Weinstein, Fred, 101, 119-122, 139
"Wellfleet Gatherings," 108
Wells, H. G., birthday committee, 43
"Why Psychoanalysis needs the Social Scientist and the Historian," 5
Winnicott, Donald W., British school, 129, 133-134
wish fulfillment, dreams as, 23
Wish To Be Free, The: Society, Psyche, and Value Change, 119
Wolf, Ernest S., AHA, 151, 153-154
Woodrow, Wilson, 58
  psychohistorians on, 172, 182-185
Woodrow Wilson and Colonel House: A Psychological Study, 183
"Woodrow Wilson Revisited: The Prepolitical Years," 184
Woolf, Virginia, birthday committee, 43

working alliance, managed care impact on, 236
Wretched of the Earth, 195

Y
Yeltsin, Boris, 239
young adult, Erikson stage, 90
Young Man Luther: A Study in Psychoanalysis and History, 53, 86, 91–98
　critique of, 104, 106–107, 157
Young Radicals, The, 109
Young Richelieu, The: A Psychoanalytic Approach to Leadership, 200–201
Youth and Dissent, 109

Z
Zanuck, Darryl, 187
Zock, Hetty, 105
Zoloft, use of, 232
Zweig, Stefan, birthday committee, 43